ASSET
PRICING

Frontiers of Real Estate Finance

Vol. 1

ASSET PRICING

Editors

Jianping Mei
New York University, USA

Hsien-hsing Liao
National Taiwan University

World Scientific
New Jersey • London • Singapore • Hong Kong

Published by

World Scientific Publishing Co. Pte. Ltd.

5 Toh Tuck Link, Singapore 596224

USA office: Suite 202, 1060 Main Street, River Edge, NJ 07661

UK office: 57 Shelton Street, Covent Garden, London WC2H 9HE

British Library Cataloguing-in-Publication Data
A catalogue record for this book is available from the British Library.

ASSET PRICING

ISBN 981-02-4563-7

This book is printed on acid-free paper.

Printed in Singapore by Mainland Press

List of Contributors

CROCKER H. LIU, *Associate Professor of Finance, New York University, Stern School of Business, Department of Finance, 900 Tisch Hall, New York, NY 10003*

JIANPING MEI, *Associate Professor of Finance, New York University, Stern School of Business, Department of Finance, 900 Tisch Hall, New York, NY 10003*

ANTHONY SAUNDERS, *Leonard N. Stern School of Business, New York University, 900 Tisch Hall, New York, NY 10003*

KEVIN WENLI LU, *Corporate Finance Division, Global Risk Advisors, 845 Third Avenue, 20 Floor, New York, NY 10022*

JIAWEI HU, *Stern School of Business*, New York University

HSIEN-HSING LIAO, *Associate Professor, Department of Finance, National Taiwan University, Taipei, Taiwan*

BIN GAO, Associate Professor, *Department of Finance, Kenan-Flagler Business School, The university of North Carolina at Chapel Hill*

Contents

CHAPTER 1

Introduction: Real Estate Analysis in a Dynamic Risk Environment

Few academic studies have exerted such a powerful influence on peoples' daily lives as modern finance. Financial innovations have revolutionized the way we invest our savings. The Modern Portfolio Theory has created a \$2 trillion mutual fund industry. The Black-Scholes option pricing model has helped to create thousands of derivative products, making it possible for risk hedging. Recent developments in present value studies have also greatly improved our understanding of security valuation and market volatility.

While this financial revolution has greatly changed many sectors of the financial industry, it has made little impact on real estate development and investment practice. Despite its huge share in world wealth, real estate investment is still a poorly researched subject. As a result, the industry remains dominated by traditional property analysts with little understanding of capital markets. These people spend too much time worrying about local conditions of space supply and demand while losing sight of the ever-changing capital market situations. This "seeing the trees and missing the woods" handicap makes them ill prepared to handle real estate market cycles. For example, a lot of analysts were caught completely off-guard when property values improved recently across many parts of the U.S. as a direct result of declining interest rates. They also failed to predict an increase in investor interest in Real Estate Investment Trust (REIT) as the spread between REIT yield and long-term bond rates widen.

Risk management in real estate is still mostly based on experience and "gut feelings" rather than solid analysis. Despite their huge real estate holdings, few financial institutions have integrated real estate

into their overall investment strategies, and few people understand
the relationship between their real estate assets and other assets in
their portfolios. As a result of this poor risk management, many large
banks and insurance companies overexposed their portfolios to real
estate risk at the peak of the last real estate cycle and suffered huge
losses when the market hit the bottom, causing serious problems of
financial survival. The 1997 Asian financial turmoil is the recent and
most obvious example.

Traditional development financing offers little relief to the real
estate industry when the market is in recession. As a result of the
sluggish economy and a large inventory of vacant space, many traditional lenders have stopped making real estate loans. Desperate
to stay above water, developers are increasingly looking to financial
market for capital. This is dramatically transforming the $3 tril-
lion commercial real estate industry in the U.S. from "often secretive
family-dominated fiefs into public companies beholden to thousands
of shareholders."[1]

This massive securitization of real estate assets has created a huge
demand for integrating traditional property analysis with financial
analysis. This is because as securitized real estate assets, their value
will be directly affected by local demand for space as well as world
capital market conditions, such as interest rates and returns of various assets in other countries. To succeed in this environment, investors need to creatively combine two bodies of knowledge, real
estate and finance, and develop a set of strategies towards real estate
valuation and risk management.

The objective of this book is to bridge the gap between real estate
and finance. It collects a series of studies conducted by the authors
and their colleagues, in which we demonstrate how modern finance
can be applied to obtain new insights into real estate risk and valuation. We also show that, by combining real estate expertise with
financial modeling, one can have a much better grasp of property

---

[1] New York Times, July 8, 1994, "Secretive property empires made public by stock
sales".

market cycles. As a result, one can achieve better investment performance through improved market timing.

Within the context of modern finance, the studies included in this book are grouped into five parts. The first part includes studies examining risk and return behaviors of real estate investment. The second part contains short-term trading strategy of securitized real estates. The third part is composed of studies analyzing the impacts of real estate investment on the value of institutional investors. The last part contains studies that look into the risk exposure and diversification benefits of international real estate investment.

More specifically, part I uses a multi-factor model to address the following issues:

(i) Is real estate market predictable?
(ii) How does the real estate risk premium vary over time?
(iii) What is the relationship between real estate returns and other asset returns?

Part II studies the short-term price behaviors of securitized real estate assets and explores the possibility of trading profits based on price reversal. Part III discusses the impact of real estate holdings on financial institution's equity price. Part IV examines the risk and return behaviors and benefits of international real estate diversification.

The rest of this introduction is divided into four sections. Each section provides a concise discussion for the studies included in each part of this book.

1.1   Time-varying Risk Premium of Real Estate

Section 1.1 consists of three studies examining the issue of time-varying risk premium in real estate:

(i) The Predictability of Returns on Equity REITs (EREITs) and their Co-movement with other Assets (by Liu and Mei, 1992).
(ii) Predictability of Real Estate Returns and Market Timing (by Mei and Liu, 1994).

(iii) A Time-varying Analysis of Equity and Real Estate Markets in the U.S. and Japan.

1.1.1   *The Predictability of Returns on EREITs and their Co-movement with other Assets*

One issue at the center of real estate finance is whether real estate risk varies over time and how does that variation affect real estate asset pricing (i.e., risk premium). To be more specific, we want to understand the following questions:

(i) Is variation of risk premiums on real estate related to business conditions?
(ii) Do expected returns (risk premiums) on stocks, bonds, and real estate move together?
(iii) To what extent do REITs resemble stocks with large capitalization, stocks with small capitalization, and bonds?
(iv) Do cap rates carry information about the variation of risk premiums for all assets in the economy?

Liu and Mei (1992) employs a multifactor, latent-variable model to answer these questions. The model allows the time variation of expected excess returns on different asset classes. The intuition behind the model is that all financial assets are affected by some common systematic factors. These systematic risks are not diversifiable so that investors need to be compensated for taking the risks. These compensations vary over time based on capital market conditions. In general, when there is high risk of economic recession, risk premiums (compensation) tend to be high. On the other hand, when there is little risk of recession, risk premiums (compensation) tend to be low.

This methodology has several distinct advantages over previous studies. First, it allows for time-varying risk premiums in contrast to the existing methodology which generally assumes constant risk premiums. Thus, it is designed to capture the time variation not only in *unexpected* excess returns but also in *expected* excess returns. It addresses the issue of the resemblance of asset returns by comparing the similarities among assets by their return variation patterns. Second, it makes no assumptions about the observability of systematic

Non-constancy of the variance of a measure over the levels of the factor under study

factors in the economy. Third, few distributional assumptions are required except those associated with Generalized Method of Moments (GMM). The estimation procedure adjusts for heteroskedasticity in the error terms. It also allows contemporaneous correlation among error terms across securities to exist. The GMM procedure also could adjust for a moderate amount of serial correlation in the returns as a result of nonsynchronous trading.

Their main finding is that the expected excess returns vary over time as a result of changing economic conditions. This variation is more predictable for real estate (EREITs) than for small cap stocks, value-weighted stocks, and bonds. They find that this variation is highly influenced by the short-term interest rate, the dividend yield, and the real estate cap rate. This suggests that the cost of capital for real estate is highly affected by changing capital market and real estate market conditions. It implies that, to be successful in real estate financing and pricing, one has to understand capital markets and the changing needs of investors. Otherwise, investors may find that real estate as an asset class cannot offer adequate returns for their capital and so they may take the money elsewhere.

Their graphical evidence indicates that the risk premiums vary substantially over time. This suggests that in certain time periods the market may have overreacted to certain economic news so that real estate may be over- or under-valued because of mispricing. Thus, from the investors' perspective, market timing might prove to be a fruitful endeavor.

While prior studies have found that EREITs return resemble large cap stocks, they find that returns on EREITs move more closely with small cap stocks. Interestingly, they also find that real estate market conditions influence small cap stocks in addition to EREITs. In addition, they find evidence that EREIT returns do not resemble bond returns even though the cash flow portion of equity REITs resembles interest payments on bonds. Moreover, to some extent, EREITs are actually less similar to bonds than to small cap stocks. This result is informative because it suggests that we can improve our understanding of real estate assets (EREITs) by using our knowledge in small stocks. It also suggests that the cost of capital for real estate may be more closely related to equity market than to the bond market.

Another finding of the study is that these preceding results are consistent with the view that the changing risk premiums of equity and bond market factors are important determinants of expected asset returns. Liu and Mei find little evidence of the presence of a risk premium associated with real estate investment. The only benefit associated with real estate investment appears to be pure portfolio diversification.

1.1.2   *Predictability of Real Estate Returns and Market Timing*

The previous study suggests that the variation in expected excess real estate returns over time is predictable and is the result of changes in business conditions. Moreover, one of these studies finds that real estate returns are more predictable relative to the returns on other assets. This raises the possibility that real estate might exhibit superior investment performance when compare to other assets if an investor is successful in market timing. The purpose of the Mei and Liu (1994) paper, therefore, is to explore whether superior real estate investment performance is possible through a market timing strategy given that we are able to forecast real estate returns. The ability to successfully use market timing to achieve superior performance is of interest to practitioner, because it suggests a more productive method of allocating investment funds.

This chapter focuses on testing for the existence of market timing ability out of the sample, instead of testing within the sample. As a result, it offers a convincing study of whether the degree of pre-dictability associated with various asset returns, with real estate in particular, is sufficient to allow an investor to construct a market timing strategy that will lead to superior investment performance.

The study uses a conditional excess return model derived from Liu and Mei (1992) to predict the time variation of expected excess returns on various asset classes. To prevent the in-sample bias problem of using the same data to both estimate the parameters and test the model, a 10-year rolling regression is used to form out-of-sample excess return forecasts. Given these return forecasts, three invest-ment portfolios are formed for each asset class including a passive buy-and-hold portfolio, a portfolio of long and short positions, and a portfolio of long positions only. These investment strategies are then examined for the overall period performances as well as bull market and bear market performances.

This methodology has several distinct advantages over previous investment performance studies that test for the presence of market timing ability. First, it allows for time-varying risk premiums in contrast to the existing methodology of Henriksson-Merton (1981) which assumes that risk premiums are stationary. Their emphasis is on the *economic significance (trading profits)* rather than on the reliability of return forecast.

The most important finding of the study is that the level of predictability associated with real estate is sufficient for successful market timing to occur. However, this is not necessarily so for the other asset classes examined. In addition, returns on a portfolio of exchange-traded real estate firms appears to outperform large cap stocks, small cap stocks, bonds, and the S&P500 benchmark portfolio over the entire out-of-sample period as well as when this period is subdivided into up and down markets. This implies that fund managers can improve their fund performance by strategically adding or reducing real estate securities in their portfolios.

1.1.3   *A Time-varying Analysis of Equity and Real Estate Markets in the U.S. and Japan*

Applying the present value model of Campbell (1988, 1991), the purpose of this study is to compare the price movements of Japanese equity and real estate stocks to those of their U.S. counterparts. The model used allows the expected discount rate to vary through time in conjunction with a vector autoregressive (VAR) process.

The key issue examined in the study is whether the relative influence of the variance in news about future returns and the variance in news about future dividends for Japanese equity and real estate markets is similar to that for U.S. markets. In particular, are movements in the Japanese capital markets driven primarily by news about the future expected return (discount rate) or by news about future cash flows? How persistent over time are changes in the expected rate of return. For example, for how many periods does a drift occur in expected returns? The study also investigated the issue of whether a strong negative serial correlation exists for Japanese equity and real estate returns, given the evidence that investors can successfully profit from using a contrarian investment strategy for the U.S. capital market in the short run.

The study finds that Japanese stocks and real estate differ in several important respects from their U.S. counterparts. The first difference is that current Japanese stock returns are useful in predicting future expected returns on Japanese real estate, whereas existing returns on U.S. real estate are valuable in forecasting future anticipated returns on U.S. stocks. Another notable feature is that news on future cash flows accounts for a major portion of the variation in unexpected returns on Japanese stocks and real estate. News on future expected returns, by contrast, has a greater impact on returns on U.S. stocks and real estate.

A further distinction is that changes in the future expected discount rate is less persistent over time for Japanese real estate and stocks relative to their U.S. counterparts, even though returns on Japanese assets are at least as predictable as returns on U.S. assets. Consequently, changes in the future expected returns have a greater impact on current prices for U.S. relative to Japanese stocks and real estate.

The final difference the study finds is that returns on Japanese stocks exhibit weaker a negative serial correlation relative on return on U.S. stocks and real estate. Japanese real estate, by contrast, appears to have fairly strong positive serial correlations over the period examined. Thus, a contrarian investment strategy is less likely to be profitable in the short run for stocks and real estate in Japan relative to the U.S.

The study does find some parallels between stocks and real estate in the U.S. and Japan. Not only are the returns on real estate more predictable relative to stock returns, but also changes in the expected return on real estate are more persistent over time compared to stocks in both countries.

1.2 Short-term Price Behavior in Real Estate Securities Market

Section 1.2 includes the following study: Price Reversal, Transaction Costs, and Arbitrage Profits in Real Estate Securities Market (by Mei and Gao, 1995).

Recent research in real estate shows that returns for exchange-traded real estate securities are predictable at monthly and quarterly intervals (see Liu and Mei (1992, 1994), and Mei and Lee (1994)). There are two explanations for this return predictability. First, the predictability is attributed to systematic time variation of risk premiums due to changes in market conditions and investors' perception of risk. Second, it is the result of some form of market inefficiency due to market overreaction or imperfection in market microstructure. This study extends their work by documenting return reversals for real estate securities at a higher frequency level (weekly).

Return reversals at weekly intervals are interesting because they provide a simple way of differentiating the two hypotheses above on return predictablity. It is easy to imagine that economic conditions and investors' perception of risk should remain relatively unchanged at daily or weekly intervals, much less so at monthly or longer intervals. Thus, any evidence of weekly return reversals points strongly to the direction of market inefficiency rather than time-varying risk premiums.

Return reversals at weekly intervals is also interesting because they provide information in the magnitude of imperfections in the market microstructure. Since short-term return reversals often create short-term arbitrage trading profits in the absence of trading costs while they vanish in their presence, the trading profits provide a good measure of market liquidity and transaction costs.

Using the methodology developed by Lehmann (1990), this paper first documents the return reversals in real estate security markets and then constructs arbitrage portfolios (zero investment) to exploit the opportunity. Next, we adjust trading profits according to reasonable assumptions about bid-ask spread and transaction costs. We then discuss some implications of our findings for market efficiency and liquidity.

The intuition behind Lehmann's approach is fairly simple. We sell short those stocks with recent price increases and use the proceeds to buy those stocks with recent price declines. If price reversal happens frequently for most stocks in the short run, we expect to make net trading gains when we reverse our trading positions. The approach is capable of calculating the arbitrage profits that could be earned by arbitrage traders if there exist return reversals. Thus, it not only provides a statistical evidence of return reversals but also the economic significance of return reversals.

Using this approach, they find that there do exist some statistically significant return reversals in exchange-traded real estate securities. These return reversals can lead to economically significant trading profits for arbitrage traders if trading cost can be ignored. However, in the current trading environment where traders have to bear the relatively high cost of bid-ask spread due to the small capitalization of real estate securities, there are not trading profits left after taking into account the implicit cost of bid-ask spread and deducting the transaction cost. Thus, the real estate securities market is efficient in the sense that one can hardly profit from the return reversals.

The results provide some useful trading rules for long-term real estate security fund managers. Based on the weekly price reversal result, they can reduce they acquisition costs by buying a few days after a weekly rally and get higher prices by selling a few days after a downturn. This trading rule does not guarantee investment savings or gains in each transaction, but in the long run it should enhance portfolio performance.

1.3   How Real Estate Market Affects Financial Institutions

Section 1.3 consists of three studies examining financial institutions' real estate risk exposure.

(i) Bank Risk and Real Estate: An Asset Pricing Perspective (by Mei and Saunders (1995)).

(ii) The Time Variation of Risk for Insurance Companies (Mei and Saunders (1994)).

(iii) Assessing the "Santa Claus" Approach to Asset Allocation: Implication for Commercial Real Estate Investment.

1.3.1 *Bank Risk and Real Estate: An Asset Pricing Perspective*

The late 1980s posed some serious commercial real estate loan management problems for large U.S. banks. As a result of poor risk management and loan pricing, the 10 largest banks in U.S. had commercial real estate loan portfolios exceeding \$3.5 billion each, and their problem commercial real estate loan to net worth ratios exceeded 30%.

This unfolding of asset-exposure problems for major U.S. banks raises an important empirical question: Do investors demand a higher risk premium for such risks in the market? It is important for banks to understand the determinants of equity risk premium, because this premium affects not only their investment decisions but also their financing decisions. As is well known, the weighted average cost of capital (WACC) is a weighted average of the costs of debt and equity. The higher the equity risk premium, the higher the equity's required rate of return, and thus, the higher the WACC. The variation of risk premium is also of interest to regulators because it contains information about market perception of bank risk. Thus, if banks have increase their exposures to certain risks, regulators should consider actions, such as additional loss provisioning and additional capital infusion, as well as revising the required deposit insurance premium paid.

Previous studies of bank stock returns have concentrated on explaining the *ex post* behavior of bank stock returns. However, no study has formally sought to identify whether such factors are priced *ex ante*, in the sense of the APT, and/or whether the influence of such factors change over time as banks alter the nature of their loan exposures. Sweeney and Warga (1986) investigated the *ex ante* risk premiums in the pricing of public utility stocks in the presence of a market and interest rate risk factors. However, their methodology was too constraining in that their premiums were fixed (constant) through time.

In Mei and Saunders (1995), they use data for 1970–1989 on large bank stock returns to investigate the time-varying nature of three sources of risk:

(i) the market factor,
(ii) an interest rate factor, and
(iii) a real estate factor.

In the light of the problems of many large banks in the real estate market, considerable attention is given to the exposure to, and the pricing of, real estate risk in bank stock returns. Moreover, since banking is a regulated industry, they try to identify regulatory induced impacts on these risk premiums. In particular, we seek to identifying whether changes in the Federal Reserve's monetary policy regime (e.g., October 1979 to October 1982) affected the relative pricing of risk.

The study finds that the time variation in bank risk premium has been partly determined by interest rate and real estate market conditions. It also finds that the real estate factor has been most important for large non-money center banks. Moreover, the study finds that the time variation of risk premiums is consistent with changes in bank real estate lending during the sample period. These results have some interesting implications for bank asset management and lending practices. For shareholder wealth maximizing banks, the results suggest that the banks should consider their overall cost of capital (i.e., cost of equity capital, debt, and deposits) rather than simply the direct borrowing cost, such as interest paid on deposits. If the overall cost of capital increases as a result of changing business conditions, then banks should changing its lending policies by charging higher loan rates so that return to capital will be enough to cover the cost of capital. Otherwise, banks will be making negative present value loans and are doomed to lose money in the long run. The depressed bank stock prices at the end of 1990 offered a good lesson to many bank executives that investors do care about their risk management skills.

1.3.2 *The Time Variation of Risk for Insurance Companies*

It is important for insurance companies to understand the determinants of equity risk premium, because this premium affects not only their investment decisions but also their financing decisions. As is well known in the corporate finance literature, the WACC is a weighted average of the cost of debt and the cost of equity. The higher the equity risk premium, the higher the equity's required rate of return, thus, the higher the WACC. A higher equity risk premium should lead to reductions in the promised minimum rate of returns paid to some universal/variable policyholders, because certain profit levels must be maintained to ensure risk-adjusted returns to shareholders. A higher equity risk premium should also lead to adjustment of investment policies, including asset allocation and risk management, because higher returns to capital are needed to compensate shareholders.

The variation of risk premium is also interesting to regulators, because it contains information about market perception of insurance company risk and cost of capital. Thus, in states where policy premium is regulated, regulators should allow for higher policy premium increases if there is substantial increase in the equity risk premium.

Despite the importance of measuring equity risk premiums for the insurance industry, the subject is poorly researched and little understood by academics and practitioners. Although there is ample evidence that cost of capital varies over time, most studies in this area still assume constant cost of capital and use static CAPM or APT to measure cost of capital. Mei and Saunders (1994) tries to change this situation. Using a life insurance stock index, a property/liability (thereafter, PY/LY) insurance stock index, and some financial and real estate variables, we address the following issue: how do changing economic conditions affect the risk premiums on insurance stocks?

The study finds that there is substantial variation in risk premium on insurance stocks, and these variations are predictable based on a small set of economic variables, namely, the short-term interest rates, the market dividend yield, and the real estate caprate. We have some preliminary evidence that insurance companies have been perceived by the market having increased their real estate risk exposure in the 1980s owing to a turbulent real estate market, although their actual holdings, as a percentage of assets, remained relatively unchanged during the period. These results are very interesting for several reasons: First, we can see that the cost of equity capital is highly variable in the insurance industry. Because of this high variation, it is probably unreasonable for the regulators to fix insurance premiums for a long time. Second, premiums need to reflect changing interest rates and stock market conditions. The insurance industry needs to stay competitive to attract not only policyholders but also equity investors. It also needs to achieve a decent return for investing its policy premiums. Third, insurance executives should pay more attention to the stock market, because the market provides information about investor perceptions on how they are running the business. These perceptions can affect stock price and change the cost of equity capital.

1.3.3   *Assessing the "Santa Claus" Approach to Asset Allocation: Implication for Commercial Real Estate Investment*

For a financial institution, the allocation of investment funds among different classes of assets, such as stocks, bonds, and real estates, is probably the most important decision. Casual observation suggests the prevalence of a "Santa Claus" approach to fund allocation, that is, giving more money to fund managers whose performance has been "nice" (good) in the recent past and giving less money to fund managers if their performance has been "naughty" (poor). However, few studies have asked the question whether the approach is consistent with rational portfolio management. The purpose of this study is to answer this question.

The study uses asset allocation data from 1973 to 1989 for commercial banks to address the issue. These institutions report on a regular and homogeneous basis. As such, they present a unique laboratory to analyze investment behavior over time and the rationality of such behavior in the light of asset pricing theories. The major objective of this study is to show that the backward-looking "Santa

Claus" approach to asset allocation is not consistent with optimal portfolio management, and that this strategy may have contributed to the poor performance of the U.S. commercial banks' real estate portfolios.

The methodology used in this study is a combination of the nonparametric market timing test developed by Heneriksson and Merton (1981) and the portfolio performance test developed by Mei and Saunders (1994). The nonparametric test is used to evaluate investors' market timing performance that only requires the observation of excess returns and the prediction of forecasters. It does not depend on knowledge of the distribution of excess returns or any particular model of security valuation. Since the prediction of forecasters is generally unobservable, later studies have tried to use *ex post* portfolio excess return to proxy for the unobservable *ex ante* prediction. However, this study uses an alternative proxy, the percentage increase in investment, to evaluate the market timing performance of various investment strategies. The intuition behind this proxy is that, in a frictionless market where commercial banks are engaged in profit-maximization and where real estate loans depend only on commercial banks' forecasts of future real estate excess returns, commercial banks will increase their positions in stocks if they forecast next period real estate return as positive or close their position if they forecast next period real estate excess return as negative. So, there is a one-to-one correspondence between real estate loan increase and commercial banks' prediction of next period real estate excess returns.

The first finding of this study is that the expected returns on real estate are time varying, generally tend to increase after a real estate market rally, and fall after a market downturn. The study finds that commercial banks' real estate investments have been driven largely by past real estate performances. It shows that a simple buy-and-hold strategy or a contrarian strategy can easily beat the "Santa Claus" strategy. It also argues that the loan-to-value ratio analysis in bank underwriting process may have contributed to this "Santa Clause" behavior.

1.4   Analysis of Emerging Real Estate Market

Section 1.4 includes the following studies:

(i) Conditional Risk Premiums of Asian Real Estate Stocks (by Mei and Hu (2000)).
(ii) Institutional Factors and Real Estate Returns — A Cross Country Study (by Liao and Mei (1999)).
(iii) The Return Distributions of Property Shares in Emerging Markets.

1.4.1   *Conditional Risk Premiums of Asian Real Estate Stocks*

Overexposure to real estate risk has been one of the major causes of the 1997 Asian financial crisis. The financial turmoil in Asia began with the adverse risk exposure to real estate loans of Thailand banks. The fear that the economy of Thailand would collapse made the Thailand Baht plunge. This produced a domino effect in the neighboring countries, including Singapore, Malaysia, Indonesia, Hong Kong, Taiwan, and South Korea (Liao and Mei (1998)).

Before the crisis, real estate investment was considered low risk because it is a real asset. The study tries to investigate the risk attributes of real estate markets in the area. The multi-factor, latent-variable model is adopted and it allows the study to relate movements in required risk premiums to currency, interest rates and real estate market conditions. The study also examines the issue of contagion in the real estate markets of this area. More specifically, why do those real estate companies that develop properties in different markets and are traded on different stock exchanges tend to rise and collapse together?

The study finds that real estate investment is actually quite risky in Asia. Conditional risk premiums vary substantially over time. As a result, better financial planning is required, because market conditions and risk premiums may change significantly. The study also finds that conditional risk premiums of these markets are driven by a similar set of world market variables. This is why the conditional equity premiums tend to move together, contributing to the phenomenon of real estate market contagion in the area.

1.4.2   *Institutional Factors and Real Estate Returns — A Cross-Country Study*

Immobility of real property and complexity of real estate transaction are the two important characteristics of real estate investments. These two characteristics are closely related to institutional environment, such as legal systems, government efficiency, economic performance, and regulations. It makes sense to hypothesize that institutional factors may exert more influence on real estate markets than other markets. However, the existing literature focus little on the influences of institutional factors on real estate returns. This study examines how the institutional factors affect the asset returns of real property as well as various measures of risks. It also examines whether economic variables, such as GDP growth and country risk rating, impact property returns and risks.

In this chapter, Liao and Mei construct a cross-country analysis of 24 countries including both developed and emerging market ones. The proxy variables for institutional factors are each country's Rule of Law index, Economic Efficiency index, Coercion of Contract, Corruption index, Institutional Investor Country Credit Rating, Economic Freedom index, and the GDP growth rate. To do the cross-country analysis, all of the return series are converted into U.S. dollar returns. They construct two *ex post* cross-sectional regressions. In the first regression, they examine the relationship between various country-specific variables and property returns controlling return volatility. This regression helps us understand how institutional variables influence property returns. In the second regression, they examine how institutional variables impact property return volatility controlling GDP growth. Since there are high correlations among these institutional factor proxies, the study uses a principal component technique to reduce these variables to a few most representative ones.

The main results show that institutional factors do influence real estate returns, and these factors are probably not fully priced. The study finds that when controlling return volatility and level of economic growth, a higher property return is expected in countries where the economy is more efficient and has more economic freedom. Our results support the view that the combination of "lumpiness" of real estate investment and the volatile nature of international capital flows may expose property investors to extra investment risk, which needs to be compensated. Our results also indicate that an improvement in a country's economic efficiency and economic freedom may reduce property variance risk.

1.4.3   *The Return Distributions of Property Shares in Emerging Markets*

Previous studies have characterized emerging market equities as having higher returns, higher volatility, and higher predictability compared with developed markets returns. The 1997 Asian crisis has once again drawn attention to the return and risk features of emerging market properties. Increasingly, the conventional wisdom about emerging markets has been questioned because of the extremely bad performance of these markets in times of adversity. Do real estate investments in emerging markets still offer attractive returns to international investors? Do correlations across different markets increase in down markets so that the more desired diversification may not be present when they are needed the most? Are real estate securities markets predictable in emerging markets? The current study tries to answer these questions by examining the behavior of the property indices' returns in 10 emerging markets.

The study uses quarterly dollar-denominated returns on property indices for 10 emerging market countries: Argentina, China, Hong Kong, Indonesia, Malaysia, Peru, Philippines, Singapore, Thailand, and Turkey. As performance benchmarks, there are 10 broad market indices as well as the S&P500 and NAREIT index.

The study found that the emerging market property indices are more volatile than both the respective market indices and the U.S. equity indices. It also found a substantial negative risk premium for the East Asian property markets during the Asian crisis. The emerging market property indices also move against exchange rate, thus creating double-squeeze in negative periods. In terms of predictability, contrary to the traditional wisdom, the study did not find overwhelming evidence for autocorrelation in the majority of these indices. The study found certain diversification benefits to invest in the emerging market property indices, but it also found the unfavorable asymmetry in the correlation between property indices and the U.S. NAREIT index.

1.5 Summary

The introduction shows that it is fruitful to apply some techniques developed in finance to real estate investment issues. Despite the large proportion of real estate assets in world wealth, real estate is still a poorly researched area. In practice, many people still treat real estate investment in isolation instead of as an integrated part of portfolio management. The introduction shows that financial institutions can improve their risk management and portfolio performance by paying attention not only to local space supply and demand conditions but also to world capital market conditions. Understanding capital market risk can not only improve institutional investors' overall market timing but also improve their individual property appraisals. The researches included in this book are just a beginning. We hope more research will be conducted in this area so that real estate investment can become an integrated part of asset management.

References

Campbell, J. Y. and R. J. Shiller, 1988, The Dividend–Price Ratio and Expectations of Future Dividends and Discount Factors, *Review of Financial Studies* **1**, 195–228.

Campbell, J. Y., 1991, A Variance Decomposition of Stock Returns, *Economic Journal* **101**, 157–179.

Henriksson, R. and R. Merton, 1981, On Market Timing and Investment Performance. II. Statistical Procedures for Evaluating Forecasting Skills, *Journal of Business* **54**, 513–533.

Lehman, B. N., 1990, Fads, Martingales, and Market Efficiency, *The Quarterly Journal of Economics*, **105** (1), 1–28.

Liao, H.-H. and J. P. Mei, 1998, Risk Attributes of Real Estate Related Securities
— An Extension of Liu and Mei (1992), *Journal of Real Estate Research*
16(3), 279–290.

Liao, H.-H. and J. P. Mei, 1999, Institutional Factors and Real Estate Returns
— A Cross Country Study, *International Real Estate Review"* **2**(1), 21–34.

Liu, C., D. Hartzell, W. Greig and T. Grissom, 1990, The Integration of the Real
Estate Market and the Stock Market: Some Preliminary Evidence, *Journal
of Real Estate Finance and Economics* **3** (3), 261–282.

Liu, C. and J. P. Mei, 1992, The Predictability of Returns on Equity REITs and
Their Co-movement with Other Assets, *Journal of Real Estate Finance and
Economics* **5**, 401–418.

Liu, C. and J. P. Mei, 1994, An Analysis of Real Estate Risk Using the Present
Value Model, *Journal of Real Estate Finance and Economics* **8**, 5–20.

Mei, J. P. and C. Liu, 1994, Predictability of Real Estate Returns and Market
Timing, *Journal of Real Estate Finance and Economics* **8**, 115–135.
Lu, K. W. and J. P. Mei, The Return Distributions of Property Shares in
Emerging Markets.

Mei, J. P. and A. Lee, 1994, Is There a Real Estate Factor Premium? *Journal of
Real Estate Finance and Economics* **9**, 113–126.

Mei, J. P. and A. Saunders, 1994, The Time Variation of Risk for Life Insurance
Companies, *Journal of Risk and Insurance* **61**, 12–32.

Mei, J. P. and A. Saunders, 1995, Bank Risk and Real Estate: An Asset Pricing
Perspective, *Journal of Real Estate Finance and Economics* **10**, 199–224.

Mei, J. P. and B. Gao, Price Reversal, Transaction Costs, and Arbitrage Profits
in Real Estate Market, *Journal of Real Estate Finance & Economics* **11**,
153–165.

Mei, J. P. and D. Geltner, 1995, The Present Value Model with Time-Varying
Discount Rates: Implications for Commercial Property Valuation and Investment Decisions, *Journal of Real Estate Finance and Economics* **11** (2),
119–135.

Mei, J. P. and J. Hu, 2000, Conditional Risk Premiums of Asian Real Estate
Stocks, *Journal of Real Estate Finance and Economics* **21**(3), 297–313.

Sweeney, R. J. and A. D. Warga, 1986, The Pricing of Interest Rate Risk: Evidence from the Stock Market, *The Journal of Finance*, **41** (2), 393–411.

CHAPTER 2

The Predictability of Returns on Equity REITs and their Co-movement with Other Assets

CROCKER H. LIU and JIANPING J. P. MEI*

*Associate Professor of Finance,
New York University, Stern School of Business, Department of Finance,
900 Tisch Hall, New York, NY 10003*

Recent evidence suggests that the variation in the expected excess returns is predictable and arises from changes in business conditions. Using a multi-factor, latent-variable model with time-varying risk premiums, we decompose excess returns into expected and unexpected excess returns to examine what determines movements in expected excess asset returns and to what extent asset returns move together. We find that expected excess returns for Equity Real Estate Investment Trusts (EREITs) are more predictable than all other assets examined, owing in part to cap rates which contain useful information about the general risk condition in the economy. We also find that the conditional risk premiums (expected excess returns) on EREITs move very closely with those of small cap stocks and much less with those of bonds.

2.1 Introduction

Recent evidence suggests that the variation in the expected excess returns over time is predictable and is the result of changes in business

*Reprint requests should be sent to Jianping Mei, at Leonard N. Stern School of Business, NYU, Department of Finance, 900 Tisch Hall, New York, NY 10003, Phone (212) 998-4182.

conditions.[1] We offer further evidence on this issue by extending the previous literature to include real estate, particularly equity real estate investment trusts (EREITs).[2] What is unique about EREITs is that it is traded as a stock on the stock exchange but represents an underlying ownership in the portfolio of real estate. This feature raises the possibility that different variables may be required to capture the time variation in its risk premiums relative to those for bond and non-REIT stocks. Another issue related to the hybrid nature of EREITs is whether EREITs are a hybrid of stocks and bonds and whether the stock component is representative of large cap stocks or small cap stocks. More specifically, the questions which this paper addresses include:

(i) Do the same variables forecast stocks, bonds and real estate returns so that the expected returns (conditional risk premiums) on these assets move together? In particular, do cap rates carry information about the conditional risk premium for EREITs but no other asset class?

(ii) Is the variation in the expected returns on EREITs related to business conditions?

(iii) To what extent do REITs resemble stocks with large capitalizations, stocks with small capitalizations, and bonds?

While Mengden and Hartzell (1986), Giliberto (1990), and Corgel and Rogers (1991), among others, have studied the hybrid nature of REITs, none of these studies focuses on the predictability of EREIT returns. Prior REIT studies have also looked at returns on broad

---

[1]See for example, Campbell (1987), Campbell and Hamao (1991), Chen'et al. (1986), Fama and French (1988, 1989), Fama and Schwert (1977), and Keim and Stambaugh (1986). These papers find that the dividend yield on the stock market, the January effect, the return on Treasury bills, and the long-term yield spread are useful in predicting excess stock returns among other variables.

[2]An EREIT is a mutual fund for investors who wish to participate in the ownership of real estate. REIT is not taxed on distributed taxable income if it satisfies certain provisions, including the fact that at least 95% (90% prior to 1980) of net annual taxable income must be distributed to shareholders.

asset market classes such as stocks and bonds to explain REIT fluctuations, rather than looking at business conditions that influence
expected returns on all asset classes.[3] Besides, these studies have
not examined small cap stocks as a hybrid component of REITs,
even though REITs have low capitalizations relative to the overall
stock market. The typical two-stage procedure used in the past to
examine the hybrid nature of REIT involved imputing a real estate
index by using the residuals from a regression of the returns on an
EREIT portfolio on a stock market proxy. EREITs were then regressed against a stock market portfolio and this real estate market
portfolio. If the beta was positive on the stock market proxy, and
zero for the real estate proxy, then the conclusion was that REITs
resemble stocks. However, several problems temper the findings of
these studies. These problems include the implicit assumption that
the returns of the "true" market indices are observable and the fact
that errors-in-variables arise as the result of the two-pass estimation
procedure. Moreover, purging the REIT portfolio of its correlation
with the broader market eliminates important real estate-related information if the arguments of Geltner (1989) and Gyourko and Keim
(1991), that common factors are likely to drive returns on both real
estate and non-real estate related assets, are valid.

Our study uses a multi-factor, latent-variable model that allows
us to study the time variation of expected excess returns on different asset classes and to address the issue of the resemblance of asset
returns by comparing the similarities among assets by their return
variation patterns. This methodology has several distinct advantages
over previous studies. First, it allows for time-varying risk premiums
in contrast to the existing methodology which generally assumes constant risk premiums. Thus it is designed to capture the time variation

---

[3]One exception to this is the study by Chan *et al.* (1990), who examine EREITs
using an APT framework. However, it does not specifically focus on the predictability of EREIT returns. Besides, it assumes that the risk premiums are
constant over time, whereas the current study allows the risk premiums to vary
over time. The current study also tests whether there are any priced factors that
are unobservable/latent, using the technique in Campbell and Hamao (1991).

not only in *unexpected* excess returns but also in *expected* excess returns. Second, it makes no assumptions about the observability of systematic factors in the economy. Third, no other distributional assumptions on the error terms is required except those associated with Hansen's (1982) Generalized Method of Moments (GMM). The estimation procedure adjusts for heteroskedasticity in the error terms and permits contemporaneous correlation among the error terms across securities to exist. The GMM procedure also could adjust for a moderate amount of serial correlation in the returns, which mitigates against the possibility that the predictability of asset returns is partly induced by serial correlation as a result of non-synchronous trading.

The most interesting finding of our study is that expected excess returns for EREITs are more predictable than large cap stocks, small cap stocks, and bonds. Returns on small cap stocks also exhibit a high degree of predictability. This increased predictability for EREITs and small cap stocks is due in part to movements in the cap rate, a real estate business condition variable not used in studies till now. Besides, we find that movements in the cap rate provide information different from that contained in dividend yield fluctuations with respect to EREITs, even though this is not necessarily so with the other asset classes that we examined. We also find that EREITs resemble small cap stocks and to a lesser extent large cap stocks, but have less in common with bonds. This implies that EREITs do not resemble bonds, and therefore bonds are not part of the hybrid nature of EREITs. Our study also finds that either a single factor or a two-factor, latent-variable model is representative of the data, depending on the level of significance used.

The rest of the paper is organized as follows. Section 2.2 describes the asset pricing framework while a description of the estimation procedure is contained in Sec. 2.3. Section 2.4 describes the data set used. The existence of predictable excess EREIT returns is documented in Sec. 2.5, together with the extent to which EREITs are a hybrid of large cap stocks, small cap stocks, and bonds. We also discuss the results of our latent-variable model that restricts the expected excess returns on value-weighted stocks, small cap stocks, EREITs, and bonds to move together. Section 2.6 concludes the study.

2.2 The Asset Pricing Framework

The asset pricing framework used in this study assumes that capital markets are perfectly competitive and frictionless, with investors believing that asset returns are generated by the following K-factor model:

$$\tilde{r}_{i,t+1} = E_t[\tilde{r}_{i,t+1}] + \sum_{k=1}^{K} \beta_{ik}\tilde{f}_{k,t+1} + \tilde{\varepsilon}_{i,t+1}. \qquad (2.1)$$

Here $\tilde{r}_{i,t+1}$ is the excess return on asset i held from time t to time $t+1$, and represents the difference between return on asset i and the risk-free rate of interest. $E_t[\tilde{r}_{i,t+1}]$ is the expected excess return on asset i, conditional on information known to market participants at the end of time period t. We assume that $E_t[\tilde{f}_{k,t+1}] = 0$ and that $E_t[\tilde{\varepsilon}_{i,t+1}] = 0$. The conditional expected excess return is allowed to vary through time in the current model, but the beta coefficients are assumed to be constant through time.

This ability of $E_t[\tilde{r}_{i,t+1}]$ to vary through time is absent in prior REIT studies.[4] However, if $E_t[\tilde{r}_{i,t+1}]$ is not restricted to be constant, then we need to look not only at the closeness of beta(s) but also at the co-movement of $E_t[\tilde{r}_{i,t+1}]$ through time in analyzing the co-movement of excess returns on two or more assets. In other words, it is possible for the risk premiums and excess returns of two assets to not move together, even though they have similar betas. However, this problem will not occur if the following linear pricing relation-

---

[4]Prior studies have concentrated on the second and third components on the right-hand side of Eq. (2.1) assuming that $E_t[\tilde{r}_{i,t+1}]$ is constant. These focus on the closeness of EREITs to stocks in terms of beta (β), that is, in terms of similar sensitivity towards the systematic forces. The idiosyncratic term is generally ignored here because the risk can be diversified and should not affect risk premiums.

ship holds:

$$E_t[\tilde{r}_{i,t+1}] = \sum_{k=1}^{K} \beta_{ik}\lambda_{kt}, \qquad (2.2)$$

where λ_{kt} is the "market price of risk" for the kth factor at time t.[5]

Now suppose that the information set at time t consists of a vector of L forecasting variables X_{nt}, $n = 1, \ldots, L$: (where X_{1t} is a constant), and that conditional expectations are a linear function of these variables. Then we can write λ_{kt} as

$$\lambda_{kt} = \sum_{n=1}^{L} \theta_{kn}X_{nt}, \qquad (2.3)$$

and therefore Eq. (2.2) becomes

$$E_t[\tilde{r}_{i,t+1}] = \sum_{k=1}^{K} \beta_{ik} \sum_{n=1}^{L} \theta_{kn}X_{nt} = \sum_{n=1}^{L} \alpha_{in}X_{nt}. \qquad (2.4)$$

Equations (2.1) and (2.4) combined are sometimes called a multi-factor, "latent-variable" model.[6] The model implies that expected excess returns are time varying and can be predicted by the forecasting variables in the information set. From Eqs. (2.3) and (2.4), we can see that the model puts some restrictions on the coefficients of Eq. (2.4), which is that

$$\alpha_{ij} = \sum_{k=1}^{K} \beta_{ik}\theta_{kj}. \qquad (2.5)$$

Here, β_{ik} and θ_{kj} are free parameters. Normally, the (α_{ij}) matrix should have a rank of P, where P is defined as $P = \min(N, L)$. Equation (2.5) restricts the rank of the (α_{ij}) matrix to be K, where

---

[5]Equation (2.2) states that the conditional expected rate of return should be a linear function of factor risk premiums, with the coefficients equal to the betas of each asset. This type of linear pricing relationship can be generated by a number of intertemporal asset pricing models, under either a no-arbitrage opportunity condition or through a general equilibrium framework. See for example, Ross (1976), Campbell (1990), Connor and Korajczyk (1988).

[6]For more details on this model, see Hansen and Hodrick (1983), Gibbons and Ferson (1985), Campbell (1987), and Ferson and Harvey (1990).

K is smaller than P. To test the restriction in Eq. (2.5), we first renormalized the model by setting the factor loadings of the first K assets as follows: $\beta_{ij} = 1$ (if $j = i$) and $\beta_{ij} = 0$ (if $j \neq i$) for $1 \leq i \leq K$. Next, we partition the excess return matrix $R = (R_1, R_2)$, where R_1 is a $T \times K$ matrix of excess returns of the first K assets and R_2 is a $T \times (N - K)$ matrix of excess returns on the rest of the assets. Using Eqs. (2.4) and (2.5), we can derive the following regression system:

$$
\begin{aligned}
R_1 &= X\Theta + \mu_{1,2}, \\
R_2 &= X\alpha + \mu_2
\end{aligned}
\tag{2.6}
$$

where X is a $T \times L$ matrix of the forecasting variables, Θ is a matrix of θ_{ij}, and α is a matrix of α_{ij}. If the linear pricing relationship in Eq. (2.2) holds, the rank restriction implies that the data should not be able to reject the null hypothesis $H_0 : \alpha = \Theta B$, where B is a matrix of β_{ij} elements. The objectives of the paper are to use the regression system in Eq. (2.6) in order to see to what extent the forecasting variables, X, predict excess returns and to test the rank restriction. If the rank restriction is not rejected by the data, then we can use the beta estimates to address the asset resemblance issue.

2.3 The Estimation Procedure

The regression system of Eq. (2.6), given the restriction in Eq. (2.5), can be estimated and tested using Hansen's (1982) GMM, which allows for conditional heteroskedasticity and serial correlation in the error terms of excess returns. A more detailed discussion of this estimation procedure is provided in the Appendix.

In our empirical work we use forecasting variables X_{nt} which are known to the market at time t. They include a constant term, a January dummy, the yield on 1-month Treasury bill, the spread between the yields on long-term AAA corporate bonds and the 1-month Treasury bill, the dividend yields on the equally weighted market portfolio, and the cap rate on real estate. The yield variable describes the short-term interest rate. The spread variable tells us the slope of the term structure of interest rates, and the dividend yield variable captures information on expectations about future cash flows and required returns in the stock market. These three variables have been used by Campbell (1987), Campbell and Hamao (1991), Fama and French (1988, 1989), Ferson (1989), Ferson and Harvey (1989), Keim and Stambaugh (1986), among others.[7] In addition, we also include the cap rate which captures information on expected future cash flows and required returns in the underlying real estate market.[8]

In general, we do not wish to assume that we have included all the relevant variables that carry information about factor premiums. Fortunately, the methods described above are robust to omitted information.[9] It is also worth mentioning that this methodology has several distinct advantages. First, the model allows for time-varying risk premiums.[10] Second, we need no other distributional assump-

---

[7]Fama and French (1989) also use the spread between yields of a low-grade, long-term corporate bond and a long-term treasury bond to capture the default risk in the financial market. But they find the variable to be capturing the same information as the dividend yield. Thus we include only dividend yield in the study.

[8]Nourse (1987) uses the cap rate in testing the impact of income tax changes on income property. He uses the Ellwood representation of the cap rate in which the cap rate represents a weighted average cost of capital with an adjustment for equity buildup and an adjustment for anticipated increases or decreases in value.

[9]By taking conditional expectations of Eq. (2.2), it is straightforward to show that the rank restrictions hold in the same form when a subset of the relevant information is used. Thus, if the coefficients in Eq. (2.4) are subject to the restrictions in Eq. (2.5) under the true information vector used by the market, they will be subject to the same form of restrictions in Eq. (2.5) if a subset of this vector is included in the information set. Similarly, if the test using the full set of the market information does not reject the K-factor model, then the test using a subset of the market information should not reject the model either. An elaboration of this robustness issue is given in Campbell (1987) and Ferson (1989).

[10]This is a significant improvement over the existing methodology which generally assumes constant risk premiums. This assumption is in contrast to a large body of evidence on time-varying risk premiums, which has been documented extensively by Campbell (1987), Fama (1990), Fama and French (1989), Ferson *et al.* (1987), Kandel and Stambaugh (1990), among others. It is certainly possible that the poor performance of the multi-factor model discovered by previous studies may due to the imposition of this restrictive assumption.

tions on the error terms except those made at the beginning of this section. Besides, the estimation procedure adjusts for heteroskedasticity in the error terms, and also allows for contemporaneous correlation among the error terms across securities. The procedure also tolerates a moderate amount of serial correlation in returns which mitigates against serial correlation, accounting for a portion of the predictability in asset returns.

2.4 Data

Stock prices, dividends, and returns on long-term U.S. government bonds are taken from the monthly stock tape of the Center for Research on Security Prices (CRSP). We study a value-weighted stock index consisting of all New York Stock Exchange (NYSE) and American Stock Exchange (AMEX) stocks. This value-weighted stock index is biased towards stocks with large market capitalizations. To adjust for this bias, we also include a small cap stock index in our study. Both the value-weighted stock index and the small cap stock index are obtained from the Ibbotson and Associates *Stocks, Bonds, Bills, and Inflation* series on CRSP. The government bond return series is from the data source, which is formed by a portfolio of treasury bonds with an average maturity of 20 years and without call provisions or special tax benefits. Finally, we construct equally weighted EREIT return series using all EREITs on the CRSP from January 1971 to December 1989. All EREITs are included, not just those having a continuous price history over the period in question, in order to avoid the problem of survivorship bias. The use of an EREIT portfolio (in addition to the GMM procedure) minimizes the problem of non-synchronous trading, since any autocorrelation associated with individual REIT returns is minimized. The EREIT portfolio consists of 50 EREITs on an average. Non-synchronous trading can be a problem because it increases the predictability of asset returns when it is present. An REIT is deemed to be an EREIT if it is listed as such on at least two of the following three sources:

(i) *REIT Sourcebook* published by the National Association of Real Estate Investment Trusts, Inc.,

(ii) *The Realty Stock Review* published by Audit Investments,
(iii) Moody's *Bank and Finance Manual, Volume 2.*

The yield on the 1-month Treasury bill, the spread between the yields on long-term AAA corporate bonds and the 1-month Treasury bill, and the dividend yields on the equally weighted market portfolio are obtained from Federal Reserve Bulletin and Ibbotson and Associates (1989). Monthly cap rates on real estate are taken from the American Council of Life Insurance publication *Investment Bulletin: Mortgage Commitments on Multifamily and Nonresidential Properties Reported by 20 Life Insurance Companies.*[11] The cap rate is defined as the ratio of net stabilized earnings to the transaction price (or market value) of a property. Net stabilized means that the income figure used in the numerator of the ratio assumes that full lease-up of the building has occurred such that the building's vacancy is equal to or less than the vacancy of the market. Alternatively, the cap rate can be thought of as the earnings-price ratio on direct real estate investment. We include the cap rate as a forecasting variable, since we hypothesize that movements in the cap rate do not necessarily contain the same information as fluctuations in the dividend yield on the stock market. Although both the cap rate and dividend yield are measures of income-to-value ratio, the cash flows of buildings are not identical to the cash flows of firms that occupy space in the buildings. The cash flows of tenants are likely to be more variable than the cash flows for the buildings they occupy since rents are a fixed cost to tenants in the short run, given the long-term nature of most leases.[12]

---

[11]Unfortunately, the ACLI does not break down monthly cap rates by the type of real estate. This is done only with respect to quarterly cap rates. The ACLI data used in the current study differs from that of Nourse (1987) in that Nourse uses quarterly cap rates as opposed to the monthly cap rates used in the current study. Critics of quarterly cap rate studies point out that one does not know which of the three months comprising a quarter that the quarterly cap rates are reflecting. This is not a problem with monthly cap rates.

[12]We thank an anonymous reviewer for his valuable insight on this point.

Table 1. Summary statistics.

	Mean	S.D.	ρ_1
Dependent variables			
Excess return on value-weighted portfolio (VW)	0.268	4.866	0.055
Excess return on REITs portfolio (REITs)	0.729	4.964	0.112
Excess return on government bond portfolio (Bond)	0.022	3.327	0.058
Excess return on small stock portfolio (SS)	0.628	6.695	0.113
Forecasting variables			
Yield on 1-month T-bill (TB)	7.537	2.775	0.913
Yield spread between AAA bond and T-bill (Spread)	2.336	1.851	0.750
Dividend yield on equal-weighted portfolio (DivYld)	3.105	0.605	0.932
Capitalization rate on EREITs (CapR)	10.46	1.166	0.957

	EW	REITs	Bond	SS
Correlations among dependent variables				
EW	1.000	0.655	0.322	0.849
REITs		1.000	0.179	0.802
Bond			1.000	0.181
SS				1.000

	TB	Spread	DivYld	CapR
Correlations among independent variables				
TB	1.000	−0.558	0.473	0.704
Spread		1.000	−0.393	−0.317
DivYld			1.000	0.546
CapRate				1.000

Notes: The sample period for this table is January 1972–April 1989, with 208 observations. Units on excess returns are percentage per month. Units on 1-month T-bill rate, yield spread, and dividend yield are percentage per annum. ρ_1 is the first autocorrelation of the series.

2.5 Empirical Results

Table 1 provides summary statistics on the behavior of the excess return for each of our four asset classes as well as on our forecasting variables. For each variable, we report the mean, standard deviation, and the first-order autocorrelation. An inspection of Table 1 reveals that EREITs have a much higher excess return relative to all other stocks and government bonds. More specifically, the mean excess returns on EREITs are 10 basis points higher than small cap stocks and

46 basis points higher than large cap stocks per month. Moreover, more than 70 basis points separate returns on EREITs from returns on government bonds. Not only is the mean excess return on ERE-ITs higher on an average, but the standard deviation is also lower than all other assets examined except for government bonds. In other words, EREITs have a higher mean excess return on an average but smaller total risks (as measured by standard deviation) relative to all other assets, which is consistent with prior research. In addition, the returns on all assets exhibit positive first-order autocorrelation. This is also consistent with prior studies, which show that the excess return on stock indices display short-run positive autocorrelation.

Table 1 also reports the correlations of returns among four asset classes. As expected, the excess returns on EREITs are highly correlated with small cap stocks since EREITs have relatively low market capitalizations, even though EREITs appear to be superior to small cap stocks from a risk-return standpoint. EREITs are also correlated to a lesser extent with value-weighted stocks, but have a low correlation with bonds. Although it is tempting here to conclude from the correlation matrix that EREITs are much closer to stocks than to bonds, a closer look at the return generating process reveals that the correlation between two types of assets in the economy can come from two sources: the co-movement of expected returns and the co-movement of unexpected returns. In general, it is possible for two assets to have high correlations but with neither their expected excess returns nor their unexpected excess returns moving together. Only under the null hypothesis, where the expected returns are restricted by Eq. (2.2), do high correlations imply that the two parts move together across the two assets.

Table 2 reports the results of regressing excess assets returns on five forecasting variables and a constant term — a January dummy, returns on Treasury bills, the spread, the dividend yield on the equally weighted market portfolio, and the cap rate. The first four variables have been used in previous studies for forecasting U.S. stock returns with regression system (2.6) employed without the rank restriction. The most interesting finding in this table is that a larger component of the excess return on EREITs is predictable relative to all other assets. In particular, approximately 17.5% of

Table 2.   Regression of the returns on each asset class at time $t+1$ on a January dummy, the yield on T-bills, the spread between the yield on AAA corporate bonds and the yield on T-bills, the dividend yield for the overall stock market, and the cap rate on real estate all at time t. Regression coefficients are given by the first line of each row, while the t-statistics are given in parenthesis in the second row. The incremental contribution of each independent variable to the explained variance of the returns for each asset class is reported in the third row.

Model: $\text{Asset}_{i,t+1} = \text{Constant} + \beta_1 \text{Jandum} + \beta_2 \text{TB}_t + \beta_3 \text{Spread}_t + \beta_4 \text{Mkt. DivYld}_t + \beta_5 \text{CapR}_t + \tilde{\varepsilon}_i$

Asset class	Constant	Jandum	TB	Spread	DivYld	CapR	DW	$\bar{R}^2$	$\bar{R}^2$(DivYld)	$\bar{R}^2$(CapR)	F-Test
VW stocks	-7.346	1.841	-0.583	0.021	1.429	0.703	1.86	0.087	0.075	0.067	0.619
	(-2.10)	(1.57)	(-3.02)	(0.10)	(2.12)	(1.64)					(0.43)
		0.130	1.272	0.001	0.363	0.003					
Equity REITs	-9.451	5.277	-0.633	-0.094	0.962	1.121	1.79	0.175	0.146	0.166	8.500*
	(-2.79)	(4.63)	(-3.38)	(-0.44)	(1.47)	(2.69)					(0.00)
		0.512	0.718	0.007	0.079	0.397					
Government bonds	-1.932	-0.668	0.121	0.404	1.447	-0.414	1.89	0.066	0.056	0.021	0.030
	(-0.80)	(-0.82)	(0.90)	(2.63)	(3.11)	(-1.39)					(0.86)
		0.049	0.155	0.770	1.056	0.321					
Small stocks	-13.237	5.398	-0.885	-0.097	2.659	1.150	1.76	0.165	0.148	0.128	1.550
	(-2.88)	(3.49)	(-3.49)	(-0.33)	(3.00)	(2.03)					(0.22)
		0.312	0.818	0.004	0.351	0.244					

Notes:

(1) The summation of the incremental variance terms might exceed one due to the omission of the covariance terms. The incremental contribution of each independent variable to the explained variance of the returns for each asset class is computed using the following equation:

$$\text{Incremental contribution to explained variance(\%)} = \sum_{i=1}^{5} \frac{a_i^2 \sigma_i^2}{(\sigma_y^2 - \sigma_\varepsilon^2)}.$$

where the a_i's are from the regression: $y = a + a_1 x_1 + a_2 x_2 + \cdots + a_5 x_5 + \varepsilon$.

(2) DW is the Durbin–Watson statistic.

(3) $\bar{R}^2$(Div Yld) is the $\bar{R}^2$ obtained from estimating the model *excluding* the CapR variable but *including* the Div Yld.

(4) $\bar{R}^2$(CapR) is the $\bar{R}^2$ obtained from estimating the model *excluding* the Div Yld variable but *including* the CapR.

(5) F-Test: The F-test tests whether the coefficient of the CapR and the coefficient of the Div Yld are the same, e.g. tests if these two variables convey the same (identical) information.

the variation in monthly excess returns on EREITs is accounted for by our five forecasting variables. Returns on small cap stocks also exhibit a large predictability component (16.5%), whereas the returns on value-weighted stocks and government bonds are roughly 50% less predictable than those on EREITs or small cap stocks. The predictability of stocks and bonds found here is consistent with previous studies by Campbell and Hamao (1991) and Harvey (1989), among others. What is interesting is the high predictability of excess returns on EREITs and the similarity of EREITs to small cap stocks.

What accounts for this high predictability of EREITs and small cap stocks? Part of the answer lies in the fact that the cap rate variable is highly significant for EREITs and small cap stocks but is not significant for value-weighted stocks and bonds. In other words, conditions in the real estate market not only influence the returns of EREITs but also affect the returns of small cap stocks. Surprisingly, the dividend yield is not significant for EREITs even though it is significant, as expected, for all other assets. This lack of forecasting power of the dividend yield on the stock market with respect to REITs might be related to the requirement that REITs pay out almost all of their available cash flow. A positive sign exists for EREITs and small stocks on both the dividend yield and cap rate, which is consistent with *ex-ante* expectations given the assumption that the cap rate should behave in a manner similar to the dividend yield. Prior studies suggest that the major movement in the dividend yield series is related to long-term business conditions and captures the same predictable component of return as the default spread. When business conditions are weak and futures uncertain, the dividend yield forecasts high future expected returns, whereas low returns are predicted when conditions are strong. And this high future expected returns represent the compensation for holding risky assets during times of high uncertainty and economic recession. At the outset, one might suspect that this finding might be due to the correlation between the dividend yield and the cap rate. However, the relatively moderate correlation between the DivYld and the CapR state variables of $0.545(r^2 = 0.297)$ implies that the dividend yield and the cap rate series do not track similar predictable components of returns. Moreover, both the dividend yield and the cap rate are significant for small stocks, whereas only the latter forecasting variable is highly significant for EREITs.

Given the moderate correlation between the cap rate and dividend yield variables in Table 1 of 0.546, we also performed several auxiliary regressions in which we excluded the cap rate (dividend yield) but included the dividend yield (cap rate) variable to determine whether the dividend yield variable picks up all of the cap rate information for EREITs. In addition, we also performed an F-test to see if the coefficient associated with the cap rate and the coefficient corresponding to the dividend yield are identical. If they are different, then these variables contain different information. The results from the the auxiliary regressions and F-tests are reported in the last three columns of Table 2. The $\bar{R}^2$ columns reveal that movements in the cap rate contain unique information for the movements of EREITs and, to a lesser extent, movements in small cap stocks. More specifically, we can observe that the $\bar{R}^2$ decreases from 0.175 to 0.146 when the cap rate is excluded from the EREIT estimation equation, but only a minimal decrease in R^2 is evident when the dividend yield variable is omitted from the model. In contrast, fluctuations in the dividend yield are more informative in accounting for movements in the returns on bonds and stocks, especially small cap stocks. When the model is estimated without dividend yields, the amount of variation accounted for by the model drops anywhere from 0.02 to 0.045 for stocks and bonds. Moreover, the results of the F-test show that we cannot reject the hypothesis that the coefficients associated with the cap rate and dividend yield variables are the same for large cap stocks, bonds, and small cap stocks. However, we can reject this proposition for EREITs. In other words, fluctuations in the cap rate do incorporate uniquely real estate-related information at least with respect to EREITs but not necessarily for other asset classes.

To facilitate a better understanding of dividend yields and the cap rate, we also plot the two series in Fig. 4. It is easy to see that the dividend yield displays a stronger high frequency variation than cap rate, whereas the latter exhibits a lower frequency variation. Thus the two variables contain different information on the state of the economy and play different roles in predicting asset returns.

The spread variable, which tracks in part a maturity premium in expected returns, is highly significant for bonds but not significant for other assets including EREITs. This observation, together with the result that DivYld is the only other variable significant for bonds, suggests that the forecasting variables responsible for the predictable component of bond returns do not predict EREIT returns. This suggests that EREITs do not resemble bonds and that bonds therefore are not part of the hybrid nature of EREITs.

As expected, the T-bill variable is significant for all stock categories but not for bonds, which is consistent with the studies of Fama and Schwert (1977) and Campbell (1987). The nature of this relationship is negative, suggesting that stocks inclusive of EREITs exhibit "perverse" inflation behavior. This finding supports the results of Chan *et al.* (1990). The addition of a dummy variable to capture the January seasonality impact has an important positive effect on EREITs and small cap stocks, but this January effect is not evident for value-weighted stocks or bonds. More specifically, the January effect accounts for 5% of the excess returns per year in EREITs and small cap stocks, after taking into account the time variation in business conditions captured by the T-bill, term spread, the dividend yield; and the cap rate. This finding of a January effect is consistent with the finding of Colwell and Park (1990) and suggests that this seasonality effect cannot be explained by variations in business condition variables.

A complementary perspective on why EREITs are similar to small cap stocks is obtained from marginal effects calculations, which are reported in the third row for each asset class in Table 2. The analysis of the incremental contribution of each forecasting variable to the explained variance of the returns for each asset class reveals that the January effect, the T-bill, and the cap rate are among the most important variables for both EREITs and small cap stocks in terms of accounting for the variation in returns for these asset classes. For both EREITs and small cap stocks, fluctuations in the T-bill is the factor that is most influential on the respective movements in returns. The January effect is the next most important catalyst for EREITs, while it is the third most influential component for small cap stocks. The cap rate is the third element of relative importance for EREITs, accounting for almost 40% of the explained variation in EREIT returns. Approximately 24% of the fluctuation in small cap returns also arises from variations in the cap rate. Although deviations in the dividend yield represent the second most influential characteristic of small cap stocks, it is of relatively little importance in accounting for changes in EREIT returns. The marginal contribution analysis also reveals that while variations in the T-bill and dividend yield are also important for large cap stocks as well as small cap stocks, neither the January effect nor the cap rate acts as a catalyst for swings in large cap stocks. For bonds, the dividend yield is the most important factor, followed by the spread variable, in accounting for movements in bond returns.

In short, the evidence in Table 2 suggests that EREITs are hybrid assets similar in nature to small cap stocks. Although EREITs resemble small cap stocks, different factors are responsible for the predictable component of excess EREIT returns since dividend yields are not useful as a forecasting variable. Besides, the cap rate appears to have more of an influence on EREIT returns relative to the returns on small cap stocks. These differences result in EREITs having a larger predictable component of excess returns relative to other assets.

A visual impression of the results in Table 2 is given in Figs. 1 and 2. Figure 1 plots the actual excess returns on EREITs ($\tilde{r}_{i,t+1}$) and the conditional expected excess return [$E_t(\tilde{r}_{i,t+1})$] using a dotted line and a solid line, respectively. Figure 1 shows that the expected excess return, assumed to be constant in prior studies, does vary over time. In fact, the sign of $E_t(\tilde{r}_{i,t+1})$ changes over time, taking on negative values in some time periods and positive values in other periods. Besides, although the volatility of the actual EREIT returns is greater in the 1970s relative to the 1980s, which is consistent with prior studies, the variation in the conditional risk premium does not appear to be changing over time. This implies that, for the latter time period, a large proportion of EREIT returns is predictable with the R^2 in Table 2, revealing that the predictable portion of return, $E_t(\tilde{r}_{i,t+1})$, accounts for 17.5% of the variation in $\tilde{r}_{i,t+1}$ over the entire study period.

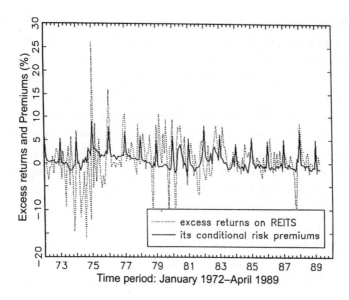

Fig. 1.   Excess returns on REITs and conditional risk premiums.

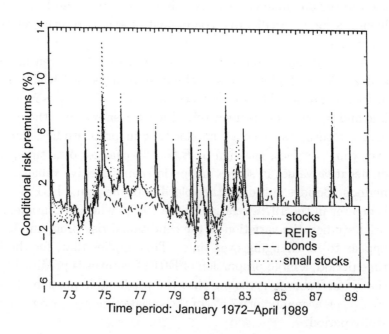

Fig. 2.   Conditional risk premiums on different assets.

Figure 2 shows the co-movement of the expected excess return, $E_t(\tilde{r}_{i,t+1})$, for value-weighted stocks, EREITs, government bonds, and small cap stocks. An inspection of this figure reveals that the conditional risk premiums for value-weighted stocks, EREITs, and small cap stocks appear to move in tandem. The strength of this co-movement is not as pronounced for bonds. Figure 2 also shows that the monthly predictable risk premiums on the EREIT can be as high as 12%. In terms of volatility in the expected excess returns, the biggest volatility in $E_t(\tilde{r}_{i,t+1})$ is associated with small cap stocks followed by EREITs, value-weighted stocks, and government bonds, respectively. The predictability in expected excess return which we document does not necessarily imply that the market is inefficient but rather that it reflects rational pricing in an efficient market under different business conditions. However, the huge variation in expected excess returns or the risk premiums is still astonishing given the seemingly stable risk tolerance of market participants and the stable payoff structure for portfolio fund managers.

A question that naturally arises from examining the excess returns on various assets relative to the five forecasting variables is the extent to which our model is well specified. Evidence appears to support the notion that our model is well specified, since the residual (ε_i) that remains after the time-varying risk premiums are accounted for has a small, if not a negligible, serial correlation.

In Table 3 we report our estimates of the restricted version of the model (Eq. (2.6)) shown in Table 2. The estimation method used is the GMM procedure of Hansen, which adjusts not only for heteroskedasticity but also for serial correlation in the error terms and allows for contemporaneous correlation among the error terms across securities. In Panel A we estimate the regression system under the assumption that there is only one "priced" systematic factor, $\tilde{f}_{1,t+1}$, in the economy ($K = 1$). With beta normalized to be 1 for value-weighted stocks, we observe that the beta for EREITs are higher than these value-weighted stocks but are smaller than small cap stocks. Not surprisingly, bonds have the lowest beta of all asset classes. The chi-square test in Table 3 indicates that a one-factor model is not rejected by the data at a 5% significance level. Figure 3 gives an alternative visual presentation of the results reported in panel A of

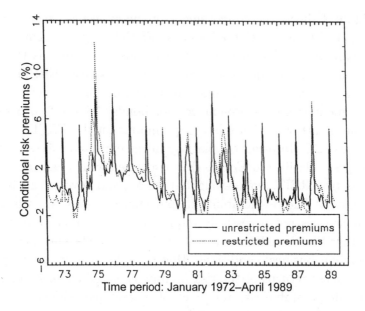

Fig. 3.   Restricted and unrestricted conditional risk premiums.

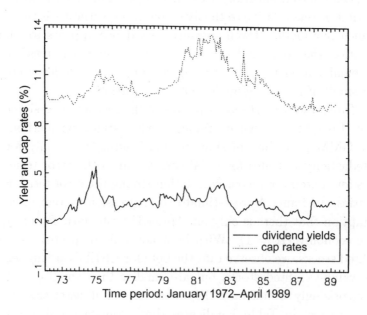

Fig. 4.   Dividend yield and cap rates.

Table 3. The figure plots the unrestricted and restricted fitted values of $E_t(\tilde{r}_{i,t+1})$ for EREITs using a solid line and a dotted line, respectively. Figure 3 shows that the expected excess returns estimated under the rank restriction closely resemble those estimated without the restriction. The figure also shows that the "single-factor", latent-variable model provides a fairly good fit of the data and results in

Table 3.   Estimation of the latent variable model (2.4) with the rank restriction of Eq. (2.5) imposed.

$$E_t[\tilde{r}_{i,t+1}] = \sum_{k=1}^{K} \beta_{ik} \sum_{n=1}^{L} \theta_{kn} X_{nt} = \sum_{n=1}^{L} \alpha_{in} X_{nt} \qquad (2.4)$$

$$\alpha_{ij} = \sum_{k=1}^{K} \beta_{ik} \theta_{kj} . \qquad (2.5)$$

	β_{i1}	S. D.		
(A) *The number of systematic factors in the economy equals 1 ($K = 1$).*				
Estimated beta coefficient for the following assets:				
Excess return on value-weighted portfolio (VW)	1.000*	–		
Excess return on REITs portfolio (REITs)	1.377	0.243		
Excess return on government bond portfolio (Bond)	0.253	0.109		
Excess return on small stock portfolio (SS)	1.783	0.198		

χ^2-statistic of the rank restriction (2.5): 24.2578 (D.F. = 15)
Significance level: $P = 0.061$

	β_{i1}	S. D.	β_{i1}	S. D.
(B) *The number of systematic factors in the economy equals 2 ($K = 2$).*				
Estimated beta coefficient for the following assets:				
Excess return on value-weighted portfolio (VW)	1.000*	–	0.000*	–
Excess return on government bond portfolio (Bond)	0.000*	–	1.000*	–
Excess return on REITS portfolio (REITS)	1.636	0.333	−0.991	0.516
Excess return on small stock portfolio (SS)	1.934	0.269	−0.317	0.518

χ^2-statistic of the rank restriction (2.5): 7.778 (D.F. = 8)
Significance level: $P = 0.455$

Notes: * indicate that these numbers are normalized to be one or zero. The sample period for this table is January 1972–April 1989, with 208 observations. The standard errors reported here have been corrected for heteroskedasticity using the GMM of Hansen (1982).

an impressive degree of movement in expected excess returns.

But the "single-factor" model is rejected if one uses a 10% significance level ($P = 0.061$). Thus we also estimate a "two-factor" model, the results of which are reported in panel B of Table 3. We normalize the value-weighted stock to have a beta of one on the first factor and a beta of zero on the second factor, and we normalize bonds to be the reverse. Under such normalization, we see that small cap stocks are more sensitive than EREITs to pervasive forces that affect value-weighted stocks, whereas EREITs appear to be a better hedge instrument than small stocks against systematic shocks that affect bond excess returns. From this perspective, it is striking that EREITs are actually less similar to bonds than are small cap stocks. The rank restriction test suggests that the "two-factor" model is not rejected by data.

2.6   Summary and Conclusions

In this study we analyze the predictability of expected returns on EREITs, using a multi-factor model with time-varying risk premiums that decompose excess asset returns into two parts: expected excess returns and unexpected excess returns. In this process, the hybrid nature of EREITs is examined. Our main finding is that the expected excess returns are more predictable for equity REITs than for small cap stocks, value-weighted stocks, and bonds. Moreover, the graphical evidence indicates that the risk premiums vary substantially over time and suggests that in certain time periods it might pay to take risks. In other words, market timing might prove to be a fruitful endeavor. Whereas prior studies have found that EREIT returns resemble large cap stocks, we find that returns on EREITs move more closely with small cap stocks. Interestingly, we also find that real estate market conditions influence small cap stocks in addition to EREITs. We also find evidence that EREIT returns do not resemble bond returns, even though the cash flow portion of EREITs resembles interest payments on bonds. Moreover, to some extent, EREITs are actually less similar to bonds than are small cap stocks. Another finding is that these results are consistent with the view that the changing price of risk of a single systematic factor affecting returns on all assets is an important determinant of expected asset returns.

Acknowledgements

We thank John Campbell for letting us use his latent-variable model algorithm, and Doug Herold and Wayne Ferson for providing us data on real estate cap rates and business condition variables, respectively. We also thank William M. Gentry for his helpful comments.

Appendix: Elaboration of the Estimation Procedure

Following Hansen, we first construct a $N \times L$ sample mean matrix: $G_T = U'X/T$ where $E(U'X) = 0$ because the error term in system (2.6) has conditional mean zero given the instruments X from Eq. (2.4). Next, we stack the column vector on top of each other to obtain a $NL \times 1$ vector of g_T. A two-step algorithm is then used to find an optimal solution for the quadratic form, $g_T'W^{-1}g_T$, by minimizing over the parameter space of (Θ, α). In the first step, the identity matrix is used as the weighting matrix W. After obtaining the initial solution of Θ_0 and α_0, we next calculate the residuals μ_1 and μ_2 from the system of equations in (2.6) and construct the following weighting matrix:

$$W = \frac{1}{T}\sum_t (u_t u_t') \otimes (Z_t Z_t'), \qquad (A.1)$$

where $\otimes$ is the Kronecker product. Next, we use the weighting matrix in (A.1) to resolve the optimization problem of minimizing $g_T'W^{-1}g_T$ over the choice of (Θ, α). Hansen proved that under the null hypothesis (i.e., when the model is correctly specified), $Tg_T'W^{-1}g_T$, is asymptotically chi-square distributed, with the degrees of freedom equal to the difference between the number of orthogonality conditions and the number of parameters estimated: $N \times L - [K \times L + (N - K) \times K] = (N - K)(L - K)$, where N is the number of assets studied, K is the number of factor loadings, and L is the number of forecasting variables.

After obtaining the weighted sum of squared residuals, we perform a chi-square test to determine if the data rejects the restricted regression system (2.6). If it does not, we can use (2.6) to study how much of the variation in asset returns do these forecasting variables predict. We can also interpret the regression results as to what extent these economic conditions affect conditional factor risk premiums. Even if the overidentifying restrictions of Eq. (2.5) are rejected, the estimated coefficients may still be of interest. The fitted values from (2.5) are the best possible forecasts of asset returns, subject to the restriction that there are K major systematic factors in the economy. They can thus be interpreted as estimates of a common component in expected asset returns.

References

Campbell, J. Y., 1987, Stock Returns and the Term Structure, *Journal of Financial Economics* **18**, 373–399.

Campbell, J. Y., 1990, Intertemporal Asset Pricing Without Consumption, Working Paper, Princeton University.

Campbell, J. Y. and Y. Hamao, 1991, Predictable Stock Returns in the United States and Japan: A Study of Long-Term Capital Market Integration, Working Paper, Princeton University.

Chan, K. C., P. Hendershott and A. Sanders, 1990, Risk and Return on Real Estate: Evidence from Equity REITs, *AREUEA Journal* **18**, 431–452.

Chen, Nai-fu, R. Roll and S. Ross, 1986, Economic Forces and the Stock Market, *Journal of Business* **59**, 386–403.

Colwell, P. and H. Y. Park, 1990, Seasonality and Size Effects: The Case of Real-Estate-Related Investments, *Journal of Real Estate Finance and Economics* **3**, 251–260.

Connor, G. and R. A. Korajczyk, 1988, Risk and Return in an Equilibrium APT: Application of a New Test Methodology, *Journal of Financial Economics* **21**, 255–289.

Corgel, J. B. and R. C. Rogers, 1991, Market Trading Characteristics of REITs: Tests of the Stock Market and Hybrid Securities Hypotheses, Working Paper, Cornell University.

Fama, E. and K. French, 1988, Dividend Yields and Expected Stock Returns, *Journal of Financial Economics* **22**, 3–25.

Fama, E. and K. French, 1989, Business Conditions and Expected Return on Stocks and Bonds, *Journal of Financial Economics* **25**, 23–49.

Fama, E. and G. W. Schwert, 1977, Asset Returns and Inflation, *Journal of Financial Economics* **5**, 115–146.

Ferson, W., 1989, Changes in Expected Security Returns, Risk, and Level of Interest Rates, *Journal of Finance* **44**, 1191–1217.

Ferson, W., 1990, Are the Latent Variables in Time-Varying Expected Returns Compensation for Consumption Risk? *Journal of Finance* **45**, 397–430.

Ferson, W. and C. Harvey, 1990, The Variation of Economic Risk Premiums, *Journal of Political Economy* (Forthcoming).

Ferson, W. and C. Harvey, 1991, The Valuation of Economic Risk Preminus, *The Journal of Political Economy* **99** (2), 385–416.

Ferson, W., S. Kandel and R. Stambaugh, 1987, Test of Asset Pricing with Time-Varying Expected Risk Premiums and Market Betas, *Journal of Finance* **42**, 201–219.

Geltner, D., 1989, Risks and Returns in Commercial Real Estate: An Exploration of Some Fundamental Relationships, Ph.D. Thesis, Massachusetts Institute of Technology.

Gibbons, M. R. and W. Ferson, 1985, Testing Asset Pricing Models with Changing Expectations and an Unobservable Market Portfolio, *Journal of Financial Economics* 14, 217–236.

Giliberto, S. Michael, 1990, Equity Real Estate Investment Trust and Real Estate Returns, *Journal of Real Estate Research* 5, 259–263.

Gyourko, J. and D. Keim, 1991, What Does the Stock Market Tell Us About Real Estate Returns? Working Paper, The Wharton School.

Harvey, C. R., 1989, Time-Varying Conditional Covariances in Tests of Asset Pricing Models, *Journal of Financial Economics* **24**, 289–317.

Keim, D. B., 1983, Size Related Anomalies and Stock Return Seasonality: Empirical Evidence, *Journal of Financial Economics* **12**, 13–32.

Keim, D. and R. Stambaugh, 1986, Predicting Returns in the Stock and Bond Markets, *Journal of Financial Economics* **17**, 357–390.

Mei, J. P., 1990, New Method for the Arbitrage Pricing Theory and the Present Value Model, Ph.D. Dissertation, Princeton University.

Mengden, A. and D. J. Hartzell, 1986, Real Estate Investment Trusts — Are They Stocks or Real Estate? *Stock Research-Real Estate*, Solomon Brothers Inc.

Nourse, H. O., 1987, The "Cap Rate," 1966–1984: A Test of the Impact of Income Tax Changes on Income Property, *Land Economics* **63**, 147–152.

Roll, R. and S. A. Ross, 1980, An Empirical Investigation of the Arbitrage Pricing Theory, *Journal of Finance* **35**, 1073–1103.

Ross, S., 1976, The Arbitrage Theory of Capital Asset Pricing, *Journal of Economic Theory* **13**, 341–360.

White, H., 1980, A Heteroskedasticity-Consistent Covariance Matrix Estimator and a Direct Test for Heteroskedasticity, *Econometrica* **48**, 817–838.

CHAPTER 3

The Predictability of Real Estate Returns and Market Timing

JIANPING J. P. MEI and CROCKER H. LIU*

*Associate Professors of Finance,
Department of Finance, Stern School of Business, New York University,
New York, NY 10012*

Recent evidence suggests that all asset returns are predictable to some extent with excess returns on real estate relatively easier to forecast. This raises the issue of whether we can successfully exploit this level of predictability using various market timing strategies to realize superior performance over a buy-and-hold strategy. We find that the level of predictability associated with real estate leads to moderate success in market timing, although this is not necessarily so for the other asset classes examined in general. Besides, real estate stocks typically have higher trading profits and higher mean risk-adjusted excess returns when compared to small stocks as well as large stocks and bonds, even though most real estate stocks are small stocks.

3.1 Introduction

Prior research on exchange-traded real estate firms have found that these firms do not earn abnormal returns. Recent evidence, however, suggests that the variation in the expected excess real estate returns over time is predictable and is the result of changes in business

---

*Reprint requests should be sent to Jianping Mei, at Department of Finance, Stern School of Business, NYU, 44 West 4th Street, New York, NY 10012-1126, Phone (212) 998-0354 or Fax (212) 995-4233.

conditions.[1] Moreover, one of these studies finds that real estate returns are more predictable than returns on other assets. This raises the possibility that real estate might exhibit superior investment performance when compared to other assets if an investor is successful in market timing. The purpose of the present study, therefore, is to explore whether superior real estate investment performance is possible through a market timing strategy given that we are able to forecast real estate returns. The present study is different from prior real estate investment studies in that no other study that we know of addresses explicitly the ability to market time in exchange-traded real estate firms, although Glascock (1991) does use a model similar in spirit to a market timing model to test for changes in portfolio betas during up markets and down markets. The ability to successfully use market timing to achieve superior performance is of interest to practitioners, because it suggests a more efficient method of allocating investment funds. Market timing is also of interest to academics not only because of the theoretical implications associated with the optimal amount of real estate to hold in a portfolio, but aslo because the findings of Gyourko and Keim (1991) show that returns on real estate investment trusts (REITs) and real estate related companies can *predict* returns on the Frank Russell Company (FRC) appraisal-based return index of unlevered institutional grade properties that most institutional investors use as the return benchmark for direct real estate investment.

The present study is also different from the previous finance literature on market timing in that prior studies have focused on testing for the existence of market timing ability *within* the sample. More specifically, the issue investigated is whether differential investment performance is due to stock selection (microforecasting) or the ability to market time (macroforecasting). The current study, in contrast, focuses on the related issue of whether the degree of predictability associated with various asset returns and real estate in particular is

---

[1]See for example Gyourko and Keim (1991) and Liu and Mei (1992) who find that common factors are likely to drive returns on both real estate and non-real estate related assets.

sufficient to allow an investor to construct a market timing strategy that would lead to superior investment performance.[2]

Our study uses the multi-factor, latent-variable model of Liu and Mei (1992) to predict the time variation of expected excess returns on various asset classes. To prevent the in-sample bias problem of using the same data to both estimate the parameters and test the model, a 10-year rolling regression is used to form out-of-sample excess return forecasts. Given these return forecasts, three investment strategy portfolios are formed for each asset class including a passive buy-and-hold portfolio, a portfolio of long and short positions, and a portfolio of long positions. This methodology has several distinct advantages over previous investment performance studies which test for the presence of market timing ability. First, it allows for time-varying risk premiums in contrast to the existing methodology of Henriksson–Merton (HM) (1981), which assumes that risk premiums are stationary. Another problem with the HM model that our methology obviates is the possibility of misspecification of the return-generating process due to a misspecification of the market portfolio, because the present model makes no assumptions about the observability of systematic factors in the economy. Besides, our model appears to be relatively robust to which set of factors are used to forecast returns in contrast to Henriksson (1984), who finds that omission of relevant factors is influential in explaining the behavior of returns. Our model also differs from the HM model and the Cumby–Modest (1987) extension of the HM model in that we explicitly develop market timing strategies according to whether the excess return forecast for an asset is positive or negative. In the market timing model of Henriksson and Merton (1981), on which most

---

[2]The market timing studies of Henriksson (1984) and Chang and Lewellen (1984) find that few mutual fund managers are able to successfully use market timing to outperform a passive buy-and-hold investment strategy using the Henriksson and Merton (1981) market timing modification to the model of Jensen (1968). More recently, Cumby and Modest (1987) generalize the Henriksson–Merton model by relaxing the assumption that the probability of a correct forecast and the magnitude of subsequent market returns need to be independent of each other and find strong evidence that portfolio managers exhibit market timing ability.

empirical studies are based, the emphasis is on the *probability* of a correct return forecast, while our model emphasis is on the *economic significance* (*trading profits*) of return forecasts.

The most important finding of our study is that the level of predicability associated with real estate is sufficient for successful market timing to occur. However, this is not necessarily so for the other asset classes examined. In addition to this, the mean risk adjusted excess returns on a value-weighted portfolio consisting of various categories of exchange-traded real estate firms appear to outperform large cap stocks, small cap stocks, bonds, and the S&P500 benchmark portfolio as well as the passive buy-and-hold real estate portfolio over the entire out-of-sample period when an active market timing strategy is used. In terms of individual real estate stocks, homebuilders have the highest mean risk adjusted excess return when either active trading tactic is chosen with a phenomenal 2.2% excess return per month on an average realized using a long and short trading scheme. More moderate mean excess returns are obtained (at least 0.78% per month) in contrast to mortgage REITs which have the poorest performance of all the real estate categories.

The rest of the paper is organized as follows: Section 2 briefly outlines the framework used for predicting asset returns. Section 3 describes the data used, while the empirical results are found in Sec. 4. Section 5 presents our summary and conclusions.

3.2 Method for Predicting Asset Returns

The condition excess return forecast model used in the current study follows from Liu and Mei (1992, 2002) and assumes that the expected excess return conditional on information at time t, $E_t[\tilde{r}_{i,t+1}]$, is linear in the economic state variables known to investors at time t.[3]

---

[3]A more rigorous derivation of Eq. (3.1) using a multi-factor, latent-variable model is found in Campbell (1987), Ferson (1989), and Liu and Mei (1992) (see Appendix). Alternatively, Eq. (3.1) is also derivable from a VAR process for asset returns as in Campbell (1991), Campbell and Mei (1991).

Mathematically,

$$E_t[\tilde{r}_{i,t+1}] = \sum_{n=1}^{L} \alpha_{in} X_{nt}, \qquad (3.1)$$

where X_{nt}, $n = 1, \ldots, L$, is a vector of L forecasting variables (X_{1t} is a constant) which are known to the market at time t. A more detailed discussion of the methodology is given in the Appendix. The forecasting variables used in the current study include a constant term, a January dummy, the yield on 1-month Treasury bill, the spread between the yields on long-term AAA corporate bonds and the 1-month Treasury bill, the dividend yields on the equally weighted market portfolio, and the cap rate on real estate. The yield variable describes the short-term interest rate, while the spread variable depicts the slope of the term structure of interest rates, and the dividend yield variable captures information on expectations about future cash flows and required returns in the stock market. In addition, we also include the cap rate which captures information on expected future cash flows and required returns in the underlying real estate market. Campbell (1987), Campbell (2002) and Hamao (2002), Fama and French (1988, 1989), Ferson (1989), Ferson and Harvey (2002), Keim and Stambaugh (1986), among others, have used the first three variables in examining the predictability of stocks. Liu and Mei (1992, 2002) also find that the cap rate in addition to the preceding three forecasting variables is useful in predicting returns, especially on real estate and small cap stocks.[4]

---

[4]The cap rate is defined as the ratio of net-stabilized earnings to the transaction price (or market value) of a property. Net-stabilized income assumes that full leaseup of the building has occurred such that the building's vacancy is equal to or less than the vacancy of the market. As such, the cap rate is analogous to the earnings–price ratio on direct real estate investment. Another interpretation of the cap rate is that it represents the weighted average cost of capital (band of investment) for real estate. For example, Nourse (1987) uses this weighted average cost of capital interpretation of the cap rate in testing the impact of income tax changes on income property. We include the cap rate as a forecasting variable, because movements in the cap rate do not necessarily contain the same information as fluctuations in the dividend yield on the stock market, for example although both the cap rate and dividend yield are measures of income-to-value, the cash flows of buildings are not identical to the cash flows of firms which

Although the preceding variable list does not necessarily include all relevant that carry information about factor premiums, the methodology we use is relatively robust to omitted information. A Generalized Method of Moments (GMM) approach, similar to Campbell (1987) and Ferson (1989), is used to estimate Eq. (3.1) in order to obtain the *ex ante* risk premiums on various asset portfolios. Out-of-sample *ex ante* excess return forecasts are formed using 10-year rolling GMM regressions with the forecasting variables. For any time period t, we estimate Eq. (3.1) using data from $t-1$ to $t-120$. Then the regression is used to form an excess return forecast, $E_t[e_{i,t+1}]$, using X_{pt}. The excess return forecasts (expected excess return) are calculated for the time period of February 1981–April 1989. A passive buy-and-hold portfolio together with two active portfolios are constructed based on this return forecast: a Long $(+)$ portfolio, and a Long $(+)$ and Short $(-)$ portfolio.

The formation of a buy-and-hold portfolio for each asset class involves assuming that a particular asset category is held over the entire February 1981–December 1989 period. Construction of the Long $(+)$ portfolio, on the other hand, entails taking a long position in a particular asset class whenever the excess return forecast for that asset class is positive, while closing the position and putting the proceeds in treasury bills whenever the excess return forecast for that asset group is negative. Finally, the Long $(+)$ and Short $(-)$ portfolio strategy takes a long position in a particular asset whenever the excess return forecast for that asset is positive, and closing the position and "selling short" (putting the proceeds from short sales in treasury bills) whenever the excess return forecast on that asset is negative.

3.3   Data

Asset returns on stocks, bonds, and exchange-traded real estate firms are obtained from the monthly stock tape of the Center for Research on Security Prices (CRSP) for the period starting January 1971 and

---

occupy space in the buildings.

ending April 1989. We use two stock return series. A value-weighted stock index consisting of all New York Stock Exchange (NYSE) and American Stock Exchange (AMEX) stocks is used as a proxy for stocks with large market capitalizations. We also include a value-weighted small cap stock index in our study. Both stock return series are taken from the Ibbotson and Associates *Stocks, Bonds, Bills* and *Inflation* (SBBI) series on CRSP. The government bond return series is also obtained from SBBI and represents a portfolio of treasury bonds having an average maturity of 20 years and without call provisons or special tax benefits.

Four value-weighted real estate stock return series are constructed as our proxies for real estate asset returns. Equity real estate investment trusts (EREITs), real estate building companies (builders), real estate holding companies (owners), and mortgage real estate investment trusts (mortgage) comprise the four real estate portfolios. The value-weighted equity and mortgage REIT series are obtained from the National Association of Real Estate Investment Trusts while the builder and owner series consist of all real estate companies in the Audit Investment publication *The Realty Stock Review*.[5] Besides this, we construct a value-weighted as well as an equally weighted portfolio consisting of all four types of real estate securities.

In addition to the returns on four real estate portfolios, monthly returns on the S&P500 is used to proxy for the market portfolio and is also used as a comparison benchmark in analyzing the relative behavior of real estate asset returns. The yield on the 1-month Treasury bill, the spread between the yields on long-term AAA corporate bonds and the 1-month Treasury bill, and the dividend yields on the equally weighted market portfolio are obtained from the Federal

---

[5]Two primary classifications exist for a REIT — equity and mortgage. An EREIT differs from a mortgage REIT in that the former acquires direct equity ownership in the properties, while the latter type of REIT purchases mortgage obligations secured by real estate. Both types of REITs are constrained in both the type of real estate activities they can pursue and the management of investments. In contrast to builders, for example, REITs are not allowed to develop properties. In contrast to owners, on the other hand, REITs are constrained in the number of properties that they can sell in any one period. The list of builders and owners is available from the authors on request.

Reserve Bulletin and Ibbotson and Associates (1989). The cap rates estate are taken from the American Council of Life Insurance publication *Investment Bulletin: Mortgage Commitments on Multifamily and Nonresidental Properties Reported by 20 Life Insurance Companies.*

3.4 Empirical Results

Table 1 reports the summary statistics for each of our asset classes and forecasting variables. An inspection of ths table reveals that none of the real estate categories has a higher mean excess return relative to small stocks, although both EREITs and real estate owners have higher excess returns relative to value-weighted stocks and government bonds. In contrast, the average return for builders and mortgage REITs are lower than that for stocks and bonds. Within the real estate subgroup, real estate owners have the highest mean excess returns followed by EREITs. Not surprisingly, the excess returns associated with real estate owners are more volatile relative to small cap stocks, large cap stocks, and bonds. However, homebuilder returns have the widest fluctuations over time. For the study period used, the standard deviation associated with EREITs is similar to that of large cap stocks, while the total volatility of mortgage REITs is greater than large cap stocks but less than small stocks. This suggests that any increase in the predictability of various real esate return classes relataive to other assets does not arise from relatively lower variations in returns, at least in the current study. Thus, this negates the argument that superior performance, if any, of real estate relative to other assets arising from market timing is attributable to exchange-traded real estate firms having a relatively lower variance. Table 1 also reveals that the returns on all assets exhibit positive first-order autocorrelation which is consistent with prior studies.

Table 1 also reports the correlations of returns among four asset classes. As expected, the excess returns on EREITs are highly correlated with small cap stocks given the prior findings of Liu and Mei (1992). Excess returns for builders, owners, and mortgage REITs also show a tendency to move with excess returns on small cap stocks. In general, the correlation among asset classes is moderate to high except for government bonds which exhibit minimal correlations with all other assets.

The results of regressing excess assets returns on five forecasting variables and a constant term — a January dummy, returns on Treasury bills, the spread, the dividend yield on the equally weighted market portfolio, and the cap rate are shown in Table 2. Table 2 not only reports the predictability as measured by the R^2 for the

Table 1.   Summary Statistics.

	Mean	S.D.	ρ_1
Dependent variables			
Excess return on value-weighted stocks (VW)	0.286	4.776	0.050
Excess return on small stocks (SM)	0.582	6.642	0.122
Excess return on government bonds (GB)	0.038	3.287	0.050
Excess return on S&P500 (S&P)	0.278	4.706	0.036
Excess return on Equity REITs (EREIT)	0.403	4.281	0.082
Excess return on Builders (BLD)	−0.183	10.830	0.212
Excess return on Real Estate Owners (OWN)	0.518	7.100	0.190
Excess return on Mortgage REITs (MREIT)	−0.169	5.971	0.026
Forecasting variables			
Yield on 1-month T-bill (TB)	7.374	2.801	0.919
Yield spread between AAA bond and T-bill (SP)	2.373	1.819	0.750
Dividend yield on equal-weighted portfolio(DY)	3.722	0.750	0.945
Capitalization rate on Equity REITs (CAPR)	10.440	1.142	0.958

	VW	SM	GB	S&P	EREIT	BLD	OWN	MREIT
Correlations among dependent variables								
VW	1.00	0.84	0.32	0.99	0.65	0.79	0.75	0.56
SM		1.00	0.18	0.81	0.71	0.82	0.71	0.64
GB			1.00	0.32	0.20	0.36	0.28	0.37
S&P				1.00	0.62	0.76	0.73	0.53
EREIT					1.00	0.69	0.58	0.64
BLD						1.00	0.72	0.71
OWN							1.00	0.57
MREIT								1.00

Notes: The sample period for this table is January 1971–April 1989, with 220 observations. Units on excess returns are percentage per month. Units on 1-month T-bill rate, yield spread, and dividend yield are percentage per annum. ρ_1 is the first autocorrelation of the series. All dependent variables are value weighted.

whole sample period (denoted as in-sample prediction); it also reports the predictability as well as the variation associated with that predictability for the 10-year rolling regressions which are used for forming out-of-sample excess return forecasts. Table 2 indicates that although returns on small stocks have the largest in-sample predictability, a larger component of the excess return on builders is predictable relative to all other real estate firm classifications as well as non-real estate assets in terms of out-of-sample prediction. In particular, the five forecasting variables account for approximately 13.6% of the variation in monthly excess returns on builders. The out-of-sample predictability on returns for owners and mortgage REITs are 10.3% and 10.9%, respectively, which are greater than the return predictability for all other asset classes except builders and small stocks. By contrast, the returns on EREITs and large stocks have similar out-of-sample predictability, although more of the in-sample return variation of the former asset can be accouted for relative to the latter asset class.[6] In short, the degree to which the excess returns on stocks, bonds, and the various real estate categories are predicatable is consistent with the previous studies of Campbell and Hamao (2002), Harvey (1989), Gyourko and Keim (1991) and Liu and Mei (1992), among others. The standard deviation of the R^2 in the last column of Table 2, which is not looked at or reported in previous studies, also reveals that the degree of predictability remains relatively stable over time for all asset classes, which suggests that any successful market timing strategy will tend to remain effective over time. Moreover, Table 2 reveals that the predictability associated with the return on builders is more stationary relative to small stocks as well as other asset categories. The only exception to this is EREITs which have the greatest amount of stability of out-of-sample predictions. When the in-sample predictability is compared to the out-of-sample predictability, it is readily apparent that the

---

[6]The predictability for EREITs relative to small stocks differ somewhat from Liu and Mei (1992) because our study uses value-weighted returns for real estate while the previous study uses equally weighted real estate returns. We also use an additional year of real estate returns with the data starting in January 1971. The Liu and Mei 1992) study, in contrast, uses data beginning in January 1972.

numbers are similar for each asset class with the predictability of excess returns slightly stronger for the out-of-sample data set, which is another indication of the strength of the predictability. The most distinguishing feature of Table 2, therefore, is that the returns on builders are not only higher relative to small stocks in terms of the level of out-of-sample predictability; more stability is associated with this predictability. More importantly, the builders' portfolio is comprised primarily of large cap stocks. In contrast to this, the equity and mortgage REIT portfolios are small stock portfolios. However, Liu and Mei (1992) have shown that REITs differ from small cap stocks in that most of the variations in unexpected real estate returns is due to cash flow fluctuations, while movements in discount rate account for most of the fluctuations in the unexpected portion of small cap returns. This therefore raises the question of whether real estate stocks will differ from small stocks in market timing, given that they are similar in predictability but differ in what accounts for the variations in their respective unexpected returns.

A visual impression of the results in Table 2 is given in Fig. 1. Figure 1 plots the conditional expected (predicted) excess return $[E_t(\tilde{r}_{i,t+1})]$ for Standard & Poor's 500, EREITs, homebuilders, property owners, and mortgage REITs. The graph shows that the expected excess returns vary over time, sometimes taking positive values and sometimes taking negative values as expected. The most interesting aspect of Fig. 1 is that the *monthly* predictable excess returns for homebuilders can reach a maximum of 18%. The high expected return at the beginning of each year reflects the well-documented "January Effect" for stocks and EREITs (see, for instance, Keim (1983), and Liu and Mei (1992)). In terms of volatility in the expected excess returns, the biggest volatility in $[E_t(\tilde{r}_{i,t+1})]$ is associated with homebuilders as well. The predictability in the expected excess returns which we document can come from two major sources. First, it can just reflect rational pricing in an efficient market under different business conditions. Second, it can come from market inefficiency as a result of investor overreaction (for instance, see DeBondt and Thaler (1987)). In any case, the huge variation in expected excess returns creates market timing opportunities for long-term investors.

Table 2. Regression of the value-weighted returns on each asset class at time $t+1$ on a January dummy, the yield on Treasury bills, the spread between the yield on AAA corporate bonds and the yield on T-bills, the dividend yield for the overall stock market, and the cap rate on real estate all at time t. Regression coefficients are given by the first line of each row, while the t-statistics are given in parenthesis in the second row. To compute out-of-sample predictions, a 10-year rolling regression technique is employed. For any time period t, we estimate Eq. (3.1) using data from $t-1$ to $t-120$ and then the regression is used to form an excess return forecast. The excess return forecast (expected excess return) are calculated for the time period of February 1981–April 1989.

Model: $\text{Asset}_{i,t+1} = \text{Constant} + \beta_1 \text{Jandum} + \beta_2 \text{TB}_t + \beta_3 \text{Spread}_t + \beta_4 \text{Mkt. DivYld}_t + \beta_5 \text{CapR}_t + \tilde{\varepsilon}_i$

Asset class	Constant	Jandum	TB	Spread	DivYld	CapR	DW	In sample predictions R^2	Out-of-sample predictions $\bar{R}^2$	Out-of-sample predictions $\sigma\bar{R}^2$
VW stocks	−7.024 (−1.98)	1.846 (1.41)	−0.556 (−2.92)	0.029 (0.13)	1.032 (1.33)	0.704 (1.61)	1.88	0.057	0.081	0.026
Small stocks	−12.562 (−2.58)	5.604 (3.42)	−0.841 (−3.30)	−0.104 (−0.34)	2.014 (2.38)	1.114 (2.00)	1.76	0.133	0.131	0.026
Government bonds	−1.388 (−0.50)	−0.665 (−0.96)	0.098 (0.72)	0.376 (2.38)	1.041 (3.48)	−0.384 (−1.13)	1.89	0.032	0.059	0.023
S&P500	−6.625 (−1.91)	1.726 (1.32)	−0.534 (−2.85)	0.038 (0.17)	0.902 (1.16)	0.694 (1.60)	1.91	0.051	0.077	0.027
EREITs	−6.641 (−2.17)	2.920 (3.33)	−0.467 (−2.58)	0.135 (0.59)	0.675 (1.28)	0.710 (1.91)	1.95	0.081	0.083	0.016
Builders	−22.983 (−2.73)	6.089 (1.96)	−1.132 (−2.83)	0.417 (0.79)	4.129 (2.46)	1.369 (1.51)	1.62	0.106	0.136	0.023
Owners	−15.104 (−3.12)	1.542 (0.84)	−0.602 (−2.26)	0.584 (1.86)	2.553 (2.42)	0.866 (1.54)	1.67	0.079	0.103	0.027
Mortgage REITs	−13.427 (−3.27)	4.414 (2.65)	−0.649 (−2.67)	−0.005 (−0.02)	1.046 (0.84)	1.322 (2.52)	2.01	0.092	0.109	0.028
VW real estate	−15.317 (−3.16)	3.308 (1.78)	−0.665 (−2.59)	0.426 (1.32)	2.119 (1.87)	1.082 (1.99)	1.66	0.095	0.133	0.032

Notes:

(1) DW is the Durbin–Watson statistic.

(2) The reported R^2's are not independent for the out-of-sample predictions because a rolling regression technique is employed. However, the $\bar{R}^2$ and the standard deviation of the $\bar{R}^2$ do provide some indication that the predictability is stable over time.

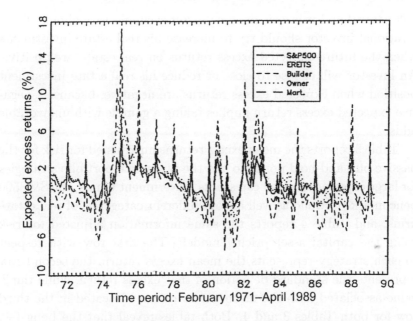

Fig. 1. Conditional risk premium on real estate assets.

Given our findings in Table 2 that all assets to some degree are predictable and that this predictability is relatively stationary over time, we now turn to the central focus of this paper, namely, to what extent we can exploit the degree of predictability and the stability of this predictability in asset returns to obtain superior investment returns through market timing. To evaluate the success or failure of market timing performance, we construct three trading strategies. More specifically, we form two active portfolios: a Long (+) portfolio and a Long (+) and Short (−) portfolio as well as a passive buy-and-hold portfolio. These portfolios are explained in greater detail subsequently. The passive buy-and-hold portfolio is used as our benchmark for finding out whether superior returns are possible. The unadjusted and risk-adjusted excess returns from each asset class are compared against each other as well as the S&P500 benchmark over various trading strategies to determine not only the relative asset investment performance but also the consistency of that performance. In undertaking this analysis, we assume that the *ex ante* expected excess returns on its investments over the holding period is all that a risk neutral and value maximizing investor should care about. Thus, a rational investor should try to increase his real estate investments when the future expected excess returns on real estate are positive. An investor will choose to close or reduce his real estate investment position when expected excess returns are negative, because a negative expected excess return implies taking a gamble with unfavorable odds.

Table 3 reports the mean excess returns unadjusted for risk for the passive buy-and-hold portfolio and the two active portfolio strategies for large cap stocks, small cap stocks, government bonds, the S&P500 benchmark portfolio as well as four different categories of real estate firms, and Table 4 reports the same information adjusted for risk using the capital asset pricing model. The first row with respect to each strategy represents the mean excess return, the second row represents the standard deviation of that excess return, while the T value associated with the mean excess return is located in the third row for both Tables 3 and 4. Both tables reveal that the Long $(+)$ and Short $(-)$ portfolio and also the Long $(+)$ portfolio outperform the passive buy-and-hold portfolio with respect to a value-weighted portfolio consisting of all types of real estate firms with the former actively managed strategy doing slightly better than the latter active strategy. Similar results also obtain for an equally weighted portfolio of various value-weighted real estate groupings. The T values in Tables 3 and 4 also reveal that the relative portfolio performance arising from either active trading strategy is statistically significant.

Slightly different results are obtained when individual real estate firm categories are examined in Tables 3 and 4. In both tables, the monthly mean excess returns for all real estate firm categories using either active trading strategy exceed those returns for the corresponding passive strategy except for the property owner portfolio in Table 3. However, the mean excess returns associated with the active strategies are not necessarily significant. For example, statistically greater than zero. Homebuilding stocks have the highest mean excess return from either an unadjusted or risk-adjusted perspective when a Long and Short trading strategy is implemented. More specifically, the mean risk-adjusted excess return for homebuilders exceeds 2.2% per month for the Long $(+)$ and Short $(-)$

Table 3.   Mean portfolio excess returns based on out-of-sample prediction excess returns are *not adjusted* for risk.

	Trading Strategies		
	Buy and hold	Long (+) and Short (−)	Long (+)
VW stocks	0.520	0.169	0.344
	(4.83)	(4.86)	(3.19)
	[1.07]	[0.35]	[1.30]
Small stocks	0.452	0.778	0.615
	(5.64)	(5.60)	(2.64)
	[0.80]	[1.38]	[1.92]
Government bonds	0.427	0.229	0.328
	(3.84)	(3.86)	(1.91)
	[1.11]	[0.59]	[1.71]
S&P500	0.551	0.172	0.362
	(4.87)	(4.90)	(2.72)
	[1.13]	[0.35]	[1.32]
EREITS	0.469	0.951	0.710
	(3.19)	(3.08)	(2.18)
	[1.46]	[3.07]	[3.24]
Builders	−0.109	1.850	0.870
	(9.99)	(9.82)	(5.79)
	[−0.11]	[1.87]	[1.49]
Owners	1.140	0.780	0.961
	(5.89)	(5.95)	(3.30)
	[1.93]	[1.30]	[2.90]
Mortgage REITS	−0.098	0.716	0.309
	(3.78)	(3.71)	(2.42)
	[−0.26]	[1.92]	[1.27]
VW real estate	0.710	0.766	0.738
	(5.23)	(5.22)	(3.07)
	[1.35]	[1.46]	[2.40]
EW of VW real estate	0.351	0.949	0.650
	(4.95)	(4.87)	(2.98)
	[0.71]	[1.94]	[2.17]

Note: The first row for each asset given a particular strategy represents the mean excess return, the second row represents the standard deviation of that excess return while the T value associated with the mean excess return is located in the third row. All returns are value weighted except the last return series which is the equally weighted portfolio of the four value-weighted real estate return series.

strategy. In contrast, the passive buy-and-hold homebuilder portfolio experiences negative mean risk-adjusted excess returns of −1.03%. Builder returns for both of these strategies are statistically significant

Table 4.   Mean *risk-adjusted* portfolio excess returns Based on out-of-sample prediction.

	Trading strategies		
	Buy and hold	Long (+) and Short (−)	Long (+)
VW stocks	−0.025	0.385	0.180
	(0.30)	(4.46)	(2.20)
	[−0.84]	[0.86]	[0.81]
Small stocks	−0.099	0.954	0.428
	(2.84)	(5.38)	(2.73)
	[−0.35]	[1.76]	[1.56]
Government bonds	0.270	0.257	0.263
	(3.58)	(3.85)	(1.82)
	[0.75]	[0.66]	[1.44]
S&P500	*****	0.383	0.191
	*****	(4.54)	(2.27)
	*****	[0.84]	[0.84]
EREITS	0.206	0.993	0.599
	(2.18)	(3.06)	(1.95)
	[0.94]	[3.23]	[3.07]
Builders	−1.030	2.200	0.585
	(5.83)	(9.33)	(5.22)
	[−1.75]	[2.34]	[1.12]
Owners	0.640	0.967	0.803
	(3.87)	(5.72)	(2.99)
	[1.64]	[1.68]	[2.68]
Mortgage REITS	−0.353	0.775	0.211
	(3.03)	(3.67)	(2.26)
	[−1.16]	[2.10]	[0.93]
VW real estate	0.203	0.956	0.580
	(2.70)	(4.95)	(2.73)
	[0.75]	[1.92]	[2.12]
EW of VW real estate	−0.133	1.090	0.478
	(2.49)	(4.71)	(2.56)
	[−0.53]	[2.30]	[1.86]

Note: The first row for each asset given a particular strategy represents the mean excess return, the second row represents the standard deviation of that excess return while the T value associated with the mean excess return is located in the third row. All returns are value weighted except the last return series which is the equally weighted portfolio of the four value-weighted real estate return series.

from zero. The risk-adjusted returns from holding a long position in the homebuilder portfolio, however, does not differ statistically from zero. When a long strategy is chosen, the property owner portfolio has the largest mean excess returns of all asset classes. Surprisingly, the active trading profits for all real estate categories except mortgage REITs exceed the corresponding profits for small stocks, even though Table 2 reveals that the in-sample predictability and out-of-sample predictability of small stocks exceed all real estate classes (with the exception of builders for the out-of-sample predictability scenario). This condition holds for both the case of unadjusted and risk-adjusted returns. Although the returns from implementing an active trading strategy for small stocks is larger than that for mortgage REITs in general, it is not necessarily true that they are statistically different from a zero return. What this suggests is that even though one could argue that real estate stocks are small stocks or behave like small stocks, real estate stocks outperform small stocks in returns using a market timing scheme in general. Moreover, all real estate categories exhibit higher returns from an active trading strategy relative to either large cap stocks or government bonds. However, Table 4 also reveals that a higher amount of volatility exists, the higher the level of mean excess returns, which is not surprising. Thus, homebuilders have the highest volatility while EREITs have the lowest fluctuations around their respective mean excess returns of the four real estate portfolios examined.

In contrast to real estate firms, an inspection of the non-real estate asset categories reveals that the two active trading strategies do not necessarily outperform a passive buy-and-hold strategy. This is the case for large cap stocks and government bonds when excess returns are not risk adjusted. However, the active trading strategies do outperform a buy-and-hold strategy for large stocks but not for bonds when returns are risk adjusted.

How well do the various asset classes do relative to the S&P500 benchmark? Although Table 3 indicates that the evidence is mixed when the unadjusted mean portfolio excess return for each asset class is completed to the S&P500, Table 4 clearly shows that *all* types of real estate firms outperform the S&P500 in both active trading strategies when returns are adjusted for risk. Of the non-real estate assets, Table 4 reveals that only small cap stocks consistently beat the market (S&P500) when either active trading strategy is used, which is not surprising given the relatively high level of predictability associated with small cap stocks. However, the performance of small cap stocks is less spectacular than that of the various real estate portfolios with the exception of mortgage REITs.

When Tables 3 and 4 are examined in terms of portfolio risk, the distinguishing conclusion from these tables is that the value-weighted portfolio consisting of all real estate groups has a *total* risk level similar to that of the non-real estate asset groups; yet it has higher mean excess returns in general. The only exception to this is the comparison to small stocks using a Long and Short positions when excess returns are not risk adjusted. The level of risk for each individual real estate portfolio is also comparable to that of other assets with the possible exception of homebuilders in Table 4 whose total risk is higher. However, it is unclear whether the individual real estate groupings in contrast to the value-weighted real estate portfolio necessarily have higher relative mean excess returns. This is particularly true for mortgage REITs. This suggests that the covariances among the real estate types are moderate at best, which is shown in Table 1, and therefore it pays to diversify on an intra-real estate basis in order to maximize profits from an active trading strategy.

The evidence thus far appears to indicate that as the level of predictability increases for an asset class, a higher mean excess return is associated with an active trading strategy, although this tendency is not perfectly monotonic. To determine the strength of this relationship from a statistical perspective, the predictability of excess returns as measured by the out-of-sample R^2 in Table 2 is correlated against the mean excess returns in Tables 3 (unadjusted for risk) and 4 (adjusted for risk) with the correlation results reported in Table 5. Table 5 shows that the level of predictability is positively correlated to the level of mean excess returns for both active trading strategies with relatively higher correlations existing for the Long and Short scenario. In particular, the mean excess returns using a Long $(+)$ and Short $(-)$ strategy has a 0.71 cross-sectional correlation while the Long $(+)$ strategy has a 0.40–0.58 cross-sectional correlation with the level of out-of-sample predictability. Not surprisingly, the passive buy-and-hold strategy is not correlated with the level of predictability for the various asset groups. One plausible reason why the results

Table 5. Cross sectional correlation of out-of-sample predictability with mean excess returns returns are value weighted.

Trading strategy	Mean excess returns unadjusted for risk	Mean excess returns adjusted for risk
Buy and hold	−0.20	−0.48
Long (+) and Short (−)	0.71	0.71
Long (+)	0.58	0.40

Notes:
(1) The out-of-sample predictability is the out-of-sample R^2 column in Table 2.
(2) The mean excess returns unadjusted for risk is obtained form Table 3.
(3) The mean excess returns adjusted for risk using the CAPM is taken from Table 4.

are not stronger is that only a few asset classes are explored in terms of predictability and market timing.

A key question of interest to investment managers is to what extent does portfolio wealth increase as a result of these active trading strategies? What is the actual magnitude of trading profits relative to a buy-and-hold strategy involving that particular asset or alternatively the S&P500? Do cumulative returns from the market timing of a particular portfolio exceed those from market timing the S&P500? The answers to these questions are reported in Table 6. All real estate portfolios exhibit positive net performance relative to the three cumulative wealth benchmarks for the active trading strategies except for the owner portfolio. These benchmarks are the final wealth levels associated with the buy-and-hold S&P500 (relative profit 1), a portfolio based on an appropriate actively traded S&P500 portfolio strategy (relative profit 2), and finally a passive portfolio consisting of that particular asset whose active strategy is the object of comparison (relative profit 3). Starting with an initial wealth of $100 in February of 1981, an investor would have realized a net profit of between $78 and $289 from a Long (+) and Short (−) strategy and between $34 and $141 from a Long (+) strategy depending on which real estate portfolio he invested in. These net profits on real estate exceed the net profit of $51 if the S&P500 were purchased and held. The only exception to this is the net profits from a long position in mortgage REITs. The relative net profits for EREITs, builders, and mortgage REITs also exceed the compensation from simply buying and holding each of the respective real estate portfolios (see Relative

Profit 3). However, a buy-and-hold strategy results in greater trading profits relative to a long position in the real estate owner portfolio.

When the individual real estate portfolios are examined, the most impressive gains are associated with homebuilder stocks using the Long (+) and Short (−) market timing with a $238.20 and an even greater $337.13 net profit realized over and above a passive strategy involving purchasing the S&P500 and homebuilder portfolios respectively at the start of 1981 and selling the portfolios at the end of 1989. In contrast, negative profits are obtained for the property owner portfolio when either market timing strategy is compared against the passive alternative. However, the total gain for the owner portfolio still exceeds the dollar returns achieved from the S&P500 using any of the three strategies examined. More specifically, a gain

Table 6.   Cumulative excess trading profits unadjusted for risk. All returns are value weighted from February 1981 to December 1989.

	Initial Wealth	Terminal Wealth	Final Profit	Relative Profit 1	Relative Profit 2	Relative Profit 3
I. Buy-and-hold strategy						
S&P500	100.00	151.20	51.20	0.00	0.00	***
Value-weighted stocks	100.00	147.20	47.20	−4.00	−4.00	***
Small stocks	100.00	131.50	31.50	−19.70	−19.70	***
Government bonds	100.00	150.20	50.20	−1.00	−1.00	***
Equity REITs (EREIT)	100.00	150.90	50.90	−0.30	−0.30	***
Homebuilders	100.00	52.27	−47.73	−98.93	−98.93	***
Property owners	100.00	254.20	154.20	103.00	103.00	***
Mortgage REITs (MREIT)	100.00	85.82	−14.18	−65.38	−65.38	***
VW real estate	100.00	173.00	73.00	21.80	21.80	***
EW of VW real estate	100.00	124.20	24.20	−27.00	−27.00	***
II. Long (+) and Short (−) strategy						
S&P500	100.00	104.70	4.70	−46.50	−0.01	−46.50
Value-weighted stocks	100.00	104.80	4.80	−46.40	0.09	−42.40
Small stocks	100.00	187.10	87.10	35.90	82.39	55.60
Government bonds	100.00	110.50	10.50	−40.70	5.79	−39.70
Equity REITs (EREIT)	100.00	244.40	144.40	93.20	139.69	93.50
Homebuilders	100.00	389.40	289.40	238.20	284.69	337.13
Property owners	100.00	178.90	78.90	27.70	74.19	−75.30
Mortgage REITs (MREIT)	100.00	192.60	92.60	41.40	87.89	106.78
VW real estate	100.00	184.70	84.70	33.50	79.99	11.70
EW of VW real estate	100.00	226.80	126.80	75.60	122.09	102.60

Table 6.   *Continued.*

	Initial Wealth	Terminal Wealth	Final Profit	Relative Profit 1	Relative Profit 2	Relative Profit 3
III. Long (+) strategy						
S&P500	100.00	136.60	36.60	−14.60	0.00	−14.60
Value-weighted stocks	100.00	134.90	34.90	−16.30	−1.70	−12.30
Small stocks	100.00	175.00	75.00	23.80	38.40	43.50
Government bonds	100.00	135.90	35.90	−15.30	−0.70	−14.30
Equity REITs (EREIT)	100.00	197.00	97.00	45.80	60.40	46.10
Homebuilders	100.00	199.00	99.00	47.80	62.40	146.73
Property owners	100.00	240.50	140.50	89.30	103.90	−13.70
Mortgage REITs (MREIT)	100.00	133.90	33.90	−17.30	−2.70	48.08
VW real estate	100.00	195.30	95.30	44.10	58.70	22.30
EW of VW real estate	100.00	181.20	81.20	30.00	44.60	57.00

Notes:
(1) Excess trading profits are calculated in excess of the T-bill rate.
(2) Terminal wealth is the wealth at the end of December 1989 from a portfolio having an initial wealth of $100 in February of 1981.
(3) Final profit is calculated as the difference between the terminal wealth at the end of December 1989 and the initial wealth at February 1981.
(4) Relative Profit 1 is calculated as the terminal wealth for an asset relative to the terminal wealth for the S&P500 assuming a passive buy-and-hold strategy for the S&P500.
(5) Relative Profit 2 is calculated as the terminal wealth for an asset relative to the terminal wealth for the S&P500 assuming that both portfolios use the same trading strategy.
(6) Relative Profit 3 is calculated as the terminal wealth for an asset given an active trading strategy relative to the terminal wealth for that asset assuming a passive-buy-and-hold strategy.

of $74.19 is realized when terminal wealth from an actively managed Long (+) and Short (−) owner portfolio is compared to final wealth from market timing the S&P500.

Of the non-real estate assets included in the study, only small cap stocks post positive gains when compared to the three benchmarks. However, the magnitude of these profits are smaller relative to any of the real estate portfolios except for the Long and Short strategy for the owner portfolio and the Long position for the mortgage REIT portfolio. Both value-weighted stocks and government bonds perform poorly relative to all benchmarks having minimal to negative relative wealth.

Figures 2–4 graphically present a more complete perspective of the cumulative wealth level (the Y axis on each graph) from

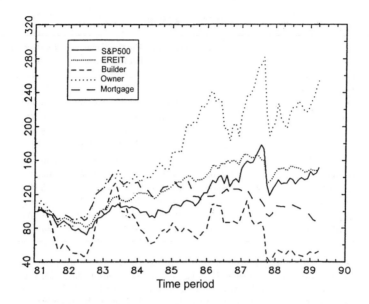

Fig. 2.   Cumulative return on the buy-and-hold strategy.

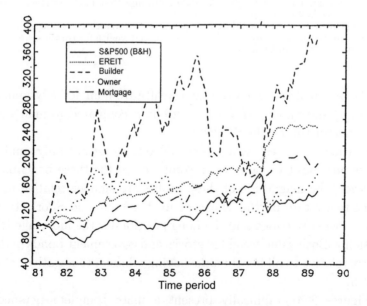

Fig. 3.   Cumulative excess return on the Long $(+)$ and short $(-)$ strategy.

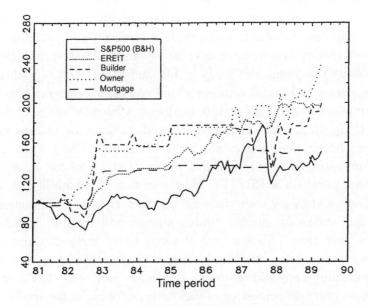

Fig. 4. Cumulative excess return on the Long (+) strategy.

implementing a buy-and-hold strategy, the long-and-short strategy, and the long strategy respectively for the four real estate portfolios. For comparison purposes, the cumulative wealth levels corresponding to buying and holding the S&P500 is also included in each graph. A comparison of these figures confirms our earlier observations that homebuilders have the most spectacular increase in wealth over time, and that of the three trading strategies, the Long (+) and Short (−) strategy results in the largest wealth levels for all real estate portfolios. In contrast, a Long scheme leads to the highest wealth accumulation for the owner group. However, Fig. 4 shows that over the period from the second quarter of 1986 to approximately the third quarter of 1987 and from the second to the third quarter of 1987, a passive buy-and-hold S&P500 strategy would have outperformed the mortgage REIT and builder portfolios, respectively.

3.5 Summary and Conclusions

Recent evidence suggests that all asset returns are predictable to some extent with excess returns on real estate relatively easier to forecast. This raises the issue of whether we can successfully exploit this level of predictability using various market timing strategies to realize superior performance over a buy-and-hold strategy. Before addressing this issue, the study of Liu and Mei (1992) is replicated using several additional value-weighted real estate categories to first determine whether their results hold over a broader range of firms. The study finds that the degree of predictability for various types of exchange-traded real estate firms is similar, albeit lower than the forecasting level which Liu and Mei (1992) find for an equally weighted portfolio of EREITs. Moreover, this predictability remains relatively stationary over time for all asset classes, which suggests that any successful market timing scheme will tend to remain effective over time. To evaluate the success of market timing performance, two active trading tactics are constrcuted together with a passive buy-and-hold strategy. Our main finding is that a value-weighted portfolio consisting of various types of exchange-traded real estate firms using either active trading strategy outperforms a passive scheme from either a unadjusted or risk-adjusted return perspective. Moreover, real estate stocks not only have higher average risk-adjusted returns but also larger trading profits with few exceptions, even though small stocks have the highest degree of out-of-sample predictability. What is even more interesting is that the builder group, which consists primarily of large cap stocks, has the highest mean excess return from either an unadjusted or risk-adjusted perspective when either active trading method is chosen with a phenomenal 2.3% excess return per month on an average using the Long (+) and Short (−) strategy. In contrast to real estate firms, the mean excess returns associated with the two active trading strategies tested do not necessarily outperform a passive buy-and-hold scheme large cap stocks and government bonds. In short, moderate evidence is found to support the proposition that we can successfully exploit the level of predictability associated with excess returns using various active market timing strategies to realize the superior performance over a buy-and-hold strategy.

Acknowledgements

We thank Doug Herold and Wayne Ferson for providing data on real estate cap rates and business condition factors respectively. We also thank John Campbell for helpful comments and Bin Gao for excellent research assistance.

Appendix: Elaboration of the Asset Pricing Framework and Estimation Procedure[7]

The asset pricing framework used in this study follows that of Liu and Mei (1992) and assumes that the following K-factor model generates assets returns:

$$\tilde{r}_{i,t+1} = E_t[\tilde{r}_{i,t+1}] + \sum_{k=1}^{K} \beta_{ik}\tilde{f}_{k,t+1} + \tilde{\varepsilon}_{i,t+1} \qquad (A.1)$$

where $\tilde{r}_{i,t+1}$ is the excess return on asset i held from time t to time $t+1$, $E_t[\tilde{r}_{i,t+1}]$ is the conditional expected excess return on asset i, conditional on information known to market participants at the end of time period t, $E_t[\tilde{f}_{k,t+1}] = 0$ and $E_t[\tilde{\varepsilon}_{i,t+1}] = 0$. The conditional expected excess return, $E_t[\tilde{r}_{i,t+1}]$, can vary through time in the current model, although the framework assumes that the beta coefficients are stationary. Since $E_t[\tilde{r}_{i,t+1}]$ is not restricted to be constant, we need to consider both the closeness of beta(s) and the co-movement of $E_t[\tilde{r}_{i,t+1}]$ through time in analyzing the co-movement of excess returns on two or more assets unless the following linear pricing relationship holds:

$$E_t[\tilde{r}_{i,t+1}] = \sum_{k=1}^{K} \beta_{ik}\tilde{\lambda}_{kt}, \qquad (A.2)$$

---

[7]This section is taken from Liu and Mei (1992).

where λ_{kt} is the "market price of risk" for the kth factor at time t and is equivalent to

$$\lambda_{kt} = \sum_{n=1}^{L} \theta_{kn} X_{nt}, \qquad (A.3)$$

if the information set at time t consists of a vector of L forecasting variables X_{nt}, $n = 1, \ldots, L$ (where X_{1t} is a constant) and that conditional expectations are a linear function of these variables. Substitution of (A.3) into (A.2) therfore results in:

$$E_t[\tilde{r}_{i,t+1}] = \sum_{k=1}^{K} \beta_{ik} \sum_{n=1}^{L} \theta_{kn} X_{nt} = \sum_{n=1}^{L} \alpha_{in} X_{nt} \qquad (A.4)$$

A comparison of Eqs. (A.3) and (A.4) reveals that the model puts the following constraints on the coefficients of Eq. (A.4):

$$\alpha_{ij} = \sum_{k=1}^{K} \beta_{ik} \theta_{kj}, \qquad (A.5)$$

where β_{ik} and θ_{kj} are free parameters. Although the (α_{ij}) matrix should have a rank of P, where P is defined as $P = \min(N, L)$, Eq. (A.5) restricts the rank of this matrix to be K where $K < P$. To test whether the restriction in Eq. (A.5) holds, we first renormalize the model by setting the factor loadings of the first K assets as follows: $\beta_{ij} = 1$ (if $j = 1$) and $\beta_{ij} = 0$ (if $j \neq 1$) for $1 \leq i \leq K$. Next, we partition the excess return matrix $R = (R_1, R_2)$, where R_1 is a $T \times K$ matrix of excess returns of the first K assets and R_2 is a $T \times (N - K)$ matrix of excess returns on the rest of the assets. Using Eqs. (A.4) and (A.5), we can derive the following regression system

$$
\begin{aligned}
R_1 &= X\Theta + \mu_1, \\
R_2 &= X\alpha + \mu_2,
\end{aligned}
\qquad (A.6)
$$

where X is a $T \times L$ matrix of the forecasting variables, Θ is a matrix of θ_{ij} and α is a matrix of α_{ij}. If the linear pricing relationship in Eq. (A.2) holds, the rank restriction implies that the data should not be able to reject the null hypothesis $H_0 : \alpha = \Theta B$, where B is a matrix of β_{ij} elements.

To estimate (A.6) we first construct a $N \times L$ sample mean matrix: $G_T = U'X/T$ where $E(U'X) = 0$ because the error term in system (A.6) has conditional mean zero given the instruments X from Eq. (A.4). Next, we stack the column vector on top of each other to obtain a $NL \times 1$ vector of g_T. A two-step algorithm is then used to find an optimal solution for the quadratic form, $g_T'W^{-1}g_T$, by minimizing over the parameter space of (Θ, α). In the first step, the identity matrix is used as the weighting matrix W. After obtaining the initial soluiton of Θ_0 and α_0, we next calculate the residuals μ_1 and μ_2 from the system of Eqs. in (A.6) and construct the following weighting matrix:

$$ W = \frac{1}{T} \sum_t (u_t u_t') \otimes (Z_t Z_t'), \tag{A.7} $$

where $\otimes$ is the Kronecker product. Next, we use the weighting matrix in (A.7) to resolve the optimization problem of minimizing $g_T'W^{-1}g_T$ over the choice of (Θ, α). When the model is correctly specified (e.g., under the null hypothesis), $Tg_T'W^{-1}g_T$, is asymptotically chi-square distributed, with the degrees of freedom equal to the difference between the number of orthogonality conditions and the number of parameters estimated: $N \times L - [K \times l + (N - K) \times K] = (N - K)(L - K)$, where N is the number of assets studied, K is the number of factor loadings, and L is the number of forecasting variables. After obtaining the weighted sum of squared residuals, we perform a chi-square test to determine if the data rejects the restricted regression system (A.6).

References

Campbell, J. Y., 1987, Stock Returns and the Term Structure, *Journal of Financial Economics* **18**, 373–399.

Campbell, J. Y., 1991, A Variance Decomposition of Stock Returns, *Economic Journal* **101**, 157–179.

Campbell, J. Y. and J. P. Mei, 1991, Where Do Betas Come From? Asset Pricing Dynamics and the Sources of Systematic Risk, New York University Working Paper.

Campbell, J. Y. and Y. Hamao, 2002, Predictable Stock Returns in the United States and Japan: A Study of Long-Term Capital Market Integration, *Journal of Finance* (forthcoming).

Chang, E. C. and W. G. Lewellen, 1984, Market Timing and Mutual Fund Investment Performance, *Journal of Business* **57**, 57–72.

Chen, N., R. Roll and S. Ross, 1986, Economic Forces and the Stock Market, *Journal of Business* **59**, 386–403.

Connor, G. and R. A. Korajczyk, 1988, Risk and Return in an Equilibrium APT: Application of a New Test Methodology, *Journal of Financial Economics* **21**, 255–289.

Cumby, R. E. and D. M. Modest, 1987, Testing for Market Timing Ability: A Framework for Forecast Evaluation, *Journal of Financial Economics*, **19**, 169–189.

DeBondt, W. and R. Thaler, 1987, Further Evidence on Investor Overreaction and Stock Market Seasonality, *Journal of Finance* **42**, 557–581.

Fama, E. and K. French, 1988, Dividend Yields and Expected Stock Returns, *Journal of Financial Economics* **22**, 3–25.

Fama, E. and K. French, 1989, Business Conditions and Expected Return on Stocks and Bonds, *Journal of Financial Economics* **25**, 23–49.

Fama, E. and G. W. Schwert, 1977, Asset Returns and Inflation, *Journal of Financial Economics* **5**, 115–146.

Ferson, W., 1989, Changes in Expected Security Returns, Risk, and Level of Interest Rates, *Journal of Finance* **44**, 1191–1217.

Ferson, W., 1990, Are the Latent Variables in Time-Varying Expected Returns Compensation for Consumption Risk? *Journal of Finance* **45**, 397–430.

Ferson, W. and C. Harvey, 1991, The Variation of Economic Risk Premiums, *Journal of Political Economy* (Forthcoming) **99** (2), 385–416.

Ferson, W., S. Kandel and R. Stambaugh, 1987, Test of Asset Pricing with Time-Varying Expected Risk Premiums and Market Betas, *Journal of Finance* **42**, 201–219.

Gibbons, M. R. and W. Ferson, 1985, Testing Asset Pricing Models with Changing Expectations and an Unobservable Market Portfolio, *Journal of Financial Economics* **14**, 217–236.

Giliberto, S. M., 1990, Equity Real Estate Investment Trust and Real Estate Returns, *Journal of Real Estate Resarch* **5**, 259–263.

Glascock, J. L., 1991, Market Conditions, Risk, and Real Estate Portfolio Returns: Some Empirical Evidence, *Journal of Real Estate Finance and Economics* **4**, 367–373.

Gyourko, J. and D. Keim, 1991, What Does the Stock Market Tell Us About Real Estate Returns? Working Paper, The Wharton School.

Harvey, C. R., 1989, Time-Varying Conditional Covariances in Tests of Asset Pricing Models, *Journal of Financial Economics* **24**, 289–317.

Henriksson, R. D., 1984, Market Timing and Mutual Fund Performance: An Empirical Investigation, *Journal of Business* **57**, 73–96.

Henriksson, R. D. and R.C. Merton, 1981, On Market Timing and Investment Performance. II. Statistical Procedures for Evaluating Forecasting Skills, *Journal of Business* **54**, 513–533.

Jensen, M. C., 1968, The Performance of Mutual Funds in the Period 1945–1964, *Journal of Finance* **23**, 389–416.

Keim, D. B., 1983, Size Related Anomalies and Stock Return Seasonality: Empirical Evidence, *Journal of Financial Economics* **12**, 13–32.

Keim, D. and R. Stambaugh, 1986, Predicting Returns in the Stock and Bond Markets, *Journal of Financial Economics* **17**, 357–390.

Liu, C. and J. P. Mei, 1992, Predictability of Returns on Equity REITs and Their Co-Movement with Other Assets, *Journal of Real Estate Finance and Economics* **5**, 401–408.

Liu, C. and J. P. Mei, 1994, An Analysis of Real Estate Risk Using the Present Value Model, *Journal of Real Estate Finance and Economic* (Forthcoming)**8**, 5–20.

Mei, J. P., 1993, A Semi-Autoregressive Approach to the Arbitrage Pricing Theory, *Journal of Finance* (Forthcoming) **48**, 599–620.

Mei, J. P. and A. Saunders, 1995, Bank Risk and Real Estate: An Asset Pricing Perspective, *Journal of Real Estate Finance and Economics* **10**, 199–224.

Nourse, H. O., 1987, The "Cap Rate," 1966–1984: A Test of the Impact of Income Tax Changes on Income Property, *Land Economics* **63**, 147–152.

White, H., 1980, A Heteroskedasticity-Consistent Covariance Matrix Estimator and a Direct Test for Heteroskedasticity, *Econometrica* **48**, 817–838.

CHAPTER 4

A Time-varying Risk Analysis of Equity and Real Estate Markets in the U.S. and Japan

CROCKER H. LIU and JIANPING MEI*

Associate Professors of Finance, Leonard N. Stern School of Business, New York University

Previous studies have found that the return behavior on Japanese assets is consistent with the existing evidence on U.S. stocks in general. The current study offers new insights which suggest that Japanese equity and real estate markets might not necessarily behave in a parallel manner to U.S. capital markets. These insights are obtained from an examination of the nature of expected and unexpected movements in the returns of Japanese assets and U.S. assets, using a present value model which allows for a time-varying expected discount rate in conjunction with a Vector Autoregressive (VAR) process. One distinct difference is that changes in the future expected return for Japanese real estate and stocks are less persistent over time than their U.S. counterparts, even though returns on Japanese real estate (stock) is relatively more predictable than (similar to) returns on U.S. stocks and real estate. A further difference in U.S.–Japan returns is that there is no sign of negative serial correlation (or mean reversion) for returns on Japanese real estate within a 7-year horizon. Returns on Japanese stocks also exhibit a weaker mean reversion process relative to returns on U.S. stocks and U.S. real estate.

*Any comments can be sent to the authors at: 44 West 4th Street, Suite 9-100, New York, NY 10012-1126, Phone (212) 998-0353 and (212) 998-0354 respectively. We thank John Campbell for letting us use his variance decomposition algorithm and Sanjiv Gupta for providing data on Japanese stock price indices by industry.

77

4.1   Introduction

Previous studies on the return behavior of Japanese assets have focused on whether the findings for U.S. securities are robust when a parallel analysis is performed of Japanese financial markets. Most notably, one area of academic interest is whether innovations in macroeconomics factors which serve as proxies for underlying risk factors that drive U.S. stock returns are portable to the Japanese equity market.[1] A related area of interest for which little evidence exists, either for the U.S. or Japan, involves what moves capital markets. For example, why do prices change in a given manner?[2] More specifically, what proportion of the variation in total returns is attributable to the variance of contemporaneous expected returns and what percentage is associated with the variance of unexpected returns? To what extent do cash flow risk and discount rate risk account for movements in unexpected returns?

---

[1]For example, Elton and Gruber (1990) find that four factors associated with macroeconomic variables are evident in Japanese stock returns, although none of the factors appear, to imply positive risk premia. Hamao (1990) finds that similar macroeconomic factors influence both the U.S. and Japanese markets. In particular, changes in expected inflation, unanticipated changes in risk premium and in the term structure's slope, changes in monthly production, and terms of trade are associated with positive risk premia, while oil price changes and unanticipated changes in foreign exchange are not priced in the Japanese equity market. Brown and Otsuki (1990) also find evidence that six to seven macro-factors are priced sources of risk in the Japanese market, using the paradigm of McElroy and Burmeister (1988) together with a VAR process. Campbell and Hamao (1989) in a related paper find that excess returns on both U.S. and Japanese stocks are predictable using similar sets of macroeconomic variables.

[2]One of the few studies which address this issue is Campbell (1991) who decomposes movements in unexpected U.S. stock returns into the variance in news about future cash flows and the variance in news about future returns, using a vector autoregressive system together with a present value model. Campbell finds that the variance of news about future cash flows accounts for only 33–50% of the fluctuations in unexpected returns with the remainder attributable to variations in news about future expected returns. Campbell and Ammer (1991) extend Campbell (1991) to address the question of what moves stock and bond markets, while Liu and Mei (1992) examine the extent to which cash flow risk, discount rate risk, and the covariance between these two types of risk are different for large stocks, small stocks, and real estate in the U.S. market.

The purpose of the current study is to examine movements in the prices of Japanese equity and real estate stocks and to compare these movements with price fluctuations for their U.S. counterparts, using the present value model of Campbell (1987, 1991) which allows the expected discount rate to vary through time in conjunction with a Vector Autoregressive (VAR) process. One key issue explored is whether the relative influence of the variance in news about future returns and the variance in news about future dividends for Japanese equity and real estate markets is similar to that for U.S. markets. In particular, are movements in the Japanese capital markets driven primarily by news about the future expected return (discount rate) or by news about future cash flows? How persistent over time are changes in the expected rate of return. For example, for how many periods does a drift occur in expected returns? Another related issue investigated is whether strong negative serial correlation exists for Japanese equity and real estate returns, given the evidence that investors can successfully profit from using a contrarian investment strategy for U.S. capital markets in the short run. We analyze real estate in addition to stocks, because prior studies such as Hamao and Hoshi (1991) and Liu and Mei (1992) find that the return characteristics of stocks are not necessarily similar to real estate returns. Moreover, the value of land represents a major portion of the market wealth in every country. Bonne and Sachs (1989) report that not only is the land value of Japan three times Japan's GNP, but also the average unit price for a Japanese parcel is 90 times that of comparable land in the U.S. However, Boone and Sachs also observe that the value of land relative to GNP is similar in each country.

We find that Japanese stocks and real estate differ in several important respects from their U.S. counterparts. One distinguishing intercountry aspect is that current Japanese stock returns are useful in predicting future expected returns on Japanese real estate, while existing returns on U.S. real estate are valuable in forecasting future anticipated returns on U.S. stocks. Another notable feature is that news on future cash flows account for a major portion of the variation in unexpected returns on Japanese stocks and real estate. News on future expected returns, in contrast, have a greater impact on returns on U.S. stocks and real estate. A further distinction between countries is that changes in the future expected discount rate are less persistent over time for Japanese real estate and stocks relative to their U.S. counterparts, even though returns on Japanese assets are at least as predictable as returns on U.S. assets. Consequently, changes in the future expected returns have a greater impact on current prices for U.S. relative to Japanese stocks and real estate. A final differentiating result is that returns on Japanese stocks exhibit weaker negative serial correlations relative to returns on U.S. stocks and real estate. Japanese real estate, in contrast, appears to have fairly strong positive serial correlations over the period examined. Thus, a contrarian investment strategy is less likely to be profitable in the short run for stocks and real estate in Japan relative to the U.S.

However, we do find some parallels between stocks and real estate in the U.S. and Japan. Most of the variation in total returns for these assets in both countries is attributable to the variance in *unexpected* stock returns, although the anticipated volatility in real estate returns accounts for a larger portion of the movement in returns in the U.S. and Japan. Besides this, returns on real estate are more predictable relative to stock returns in both countries. Changes in the expected return on real estate are more persistent over time compared to stocks in each country. The return on real estate also exhibits less negative serial correlations relative to stocks in both the U.S. and Japan.

The rest of the paper is organized as follows: The next section discusses the framework used to view the relationship between unexpected returns and movements in expected returns. This section also describes the VAR approach used to decompose the variance of Japanese stock returns into news about future cash flows and news about future expected returns. Section 4.3 describes our data set while our empirical results, including the extent to which variations in unexpected returns for Japanese securities are associated with different types of news, are reported in Sec. 4.4. Section 4.5 concludes the study.

4.2 The Basic Framework and Estimation Process

4.2.1 *The Relationship Between Expected Returns and Unexpected Returns*

The approximate present value model of Campbell (1991) is used to characterize the relationship between the unexpected real asset return in the next period $(t+1)$ and changes in rational expectations of future dividend growth and future asset returns. More formally, the fundamental equation is

$$h_{t+1} - E_t h_{t+1} = (E_{t+1} - E_t) \sum_{j=0}^{\infty} \rho^j \Delta d_{t+1+j}$$

$$- (E_{t+1} - E_t) \sum_{j=0}^{\infty} \rho^j h_{t+1+j}, \qquad (4.1)$$

where E_t is the expectation formed at the end of period t, h_{t+1} represents the log of the real return on an asset held from the end of period t to the end of period $t + 1$, d_{t+1} is the log of the real dividend paid during period $t + 1$, Δ denotes a 1-period backward difference, and $(E_{t+1} - E_t)$ represents a revision in expectations given that new information arrived at time $t + 1$. The parameter ρ is a constant and is constrained to be smaller than one.[3] A more detailed derivation of the model is given in the Appendix. The main point of Eq. (4.1) is that if the unexpected return on an asset is negative given that expectations are internally consistent, then it follows that either the expected future growth in dividends must decrease, the expected future returns (discount rate) on the stock must increase, or both phenomena must occur.

For our study, we will use a more compact version of Eq. (4.1) written as follows:

---

[3]The model is derived using a first-order Taylor approximation of the present value equation which relates the log of asset returns to the log of asset prices and dividends. To solve the resulting equation using a forward process, a terminal condition is imposed which does not allow the log of the dividend–price ratio to follow an explosive process.

$$\nu_{h,t+1} = \eta_{d,t+1} - \eta_{h,t+1}\,, \tag{4.2}$$

where $\nu_{h,t+1}$ is the unexpected component of the stock return h_{t+1}, $\eta_{d,t+1}$ represents news about cash flows, and $\eta_{h,t+1}$ represents news about future returns (discount rate).

4.2.2   *The Estimation Procedure*

We model eight economic state variables including the real monthly returns on stocks and real estate, the nominal return on government bills, and the dividend yield for the U.S. and Japan according to a K-order VAR process, given that the VAR process provides a useful framework to summarize data.[4] As in previous studies, we include the nominal return on government bills to capture information on the short-term interest rate, and the dividend yield which provides information on expectations about future cash flows and required returns in the stock market.[5] The real return on real estate is included in the study, given that Hamao and Hoshi (1991) find that real estate market conditions help explain the time-variation in *ex ante* Japanese equity returns and *vice versa*.

The VAR process initially involves defining a vector z_{t+1} which has k elements, the first of which are the real asset returns h_{t+1} in consideration, and additional elements in this vector are other variables which are known to the market at the end of period $t + 1$. Although we initially model asset returns under the assumption that the vector z_{t+1} follows a first-order VAR process shown in Eq. (4.3)

---

[4] The VAR approach assumes that each variable in the process is a stationary time-series and as such can be modeled using an autoregressive (AR) model. The fact that lagged state variables are present in an autoregressive process is not necessarily contradictory to market efficiency if the risk premiums paid on assets vary over time owing to changing economic conditions. If this is the case, then the lagged variables in the VAR process serve as a proxy for the economic state variables that drive the risk premium, and this also provides us some clue as to what are the relevant variabes to include in the VAR model of asset pricing dynamics.

[5] See Campbell (1990), Campbell an Hamao (1989), Campbell and Mei (1991), Fama and French (1989), and Hamao (1989).

below, we later relax this assumption:

$$z_{t+1} = Az_t + w_{t+1}. \tag{4.3}$$

Higher-order VAR models that we employ are stacked into this VAR(1) model in the same manner as discussed in Campbell and Shiller (1988a). In Eq. (4.3), the matrix A is known as the companion matrix of the VAR.

In addition to the vector z_{t+1}, we also define a k-element vector e_1, whose elements are all equal to zero except the first element which is equal to 1. The vector e_1 is used to separate out real asset returns h_{t+1} from the vector z_{t+1}, for example, $h_{t+1} = e_1' z_{t+1}$ and to extract the unexpected component of real asset returns $\nu_{h,t+1} = e_1' w_{t+1}$ from the residual vector (w_{t+1}) of the VAR process. The VAR(1) approach produces intertemporal predictions of future returns:

$$E_t h_{t+1+j} = e_1' A^{j+1} z_t. \tag{4.4}$$

From Eq. (4.4), it follows that we can define news about future returns or discount rates (the present value of the revisions in forecasted returns) as

$$\eta_{h,t+1} \equiv (E_{t+1} - E_t) \sum_{j=1}^{\infty} \rho^j h_{t+1+j} = e_1' \sum_{j=1}^{\infty} \rho^j A^j w_{t+1}$$

$$= e_1' \rho A (I - \rho A)^{-1} w_{t+1} = \lambda' w_{t+1}, \tag{4.5}$$

where $\lambda' = e_1' \rho A (I - \rho A)^{-1}$ and is a nonlinear function of the VAR coefficients. In addition to this, given that the first element of w_{t+1} is $\nu_{h,t+1} = e_1' w_{t+1}$, Eqs. (4.5) and (4.2) imply that we can write news about cash flows as follows:

$$\eta_{d,t+1} = (e_1' + \lambda') w_{t+1}. \tag{4.6}$$

We will use the expressions in Eqs. (4.5) and (4.6) to decompose the variance of unexpected asset returns ($\nu_{h,t+1}$) for each stock portfolio into the variance of the news about cash flow ($\eta_{h,t+1}$), the variance of the news about expected returns ($\eta_{h,t+1}$), and a covariance term. As in Campbell (1991), we will use the following persistence measure P_h associated with the VAR process as our measure of the persistence of expected returns:

$$P_h \equiv \frac{\sigma(\eta_{h,t+1})}{\sigma(u_{t+1})} = \frac{\sigma(\lambda' w_{t+1})}{\sigma(e_{1'} A w_{t+1})}, \tag{4.7}$$

where $u_{t+1} = (E_{t+1} - E_t)h_{t+2}$ denotes innovations in the 1-period-ahead expected return and $\sigma(x)$ denotes the standard deviation of x. This measure represents the volatility of the news about expected returns relative to the variability of the innovation in the 1-period-ahead expected return. We can interpret the persistence measure as follows: a $P_h\%$ capital loss on the stock will result given a 1% positive innovation in the expected return. The intuition underlying this persistence measure is that if changes in expected returns are temporary, then it will not impact significantly on the news about future expected returns $(\eta_{h,t+l})$. Otherwise, it will have a major impact on stock returns due to its effect on discount rates.

In addition to decomposing the variance of unexpected returns and determining to what extent expected returns persist on an intertemporal basis, we use a variance ratio test to ascertain if Japanese stock and real estate returns exhibit mean-reverting behavior similar to that for their U.S. counterparts.[6] The variance ratio statistic $V(K)$, which is defined as the ratio of the variance of K-period returns to the variance of 1-period returns, divided by K, can be calculated directly from the autocorrelations of 1-period returns by using the fact that

$$V(K) = 1 + 2 \sum_{j=1}^{K-1} \left(1 - \frac{j}{K}\right) \text{Corr}(h_t, h_{t-j}). \tag{4.8}$$

The variance ratio equals one for white noise returns(i.e., there is no serial correlation in the return series so $\text{Corr}(h_t, h_{t-j}) = 0$); it exceeds one when returns are mostly positively autocorrelated, and it is below one when negative autocorrelations dominate.

---

[6] Campbell (1990), Cochrane (1988), Lo and MacKinlay (1988) and Poterba and Summers (1988), have all used the variance ratio test to document the mean reverting behavior of stock rctums. Kandel and Stambaugh (1988) also report a number of calculations of this type.

The Generalized Method of Moments of Hansen (1982) is used to jointly estimate the VAR coefficients and the elements of the variance–covariance matrix of VAR innovations. To calculate the standard errors associated wih estimation error for any statistic, we first let γ and V represent the whole set of parameters and the variance–covariance matrix, respectively. Next, we write any statistic such as the covariance between news about future expected returns and discount rates, as a nonlinear function $f(\gamma)$ of the parameter vector γ. The standard error for the statistic is then estimated as $\sqrt{[f_\gamma(\gamma)'Vf_\gamma(\gamma)]}$.

4.3 The Data

Monthly returns on value-weighted stocks, returns on government bills, the dividend yield, and the rate of inflation for Japan are obtained from Hamao/Ibbotson and Associates *Stocks, Bonds, and Inflation 1989 Japan Yearbook* and updates to that yearbook. In addition to this, monthly returns for Japanese real estate are derived using the real estate index taken from the Nikkei Telecom News Retrieval system which reports Japanese stock price indices by industry for the first section of the Tokyo Stock Exchange.[7] Returns on this Japanese real estate security index do provide information on conditions in the underlying real estate market, given that correlations of the absolute levels of this Japanese real estate index with the Japanese CPI housing index and also the Japanese Real Estate Institute (JREI) Indices used in Hamao and Hoshi (1991) reveal correlations ranging from 0.78 for the JREI Indices to 0.97 for the CPI housing index.

Data on monthly U.S. stock returns, dividend yields, yields on 1-month Treasury bills, and the rate of inflation are taken from Ibbotson and Associates *Stocks, Bonds, Bills, and Inflation* series on

---

[7] Japanese stocks included in the real estate index include Mitsui Real Estate Development, Mitsubishi Estate, Tokyo Tatemono, Osaka Building, Sankei Building, Tokyu Land, Kakuei Construction, Daiwa Danchi, Sumitomo Realty and Development, Odakyu Real Estate, Toho Real Estate, Towa Real Estate Development, Taiheiyo Kouhatsu, Nichimo, Daikyo, TOC, and Tokyo Rakutenchi.

the CRSP tape. To proxy for real estate returns in the U.S., we use the value-weighted equity Real Estate Investment Trust (REIT) series published by the National Association of Real Estate Investment Trusts (NAREIT).[8] The NAREIT index includes all Equity REITs (EREITs), not just those having a continuous price history over the period in question to avoid the problem of survivorship bias. Gyourko and Keim (1992) have shown that lagged EREIT returns are useful in predicting appraisal-based real estate returns and that EREIT returns are contemporaneously correlated with the National Association of Realtors (NAR) existing home sales appreciation rate. Fisher *et al.* (1991) find that appraisal-based series such as the Frank Russell Company (FRC) index move very closely with the NAREIT index after "de-smoothing" the appraisal-based series, while Mei and Lee (1994) also discover that the FRC index and EREITs are driven by common real estate factors. Consequently, these studies indicate that returns on securitized real estate represent good proxies for returns to the underlying real estate.

Returns on stocks and real estate in both countries are deflated using the respective own country rate of inflation. The resulting returns on Japanese stock and real estate are then denominated in U.S. dollars. All of the series used start in February 1972 and end in February 1992.

4.4 Empirical Results

Table 1 provides summary statistics on and correlations among real returns for Japanese and U.S. value-weighted stocks and real estate securities as well as for our other forecasting variables denominated in U.S. dollars. While real estate exhibits a lower risk and higher returns relative to stocks in the U.S., which is consistent with the findings of Liu and Mei (1992), Table 1 reveals that the converse situation exists with respect to Japanese real estate and stocks. U.S.

---

[8]An EREIT is analogous to a closed-end investment company for investors who want to participate in the ownership of real estate. A REIT is not taxed on distributed taxable income if it satisfies certain provisions, including the fact that at least 95% of net annual taxable income must be distributed to shareholders.

Table 1. Summary statistics.

	Mean	S.D.	ρ_1
Dependent variables			
Real Return on U.S. stock portfolio (USStk)	0.387	4.81	0.057
Real Return on U.S. real estate portfolio (USRE)	0.392	4.13	0.128
Real Return on Japanese stock portfolio (JPStk)	0.978	6.63	0.091
Real Return on Japanese real estate portfolio (JPRE)	0.532	7.57	0.288
Nominal Return on U.S. T-Bills (USTBill)	0.079	1.61	0.738
Nominal Return on U.S. Dividend Yield (USDYld)	4.117	0.88	0.967
Nominal Return on Japanese T-Bills (JPTBill)	0.041	4.19	0.209
Nominal Return on Japanese Dividend Yield (JPDYld)	1.623	0.78	0.994

	USStk	USRE	JPStk	JPRE	USTBill	USDYld	JPTBill	JPDYld
Correlations								
USStk	1.00							
USRE	0.64	1.00						
JPStk	0.31	0.26	1.00					
JPRE	0.17	0.15	0.69	1.00				
USTBill	−0.24	−0.23	−0.07	−0.14	1.00			
USDYld	0.13	0.13	−0.08	−0.04	−0.09	1.00		
JPTBill	−0.06	−0.08	0.40	0.42	−0.03	0.04	1.00	
JPDYld	−0.05	0.04	0.02	−0.03	0.00	0.34	−0.02	1.00

Notes: The sample period for this table is February 1972– February 1992, with 240 observations. Units on returns are percentage per month with the real returns on Japanese stock and real estate denominated in U .S. dollars. ρ_1 is the first autocorrelation of the series.

real estate exhibits a lower volatility in returns relative to U.S. stocks, because EREITs are required by law to payout 95% of their earnings as dividends. Japanese real estate companies have a higher return volatility relative to stocks in contrast. This is probably due to their practice of using the run-up in the price of their underlying real estate to borrow additional money and reinvesting these funds in the stock market as a method of generating additional profits. In addition to this, both real estate and stocks in Japan have higher returns and risk on an average relative to their U.S. counterparts, which is not surprising given the spectacular rise in prices for Japanese stocks and real estate relative to U.S. stocks and real estate and the fact that Japanese firms tend to have higher debt-to-equity ratios in general relative to U.S. firms. Table 1 also reveals that the returns on all asset categories exhibit positive first-order autocorrelation with the returns on real estate securities in the U.S. and Japan having a relatively higher positive serial correlation. This suggests that the return on real estate in both countries tend to be more predictable relative to stocks. Although real estate and stock returns are moderately correlated within a particular country, intercountry correlations among asset returns are low.

The results of regressing the mean adjusted real stock returns on eight forecasting variables, the lag of the real return on U.S. and Japanese real estate and stocks in addition to the return on government bonds and the dividend yield are reported in Table 2 for a VAR(1) process. Table 2 shows that the returns for stocks and real estate in the U.S. and Japan are predictable, with real estate in both countries more predictable relative to stocks which is consistent with the positive serial correlations in Table 1. In fact, approximately 17% (7%) of the variation in returns on Japanese (U.S.) real estate securities are predictable. In contrast, U.S. and Japanese stocks are less predictable with 6.8 and 5.9% of the variation in these returns respectively being predictable. Surprisingly, the lagged return on U.S. real estate is influential in forecasting future U.S. stock returns. U.S. dividend yields lagged are also significant in predicting both future stock and real estate returns in the U.S. Neither lagged returns on U.S. stocks and real estate nor lagged returns on Japanese real estate, in contrast, have an impact on future U.S. real estate returns, although Japanese stock returns are of marginal significance in forecasting returns on U.S. real estate. The converse situation exists with respect to returns on Japanese stocks and real estate. Lagged returns on Japanese stocks are useful in predicting future returns on Japanese real estate. One plausible explanation for this as restated earlier is that profits for Japanese real estate firms are closely linked to the stock market movements, because these asset-rich companies have borrowed on their real estate equity and have invested the proceeds in the stock market to generate additional profits. The only cross-country effect is that lagged U.S. stock returns are useful in anticipating future returns on Japanese stocks, which supports the prior findings of Hamao *et al.* (1990) and Campbell and Hamao (1989) that the Japanese stock market is more sensitive to foreign

Table 2. Basic VAR results for real returns on Japanese and U.S. stocks using generalized method of moments one lag, monthly: Period February 1972 to February 1992 (T statistics in parentheses).

Dependent variable	USStk$_t$	USRE$_t$	JPStk$_t$	JPRE$_t$	USTBill$_t$	USDYld$_t$	JPTBill$_t$	JPDYld$_t$	R^2	P-value	DW
USStk$_{t+1}$	-0.127 (-1.39)	0.198 (2.18)	0.053 (0.82)	0.013 (0.20)	-0.260 (-1.38)	0.936 (2.35)	0.027 (0.34)	-0.782 (-1.81)	0.068	0.04	1.98
USRE$_{t+1}$	-0.020 (-0.28)	0.044 (0.48)	0.087 (1.55)	0.041 (0.92)	-0.279 (-1.65)	0.767 (2.02)	-0.084 (-1.17)	-0.091 (-0.22)	0.074	0.02	1.99
JPStk$_{t+1}$	0.267 (2.18)	0.031 (0.25)	-0.008 (-0.07)	0.067 (0.74)	-0.171 (-0.65)	-0.402 (-0.76)	-0.096 (-0.78)	0.323 (0.54)	0.059	0.09	2.02
JPRE$_{t+1}$	0.187 (1.52)	0.080 (0.61)	0.297 (2.60)	0.107 (1.10)	-0.428 (-1.55)	0.273 (0.51)	-0.136 (-1.07)	-0.223 (-0.36)	0.174	0.00	1.95
USTBill$_{t+1}$	0.006 (0.21)	-0.024 (-0.90)	-0.004 (-0.28)	-0.008 (-0.76)	0.709 (12.85)	-0.158 (-1.60)	-0.061 (-2.67)	0.068 (0.83)	0.589	0.00	1.94
USDYld$_{t+1}$	-0.043 (-25.34)	-0.003 (-1.91)	0.002 (2.24)	0.001 (0.55)	-0.001 (-0.16)	1.002 (129.67)	-0.003 (-1.96)	-0.010 (-1.39)	0.991	0.00	2.36
JPTBill$_{t+1}$	0.082 (1.08)	-0.025 (-0.32)	-0.124 (-2.14)	-0.098 (-1.79)	-0.100 (-0.49)	0.001 (0.00)	0.363 (4.28)	-0.082 (-0.26)	0.129	0.00	2.11
JPDYld$_{t+1}$	-0.000 (-0.37)	-0.000 (-0.31)	-0.012 (-11.94)	0.001 (2.31)	0.001 (0.77)	0.004 (0.97)	0.007 (7.52)	0.986 (163.72)	0.996	0.00	1.62

Notes: Real returns on Japanese stock and real estate are denominated in U.S. dollars. The *P*-value refers to the significance level for a test of the hypothesis that all regression coefficients are zero. DW is the Durbin-Watson statistic.

shocks compared to the U.S. stock market. The short-term Japanese bill is not an important factor in predicting returns on either U.S. or Japanese assets, while the U.S. T-bill is only marginally significant in predicting future real estate returns in both countries.

To determine the lag length used in the VAR process, we performed a joint Wald-test of including an additional lag in our VAR(1) model. Our test reveals that while a second lag of some variables is significant, the joint test cannot reject the hypothesis that the coefficients on the second lag are jointly zero.[9]

We therefore use a VAR(1) process and alternatively use a VAR(2) process to decompose the variance of real asset returns into the variance of contemporaneous expected asset returns and the variance of unexpected asset returns. A decomposition of this risk in Table 3 reveals that the variance of contemporaneous *expected* asset returns accounts for only a minimal portion of the total variation associated with the return on each asset class regardless of whether a VAR(1) or VAR(2) process is used. The only exception to this is for Japanese real estate. The volatility of contemporaneous expected returns on Japanese real estate accounts for 17.4–21.2% of the total real estate risk. Movements in contemporaneous expected returns on U.S. assets and Japanese stocks, in contrast, account for a much lower portion (5.9–11.8%) of the total risk for these asset classes. Consequently, the variance of unexpected returns accounts for most of the variance in total returns for both U.S. and Japanese assets which is consistent with the evidence in the U.S. market.

The variance of unexpected asset returns associated with each equation in the VAR system denoted σ_ε^2 is further partitioned into three components in Table 4. The three components are the news about future cash flows or cash flow risk [Var(η_d)], the *future* expected return or discount rate risk [Var(η_h)], and the covariance between future cash flow risk and discount rate risk [Cov($\eta_d\eta_h$)]. For easier interpretation, the three terms Var(η_d), Var(η_h), and -2 Cov($\eta_d\eta_h$) are given as ratios to the variance of the unexpected real returns

---

[9]A test on the significance of a VAR(3) process is not possible owing to lack of degrees of freedom. In our study, we present results for both VAR(1) and VAR(2).

Table 3. Decomposition of the *total* variance of real U.S. and Japan asset returns, (decomposed into variances of expected and unexpected asset returns).

Asset category	R^2	Total variance σ^2	Expected σ_E^2	Unexpected σ_ε^2
VAR(1) process				
U.S. stocks	0.068	23.136	1.573	21.563
U.S. real estate	0.074	17.057	1.262	15.795
Japanese stocks	0.059	43.957	2.594	41.363
Japanese real estate	0.174	57.305	9.971	47.334
VAR(2) process				
U.S. stocks	0.118	23.136	2.730	20.406
U.S. real estate	0.114	17.057	1.945	15.112
Japanese stocks	0.094	43.957	4.145	39.812
Japanese real estate	0.212	57.305	12.149	45.156

Notes: σ^2 is defined as the variance of total real returns for each asset. This variance can be decomposed into two components: σ_E^2 which is defined as the variance of expected asset returns and σ_ε^2 which represents the unexplained variance of the residual term associated with each equation in the VAR system or alternatively the variance of the unexpected asset returns. By definition, the covariance between expected and unexpected asset returns is zero. The R^2 represents the variation in total asset returns which is accounted for by the VAR(n) process where n is the number of lags.

so that they sum to 1. Table 4 reveals that although cash flow risk accounts for the largest portion of the variance in unexpected returns for all Japanese assets, it is not statistically significant owing to large estimation errors. Moreover, news about future expected returns has also no statistically significant impact on Japanese asset returns.

Returns on U.S. stocks and real estate, in contrast, are influenced by news on future expected returns, although the impact of this news is not statistically significant for real estate. News about future cash flows, however, is significant for U.S. real estate returns. This is consistent with the fact that EREITs are required to pay out 95% of their earnings. Changes in future expected cash flows for EREITs could arise in part from changing expectations in future rental rates, anticipated vacancies, and tentative absorption rates. The Corr($\eta_d \eta_h$) column of Table 4 also reveals that good news about changes in future cash flows tend to be strongly associated with increases in expected future returns (discount rate) for U.S. and Japanese securities

Table 4. Variance decomposition of *unexpected* real asset returns on Japanese and U.S. assets (standard erros are in parenthesis).

VAR specification	R^2	σ_ε^2	Var(η_d)	Var(η_h)	-2Cov(η_d, η_h)	Corr(η_d, η_h)	P_h
1 *Lag, monthly*							
U.S. stocks	0.068	21.56	0.293	0.686	0.022	-0.024	4.692
			(0.24)	(0.34)	(0.25)	(0.29)	(2.08)
U.S. real estate	0.074	15.79	0.807	1.289	-1.096	0.537	6.057
			(0.45)	(1.08)	(1.51)	(0.37)	(3.08)
Japanese stocks	0.059	41.36	1.276	0.068	-0.344	0.584	1.133
			(1.25)	(0.27)	(1.50)	(1.18)	(2.30)
Japanese real estate	0.174	47.33	1.970	0.282	-1.251	0.840	1.280
			(1.15)	(0.46)	(1.60)	(0.18)	(1.02)
2 *Lags, monthly*							
U.S. stocks	0.118	20.41	0.220	0.791	-0.012	0.014	4.143
			(0.17)	(0.30)	(0.27)	(0.32)	(1.63)
U.S. real estate	0.114	15.11	0.937	1.271	-1.207	0.553	4.804
			(0.55)	(1.02)	(1.53)	(0.33)	(2.45)
Japanese stocks	0.094	39.81	1.364	0.145	-0.509	0.572	1.663
			(1.17)	(0.26)	(1.41)	(0.87)	(1.57)
Japanese real estate	0.212	45.16	2.495	0.568	-2.063	0.867	1.604
			(1.40)	(0.68)	(2.06)	(0.13)	(0.92)

Notes: σ_h^2 represents the unexplained variance of the residual term associated with each equation in the VAR system. η_d and η_h represent news about future cash flows and news about future expected returns, respectively. They are calculated from the VAR system using Eqs (4.5) and (4.6). The three terms Var(η_d), Var(η_h), and -2Cov(η_d, η_h) are given as ratios to the variance of the unexpected asset return so from Eq. (2) they sum to 1. The persistence measure P_h is defined in Eq. (7). A typical 1% positive innovation in the expected real return is associated with a P_h% capital loss on the stock.

except for U.S. stocks for a VAR(1) process. This means that whenever there is good news about future cash flow, investors become apprehensive about the future and so demand higher expected future returns. The net effect of this phenomenon is that it dampens the shock of future cash flow news and future discount rate news to the market because they work in opposite directions. News about future cash flow is good for the current asset price, whereas news about future *expected* return is bad for the current asset price. This phenomena is consistent with stocks and real estate in the U.S. and Japan (except for U.S. stocks for a VAR(1) process). However, the correlation is significant only for real estate returns in the U.S. and Japan.

A persistence measure P_h is also computed in the last column of Table 4 using Eq. (4.7). This measure of persistence measures the capital loss on a stock given a positive innovation in the discount rate. For example, a typical 1% positive innovation in the future expected return (discount rate) is associated with a P_h% decline in value on the stock. The higher the P_h value, the more persistent over time are the changes in expected return. The measure of persistence (P_h) differs from R^2 in that R^2 measures the ability to forecast expected returns in the *next* period $(t+1)$ whereas P_h measures how persistent *over time* $(t+1, \ldots, t+T)$ are changes in the expected rate of return or discount rate. For example, for how many periods does a positive (negative) drift occur in expected returns. The persistence measure reveals that changes in the future expected return (discount rate) for Japanese stocks and real estate are less persistent over time than their U.S. counterparts (cf. Campbell, 1991). This means that even though the expected returns for Japanese assets are high today, it is unlikely that these expected returns will remain high tomorrow. The temporary nature of changes in the discount rate for Japanese assets implies that the forecasted changes in expected return will have a smaller impact on current price and therefore on current returns on Japanese stock and real estate. This is consistent with the above result in Table 4 that news about future expected return explains a small portion of σ_ε^2 in Japan.

Figures 1 and 2 provide plots of the variance ratio calculations for U.S. and Japanese asset returns using a VAR(1) and VAR(2) process, respectively. As stated earlier in this paper, the variance ratio is equal to one for white noise returns (i.e., there is no serial correlation in the return series); it exceeds one when returns are mostly positively autocorrelated, and it is below one when negative autocorrelations dominate. The variance ratios are calculated using 6-month intervals and go from 6 to 90 months. Figure 2 reveals that the variance ratios are always greater than 1 and are increasing steadily over the 7-year horizon for Japanese real estate, implying that the autocorrelations for all holding period returns are dominantly positive. However, returns on Japanese real estate display some evidence of negative serial correlation when a VAR(1) process is employed. However, returns on Japanese stock and U.S. real estate take a longer time to display

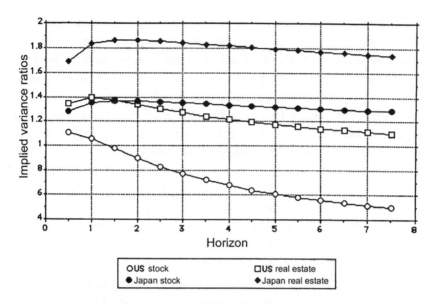

Fig. 1.   Implied variance ratios using a VAR(1) process. Variance ratios are calculated from the VAR(1) models estimated in Table 2.

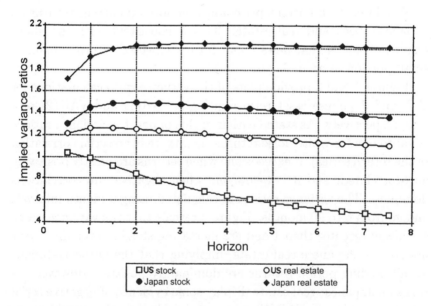

Fig. 2.   Implied variance ratios using a VAR(2) process. Variance ratios are calculated from the VAR(2) model.

negative autocorrelations relative to U.S. stock returns. In addition, the returns on Japanese assets show signs of negative autocorrelation much more slowly when compared to the mean reversion process for U.S. assets. This result is not unexpected, given our earlier finding that Japanese capital markets are driven mainly by news on future cash flows and are therefore much less influenced by news on future expected returns, which are more likely to be affected by market overreaction or the changing perception of risk by investors.[10] This finding is consistent with prior evidence for U.S. capital markets that negative autocorrelations (or mean reversion) exist for long horizon returns, even though mean reversion is much weaker for real estate relative to stocks (cf. Campbell, 1990; Cochrane, 1988; Kandel and Stambaugh, 1988; Lo and MacKinlay, 1988; Poterba and Summers, 1988; and more recently Liu and Mei, 1994).

4.5 Summary and Conclusions

The current study offers evidence that returns on Japanese stocks and real estate do not necessarily exhibit behavior parallel to those of their U.S. counterparts. In particular, we find that current Japanese stock returns are useful in predicting future expected returns on Japanese real estate. Existing returns on U.S. real estate, in contrast, are valuable in forecasting future anticipated returns on U.S. stocks. Another distinguishing intercountry aspect is that changes in the future expected returns are less persistent over time for Japanese assets relative to their U.S. counterparts, which suggests that changes in the future expected returns have a lesser impact on current prices for Japanese assets relative to U.S. assets. A final distinguishing characteristic is that the return on Japanese stocks and real estate exhibit a weaker negative serial correlation (or mean reversion) compared to returns on U.S. assets over the periods examined. However, our study does find some parallels between stocks and real estate in the U.S.

---

[10]From the perspective of market timing, this implies that contrarian strategists who want to exploit mean reversion have to be more patient with the Japanese market, because there is little evidence of negative serial correlation in the short run.

and Japan. Not only are the returns on real estate more predictable relative to stock returns, but also changes in the expected return on real estate are more persistent over time compared to stocks in both countries. The negative serial correlation for real estate is also found to be weaker compared to stocks across both the U.S. and Japan.

Appendix: The Dividend-Ratio Model

Campbell and Shiller (1988a) use a first-order Taylor series approximation of the log of the holding period return equation, $h_{t+1} = \log\left((P_{t+1} + D_{t+1})/P_t\right)$ to obtain the following equation:

$$h_{t+1} \approx k + \delta_t - \rho\delta_{t+1} + \Delta d_{t+1} \qquad (A.1)$$

where h_{t+1} is the asset return in period $t+1$, d_t is the log of the real dividend paid during period t, δ_t is the log dividend-price ratio $d_t - p_t$, p_t is the log real stock price at the end of period t, ρ is the average ratio of the stock price to the sum of the stock price and the dividend, and the constant k is a nonlinear function of ρ.[11] The log dividend-price ratio model δ_t is next obtained from Eq. (A.1) by treating Eq. (A.1) as a difference equation relating δ_t to δ_{t+1}, Δd_{t+1} and h_{t+1}, and then solving this equation forward imposing the terminal condition that δ_{t+i} does not explode as i increases ($\lim_{i \to \infty} \rho^i \delta_{t+1} = 0$) The resulting log dividend-price equation is

$$\delta_t = \sum_{j=0}^{\infty} \rho^j (h_{t+1+j} - \Delta d_{t+j+j}) - \frac{k}{1-\rho}. \qquad (A.2)$$

Equation (A.2) represents the present value of all future returns h_{t+j} and dividend growth rates Δd_{t+j}, discounted at the constant rate ρ with a constant $k/(1-\rho)$ subtracted from this result and implies that if the dividend yield is currently large, high future returns will occur unless dividend growth is low in the future. Although all of

---

[11]The equations used in the current study differ slightly from those used in Campbell and Shiller (1988a,b) owing to a difference in timing conventions. More specifically, we assume that the stock price at time t and the conditional expectation of future variables are measured at the end of period t rather than at the beginning of period t.

the variables in (A.2) are measured *ex post*, (A.2) also holds *ex ante*. Consequently, Eq. (4.1) in the paper obtains if we use the *ex ante* version of Eq. (A.2) to substitute δ_t and δ_{t+1} out of (A.1).[12]

References

Boone, P. and J. Sachs, 1989, Is Tokyo Worth Four Trillion Dollars? An Explanation for High Japanese Land Prices, Working Paper, Harvard University.

Brown, S. and T. Otsuki, 1990, Macroeconomic Factors and the Japanese Equity Markets: The CAPMD Project, in E. Elton and M. Gruber (eds.), *Japanese Capital Markets*, New York: Harper and Row.

Campbell, J. Y., 1987, Stock Returns and the Term Structure, *Journal of Financial Economics* **18**, 373–399.

Campbell, J. Y., 1990, Measuring the Persistence of Expected Returns, *American Economic Review Papers and Proceedings* **80**, 43–47.

Campbell, J. Y., 1991, A Variance Decomposition of Stock Returns, *Economic Journal* **101**, 157–179.

Campbell, J. Y. and J. Ammer, 1991, What Moves the Stock and Bond Markets? A Variance Decomposition for Long-Term Asset Returns, NBER Working Paper No. 3760, June 1991.

Campbell, J. Y. and Y. Hamao, 1989, Predictable Stock Returns in the U.S. and Japan: A Study of Long-Term Capital Market Integration, NBER Working Paper No. 3191.

Campbell, J. Y. and J. P. Mei, 1993, Where Do Betas Come From? Asset Pricing Dynamics and the Sources of Systematic Risk, *Review of Financial Studies* **6**, 567–592.

Campbell, J. Y. and R. J. Shiller, 1987, Cointegration and Tests of Present Value Models, *Journal of Political Economy* **95**, 1062–1088.

Campbell, J. Y. and R. J. Shiller, 1988a, The Dividend–Price Ratio and Expectations of Future Dividends and Discount Factors, *Review of Financial Studies 1*, 195–228.

Campbell, J. Y. and R. J. Shiller, 1988b, Stock Prices, Earnings, and Expected Dividends, *Journal of Finance* **43**, 661–676.

Elton, E. and M. Gruber, 1990, A Multi-Index Risk Model of the Japanese Stock Market, in E. Elton and M. Gruber (eds.), *Japanese Capital Markets*, New York: Harper and Row.

---

[12]This follows from the fact that δ_t is unchanged on the left hand side of Eq. (A.2) if we take expectations of Eq. (A.2), conditional on information available at the end of time period t because δ_t is in the intormation set and the right hand side of Eq. (A.2) becomes an expected discounted value. See Campbell and Shiller (1988a) for an evaluation of the quality of the linear approximation in Eqs. (A.1) and (A.2).

Fama, E. and K. French, 1989, Business Conditions and Expected Return on stocks and Bonds, *Journal of Financial Economics* **25**, 23–49.

Ferson, W. and C. Harvey, 1991, The Variation of Economic Risk Premiums, *Journal of Political Economy* **99** (2), 385–416.

Fisher, J. D., R. B. Webb and D. Geltner, 1991, Historical Value Indices of Commercial Real Estate, Working Paper, University of Indiana.

Gibbons, M. R. and W. Ferson, 1985, Testing Asset Pricing Models with Changing Expectations and an Unobservable Market Portfolio, *Journal of Financial Economics* **14**, 217–236.

Gyourko, J. and D. Keim, 1992, What Does the Stock Market Tell Us About Real Estate Returns? *AREUEA Journal* **20**, 457–486.

Hamao, Y., 1989, Japanese Stocks, Bonds, Bills, and Inflation, 1973–1987, *Journal of Portfolio Management* **15**, 20–26.

Hamao, Y. 1990, An Empirical Examination of the Arbitrage Pricing Theory: Using Japanese Data, in E. Elton and M. Gruber (eds.), *Japanese Capital Markets*, New York: Harper and Row.

Hamao, Y. 1991, Tokyo Stock Exchange, in *The New Palgrave Dictionary of Money and Finance*, London: Macmillan Press.

Hamao, Y. and T. Hoshi, 1991, Stock ana Land Prices in Japan, Working Paper, Columbia University.

Hamao, Y., R. W. Masulis and V. Ng, 1990, Correlations in Price Changes and Volatility Across International Stock Markets, *Review of Financial Studies* **3**, 281–308.

Jaffe, J. and R. Westerfield, 1985, Patterns in Japanese Common Stock Returns: Day of the Week and Turn of the Year Effects, *Journal of Financial and Quantitative Analysis* **20**, 261–272.

Kato, K. and J. S. Schallheim, 1985, Seasonal and Size Anomalies in the Japanese Stock Market, *Journal of Financial and Quantitative Analysis* **20**, 243–260.

Liu, C. H. and J. Mei, 1992, The Predictability of Returns on Equity REITS and Their Co-Movement with Other Assets, *Journal of Real Estate Finance and Economics* **5**, 401–408.

Liu, C. H. and J. P. Mei, 1994, An Analysis of Real Estate Risk Using the Present Value Model, *Journal of Real Estate Finance and Economics* **8**, 5–20.

Mei, J. P. and A. Lee, 1994, Is there a Real Estate Factor Premium? *Journal of Real Estate Finance and Economics* (Forthcoming).

Lo, A. W. and A. C. MacKinlay, 1988, Stock Market Prices do not Follow Random Walks: Evidence from a Simple Specification Test, *Review of Financial Studies* **1**, 41–66.

Matsumoto, T. 1989, *Japanese Stocks: A Basic Guide for the Intelligent Investor*, Tokyo: Kodansha International.

McElroy, M. B and E. Burmeister, 1988, Arbitrage Pricing Theory as a Restricted Nonlinear Multivariate Regression Model: Iterated Nonlinear Seemingly Unrelated Regression Estimates, *Journal of Business and Economic Statistics* **6** (1), 29–43.

Pettway, R. H., N. W. Sicherman and T. Yamada, 1990, The Market for Corporate Control, the Level of Agency Costs, and Corporate Collectivism in Japanese Mergers, in E. J. Elton and M. J. Gruber (eds.), *Japanese Capital Markets* New York: Harper and Row.

Roll, R. and S. A. Ross, 1980, An Empirical Investigation of the Arbitrage Pricing Theory, *Journal of Finance* **35**, 1073–1103.

Shimizu, R., 1980, *The Growth of Firms in Japan*, Tokyo: Keio Tsushin.

White, H. 1980, A Heteroskedasticity-Consistent Covariance Matrix Estimator and a Direct Test for Heteroskedasticity, *Econometrica* **48**, 817–838.

CHAPTER 5

Price Reversal, Transaction Costs, and Arbitrage Profits in Real Estate Securities Market **

JIANPING (J.P.) MEI*   and BIN GAO

This paper studies the return reversals of exchange-traded real estate securities using an arbitrage portfolio approach. Using the approach, we find that there exist significant return reversals in such securities. These return reversals could be exploited by arbitrage traders if trading costs can be ignored. However, the arbitrage profits disappear after deducting trading costs and taking into account the implicit cost of bid–ask spread. Thus, the real estate securities market is efficient at weekly intervals in the sense that one could not exploit the price reversals via some simple trading rules.

5.1 Introduction

Recent research in real estate shows that returns for exchange-traded real estate securities are predictable at monthly and quarterly intervals (see Liu and Mei (1992, 1994) and Mei and Lee (1994)). There are two explanations for this return predictability. First, the predictability is attributed to systematic time variation of risk premiums due to changes in market conditions and investors' perception of risk. Second, it is the result of some form of market inefficiency due to market overreaction or imperfection in market microstructure.

* Associate Professor of Finance, Department of Finance, Stern School of Business, New York University

** Associate Professor, Department of Finance, Kenan-Flagler Business School, The University of North Carolina at Chapel Hill.

We thank Crocker Liu for providing us with the security codes based on which our data are collected.

This paper extends their work by documenting return reversals for real estate securities at a higher frequency level (weekly).

Return reversals at weekly intervals are interesting because they provide a simple way of differentiating the two hypotheses above on return predictability. It is easy to imagine that economic conditions and investors' perception of risk should remain relatively unchanged at daily or weekly intervals while much less so at monthly or longer intervals. Thus, any evidence about weekly return reversals points strongly to the direction of market inefficiency rather than time-varying risk premiums.

Return reversals at weekly intervals are also interesting because they provide information on the magnitude of imperfections on the market microstructure. Since short-term return reversals often create short-term arbitrage trading profits in the absence of trading costs while they vanish in their presence, the trading profits provide a good measure of market liquidity and transaction costs.

Using the methodology developed by Lehmann (1990), this paper first documents the return reversals in real estate security markets and then constructs arbitrage portfolios (zero investment) to exploit the opportunity. Next, we adjust trading profits according to reasonable assumptions about bid–ask spread and transaction costs. We then discuss some implication of our findings for market efficiency and liquidity.

The chapter is organized as follows: Section 5.2 discusses the methodology. Section 5.3 provides some data description. Section 5.4 gives the empirical results, and Sec. 5.5 concludes.

5.2   Empirical Methods

The study of real estate market efficiency has always been an important issue in real estate financial research. However, owing to the lack of systematically collected transaction data, previous studies have largely ignored the issue. A notable exception is the two market-efficiency test papers by Hoag (1980), in which he studied the issue by using constructed real estate price series. Gau (1984) also collected data from Vancouver apartments and commercial property sales to study the time-series behavior of real estate price and found little evidence of market inefficiency.

Recently, Gyourko and Keim (1992) studied the relationship between exchange-traded real estate securities and the underlying real estate assets and found the returns on the two classes of real estate assets to be highly correlated. Their study opens some new possibilities for real estate market research, because price data on exchange-traded real estate securities are available on a daily and monthly basis, thus making it possible to use more elaborate statistical procedures. Recent examples include Chen *et al.* (1990) and Liu and Mei (1992, 1994). Unfortunately, most of these studies have concentrated on the real estate pricing behavior at monthly or quarterly intervals, while little attention is given to higher frequencies such as daily or weekly intervals. It is not difficult to imagine that the real estate market may be inefficient at daily or weekly intervals because, though there may be market overreaction, the cost of collecting and processing information at such high frequency may be prohibitively high. On the contrary, at monthly or longer intervals the lower cost of collecting and processing information may result in a fairly efficient exchange-traded real estate market.

To study the weekly return behaviors of exchange-traded real estate assets, this paper uses the arbitrage portfolio approach of Lehmann (1990). This approach complements the time-series approach of previous studies by explicitly calculating the trading profits associated with the exploitation of the existing market inefficiency. This allows us to make a distinction between statistical inefficiency and economic inefficiency. If return reversal or predictability in real estate market cannot be translated into economically significant abnormal returns, then we have to recognize that the market is still efficient in the sense that there is no "free lunch" or "easy profit" in the market. In this chapter we first document the return reversals in the real estate security prices and then construct arbitrage portfolio to see whether arbitrage trading profits exist.

The intuition behind Lehmann's costless arbitrage portfolio strategy is as follows: Building a costless portfolio in which the capital needed to cover the long position in securities which recently suffered lower-than-average returns (losers) is exactly offset by the short position in securities which lately experienced higher-than-average returns (winners), rolling the portfolio for some particular length of time, and unwinding it by the end of the period, investors can reap net positive profit without investing any money if the proper time duration that the market needs to realize return reversals can be identified.

Following Lehmann, we consider applying such a return reversal portfolio strategy to exchange-traded real estate securities.[1] Suppose there is a portfolio consisting of N stocks and extending in time dimension over T trading periods.[2] The ith stock's return in period $t - k$, where t is the current time period, is denoted to be $R_{i,t-k}$, and the corresponding return of the equally weighted stock portfolio in that period is represented by

$$\bar{R}_{t-k} = \frac{1}{N} \sum_{i=1}^{N} R_{i,t-k} \,. \tag{5.1}$$

The return reversal portfolio, at the beginning of time period t, is built from all the N stocks, while the weight of each stock in the portfolio, designated by $w_{i,t-k}$, is in direct proportion to the difference between return of that particular stock k period ahead, $R_{i,t-k}$, and the return of the equally weighted stock portfolio, $\bar{R}_{t-k}$, in that period, namely

$$w_{i,t-k} = \alpha(R_{i,t-k} - \bar{R}_{t-k}) \,. \tag{5.2}$$

Thus, the total investment of the portfolio, which is constructed at the beginning of period t based on the return information of period $t - k$, is

$$W_{t-k} = \sum_{i=1}^{N} w_{i,t-k} = \alpha \sum_{i=1}^{N} (R_{i,t-k} - \bar{R}_{t-k}) = 0 \,, \tag{5.3}$$

---

[1] This strategy, derived strictly from Lehmann's (1990), ensures that our results are based on *ex ante* information.

[2] A period is defined as a series of consecutive trading days, which is chosen to be 4, 5, 6, and 7 days, respectively, in this study.

where α is a parameter which, we argue, should subject to the following two constraints. First, to exploit the opportunity of return reversals, α must be negative, meaning long in past losers and short in past winners in order to realize profits on the return reversals. Second, it has been shown in Eq. (5.3) that the total investment in the portfolio is zero, implying equal amount of capital being invested in long and short positions. To set up a performance yardstick, the portfolio is to be normalized to $1.00 investment in each of the two positions. Under the two constraints, we are able to determine that

$$\alpha = - \left(\sum_{R_{i,t-k}-\bar{R}_{t-k}>0} (R_{i,t-k} - \bar{R}_{t-k}) \right)^{-1}, \qquad (5.4)$$

which shows that the investment in each of the long and the short position to be

$$\sum_{R_{i,t-k}-\bar{R}_{t-k}>0} |w_{i,t-k}| = \sum_{R_{i,t-k}-\bar{R}_{t-k}<0} |w_{i,t-k}| = 1. \qquad (5.5)$$

The profit of the portfolio at the end of period t is given by

$$\pi_{t,k} = \sum_{i=1}^{N} w_{i,t-k} R_{i,t} = - \frac{\sum_{i=1}^{N} (R_{i,t-k} - \bar{R}_{t-k}) R_{i,t}}{\sum_{R_{i,t-k}-\bar{R}_{t-k}>0} (R_{i,t-k} - \bar{R}_{t-k})}. \qquad (5.6)$$

Then, the average profit on this strategy over T periods is the arithmetic mean of each period's profit.

$$\bar{\pi}_k = \frac{1}{T} \sum_{t=1}^{T} \pi_{t,k}. \qquad (5.7)$$

And finally the total profit for a time horizon of M period is

$$\pi_{m,k}^{M} = \sum_{t=(m-1)(M+1)}^{mM} \pi_{t,k}. \qquad (5.8)$$

Obviously, any abnormally high return without accompanying risk is a sign of market inefficiency. In particular, for short period length, which warrants the viability of constant expectation assumption and for some time horizon M, if the strategy never loses money, we have to cast serious doubts on market efficiency.

5.3   Data, Estimation, and Problems

The chapter deals with the abnormal returns in exchange-traded real estate securities. We extracted all stocks related to real estate market of their daily returns dated from July 2, 1962 to December 31, 1990 from CRSP tape (Center for Research and Security Prices) maintained by the University of Chicago. We focus on NYSE/AMEX stocks because the number of real estate related stocks traded in OTC is quite small, not enough to yield any statistically meaningful result.

Over the whole sample period, a total of 195 exchange-traded real estate stocks are listed in NYSE/AMEX. But there are only 132 stocks trading at the end of the sample period.

The stocks fall into three categories:

(1) 61 Equity Real Estate Investment Trust (EREIT).
(2) 32 Mortgage Real Estate Investment Trust (MREIT).
(3) 39 real estate property builders and owners.

Table 1 gives some summary statistics of the samples. As the numbers show, with a total capitalization of \$42 billion, daily trading of 4 million shares, and daily capital turn-over of \$84 million, the real estate related security trading has become a sizable market. More interesting in Table 1 is the direct documentation of negative first-order autocorrelation of individual security return. Although the autocorrelation coefficient of -0.05, which is an average of those of all stocks, is small, nevertheless, it is significant with a t-value of $t = \bar{\rho}_w/\sigma_{\bar{\rho}_w} = 4.59$, and it shows that the individual real estate security return is negatively serially correlated at weekly intervals.

Several choices have to be made before we can start any testing of market efficiency with the strategy developed in Sec. 5.2: first, the period length, namely, how many trading days are proper for a period; second, the lag length, k, on the base of how far lagged period return should we compute the portfolio weight; and finally the time horizon, M, over which horizon are portfolio profits aggregated. The choice of the first two are tricky because, on the one hand, we would like to have as short a period as possible to guarantee the irrelevance of time-varying market expectation in testing the market efficiency;

Table 1.   Summary sample statistics.

Average of the last seven trading days for the year 1990	
Total capitalization (TC)	42,000,000,000
Number of daily trading shares (S)	4,096,861
Daily capital turnover (M_c)	$84,151,000
Number of stocks in trading (N_s)	132
Over the whole sample period	
Mean weekly return ($\bar{R}_w$)	0.0025
Standard deviation of weekly return (σ_w)	0.0270
Mean value of first-order autoregression coefficient ($\bar{\rho}_w$)	−0.0500
Standard deviation of first-order autoregression coefficient ($\sigma_{\bar{\rho}w}$)	0.0109

on the other hand, we want the period to be long enough to give the market enough time to correct the mispricing in order to profit from the return reversals. French and Roll's (1986) registering of return reversion for stock returns beyond a week interval suggests that a week may be a sensible choice for a period length, and one period lag is appropriate for lag length. As for the time horizons to aggregate the portfolio profits, we pick up four of them, one month, one quarter, half year, and one year, with one year as our main focus.

Unlike most previous research, we do not use the calendar week as the base period, but instead define a consecutive five trading days as a trading week. There are two reasons for this:

(i) there is no guarantee that a week is the best choice to exploit the price reversal profitability, and the use of calendar week will make it difficult to fine-tune the period length; and

(ii) as has been pointed out by French and Roll (1986), the stock price volatility over weekends and holidays is much smaller than that when the market is open. Thus the use of calendar week actually does not use the constant period length in calculating the period returns because, for those weeks which contain national holidays, there are less than five trading days for the market to correct possible market overreaction.

The individual stock's period return is the compound rate of daily returns over all the trading days inside the trading period. All stocks which have complete return information on period t and period $t - k$

are drawn together to form a return reversal portfolio. We use period $t-k$'s return information to compute the individual security's weight in the portfolio according to Eqs. (5.2) and (5.4), and then we can calculate the profit for each period from Eq. (5.6).

There could be two problems in performing the task this way. The first problem is that computing the portfolio weight on the basis of the previous period's full period return can create spurious return reversal effect because of the presence of bid–ask spread. Take two period cases as an example. Suppose period one is from day 1 to 5, and period two from day 6 to 10. Starting with a mean of bid–ask prices, a stock's price closing at below bid–ask mean price on day 5 may looks like a loser in the first period in comparison with the closing price of a mean of bid–ask price. For the next period there is a half chance that the stock price can land above the bid–ask mean price on the last day of the second period and look like a winner in the second period, thus creating an artificial return reversal effect. The problem can be mitigated if we do not use the last day's return information to compute the portfolio weight, that is, for a trading week of five days, we use the compound rate of return of first four days of previous period to compute the portfolio weight. It is argued that if the stock is sufficiently liquid, there should be no correlation between closing price at day 4 and day 5; thus artificial effect is eliminated.[3]

Another problem concerning the estimation process is the possible existence of selection effect. A loser from last period, which we could have bought and held, may be excluded from our portfolio, because it is delisted next period and gives no return information. The delisting may yield a negative return close to minus one, inflicting big losses had we engaged in a long position in the stock as our strategy suggests. The problem is alleviated somewhat when we only use stock return information several periods before its delisting; in other words, we do not trade in any stock suspected of delisting.

---

[3]For period length of four, six, or seven trading days the first three, five, or six trading days of the lagged period are used to compute the portfolio weight.

There are situations in which the existence of arbitrage opportunity is significant statistically, but not economically, because of the financial market frictions, namely transaction cost and bid–ask spread. So here market friction poses another challenge to the profitability of the strategy, especially in this strategy of rapid turnover of the stock portfolio. The requirement of quickly rebalancing the return reversal portfolio at the end of every trading week may result in buying at ask price and selling at bid price. This unfavorable situation, in addition to the transaction cost, may eat up a large chunk of profit and prevent arbitraging. In this chapter we try to incorporate all these trading costs into our trading strategy.

Assuming that the one way trading cost is c percent, building and unwinding the portfolio at the start and the end of a period would incur $2c$ percent cost. The cost has to be covered by the net profit of the trading. Since all the above equations are linear, the result of deducting trading costs will be to substitute $\pi_{t,k}$ with $\pi_{t,k}^c = \pi_{t,k} - 4c$. $4c$ is used instead of $2c$ because the profit is from a \$2 portfolio, \$1 short and \$1 long.

It is worth mentioning that such a calculation of trading cost is the upper bound, because the above consideration is to sell all the stocks in the portfolio at the end of the period and buy all the new shares at the start of next period. The corresponding trading cost is

$$
\begin{aligned}
C &= c \sum_{i=1}^{N} (|w_{i,t-k-1}| + |w_{i,t-k-1}|) \\
&= c \left(\sum_{R_{i,t-k} - \bar{R}_{t-k} > 0} |w_{i,t-k}| + \sum_{R_{i,t-k} - \bar{R}_{t-k} < 0} |w_{i,t-k}| \right. \\
&\quad + \sum_{R_{i,t-k-1} - \bar{R}_{t-k-1} > 0} |w_{i,t-k-1}| \\
&\quad \left. + \sum_{R_{i,t-k-1} - \bar{R}_{t-k-1} < 0} |w_{i,t-k-1}| \right) \\
&= 4c.
\end{aligned}
\tag{5.9}
$$

In practice, this may not be necessary because only marginal adjustment of $w_{i,t-k} - w_{i,t-k-1}$ needs to be made, thus the transaction cost

$$C^m = c \sum_{i=1}^{N} |w_{i,t-k} - w_{i,t-k-1}| \le c \sum_{i=1}^{N} (|w_{i,t-k}| + |w_{i,t-k-1}|) = 4c \,.$$

$$(5.10)$$

As Lehmann (1990) argues, bid–ask spread may not work to our disadvantage in our strategy, because there is usually a buying drive in winner stocks which we are happy to sell. We may be able to sell them at the ask price because we are providing the market the needed liquidity. The reverse is true for loser stock. In general, we may expect to achieve market price and reduce the loss due to the adverse bid–ask spread being at a minimal level.

5.4   Empirical Result and Its Implications

The results are summarized in Table 2 through Table 5. In all these tables, we report six summary statistics: the mean profit, $\bar{\pi}$, the standard deviation of profits, σ, its t-statistics, t-value , the maximum profit, π_{max}, the minimum profit, π_{min}, and the fraction of periods for which profits are positive. We also report the summary statistics for different return horizons: one period, one month, one quarter, half year, and one year.

Table 2 shows the profits of return reversal strategy based on various lengths of trading days in a period. Different number of days is used as period lengths to see the relationship between the profitability and length of a period; hopefully, a time scale of market correction to the return reversal can be spotted. The most striking feature of the result is that the profit is significantly greater than zero (t-statistics $\gg 2$) for all the period lengths and time horizons. But still there are differences in the degree of profitability. We do not compare the profitability among periods because they are of different lengths. If half year or one year is used as the time horizon for performance evaluation, the five-trading-day period (a trading week) clearly dominates all the other period lengths with semiannual return of 30.77 cents and annual return of 62.2 cents on a costless stock portfolio with $1 each in both short and long position. This result is very

Table 2. Profits on return reversal portfolio strategies (various lengths of period).

Horizon[4]	$\bar{\pi}$	σ	t-value	π_{min}	π_{max}	$N_{R>0}/N_{obs}$	N_{obs}
Weights based on first 3-day-return of previous 4-day trading period							
Four days	0.0104	0.0342	12.8799	−0.1721	0.3328	0.6406	1789
One month	0.0616	0.0897	12.9471	−0.1841	0.4613	0.7675	357
One quarter	0.1705	0.1544	11.5853	−0.1335	0.5455	0.8468	111
Half year	0.3073	0.1606	14.0660	−0.0632	0.5577	0.9818	55
One year	0.5913	0.1058	29.0381	0.3981	0.8272	1.0000	28
Weights based on first 4-day-return of previous 5-day trading period							
Five days	0.0114	0.0374	11.5121	−0.3885	0.3088	0.6478	1431
One month	0.0456	0.0896	9.5890	−0.4451	0.3469	0.7535	357
One quarter	0.1340	0.0910	15.9885	−0.0507	0.3746	0.9748	119
Half year	0.3077	0.1625	14.1720	0.0838	0.6086	1.0000	57
One year	0.6220	0.0868	37.2250	0.4725	0.8272	1.0000	28
Weights based on first 5-day-return of previous 6-day trading period							
Six days	0.0150	0.0409	12.6959	−0.1978	0.3617	0.6527	1192
One month	0.0569	0.0957	10.2386	−0.1417	0.3425	0.6946	298
One quarter	0.1201	0.1565	8.3338	−0.2435	0.5228	0.8067	119
Half year	0.2200	0.1651	9.8826	−0.0331	0.5279	0.9107	56
One year	0.4348	0.1396	16.1795	0.2197	0.7073	1.0000	28
Weights based on first 6-day-return of previous 7-day trading period							
Seven days	0.0148	0.0404	11.6661	−0.1620	0.2051	0.6650	1021
One month	0.0457	0.0876	9.6122	−0.2030	0.4182	0.6824	340
One quarter	0.1031	0.1196	9.1290	−0.2437	0.3220	0.8053	113
Half year	0.2508	0.1202	15.4741	−0.0501	0.4927	0.9643	56
One year	0.4922	0.1532	16.6973	0.1707	0.7248	1.0000	28

[4]Time horizons of month, quarter, half-year and one year is defined in a trading sense, that is 252 trading days a year, 63 trading days a quarter, and 21 trading days a month. since the whole sample period of 7168 trading days may not be the integer multiple of some horizons, the calculation of average profit in that horizon may not use the full return information of the whole sample period. That is why a 4-day trading period has higher 1-month profit and one-quarter profit but less half-year profit and 1-year profit than those of a 5-day trading period. The same problem arises in Table 3 through Table 5 as well.

close to Lehmann's (1990) result of using the entire NYSE/AMEX stocks with calendar week as his return period. The result indicates that it takes approximately a week for the market to realize return reversals, and this result is consistent with French and Roll's variance ratio test result of strong negative return autocorrelation of individual stock for time horizon beyond one week.

Table 3.   Profits on return reversal portfolio strategies (different subperiod).

Horizon	$\bar{\pi}$	σ	t-value	π_{min}	π_{max}	$N_{R>0}/N_{obs}$	N_{obs}
The first decade (1960s)							
Five days	0.0115	0.0422	5.9283	−0.3885	0.1361	0.6457	477
One month	0.0451	0.0591	8.2964	−0.0996	0.1900	0.7815	119
One quarter	0.2011	0.0908	13.6492	0.0445	0.3746	1.0000	39
Half year	0.5009	0.0539	39.4120	0.3961	0.6086	1.0000	19
One year	0.7048	0.0546	36.5014	0.6502	0.8272	1.0000	9
The second decade (1970s)							
Five days	0.0137	0.0322	9.2803	−0.1132	0.1337	0.6813	477
One month	0.0586	0.0572	11.1360	−0.0457	0.2795	0.8487	119
One quarter	0.1353	0.0513	16.2751	0.0229	0.2159	1.0000	39
Half year	0.2848	0.0532	22.7297	0.2135	0.3591	1.0000	19
One year	0.5748	0.0508	32.0320	0.5191	0.6765	1.0000	9
The third decade (1980s)							
Five days	0.0089	0.0369	5.2870	−0.1837	0.3088	0.6164	477
One month	0.0448	0.0580	8.3963	−0.0696	0.2776	0.8067	119
One quarter	0.0554	0.0651	5.2465	−0.0345	0.1860	0.7949	39
Half year	0.1180	0.0542	9.2404	0.0289	0.1974	1.0000	19
One year	0.1969	0.0275	20.2329	0.1590	0.2228	1.0000	9

To check the consistency of the strategy's performance, we break up the sample into three subperiods, roughly corresponding to the three decades from 1960s, 1970s, and 1980s. The macroeconomic environments in these three decades are very different: volatile real estate market in the first, oil shocks and high inflation in the second and bull market in the third. Nevertheless, it is easy to see, from Table 3, that the strategy consistently gives all positive returns for semiannual and annual horizons. One interesting feature of the results is that the profits become smaller and smaller from the 1960s to the 1980s, with profit in the 1980s being the smallest of the three. The feature may be partly a reflection of active arbitraging in the market during the 1980s.

Holding the length of a period unchanged, for example, a trading week in this test, Table 4 presents the strategy's profits as a function of lagged k period whose return information is used to calculated the portfolio weights. Again the result is similar to what Lehmann (1990) has found. The portfolio in which the weight is based on information of one period back's return is most profitable. The profits diminish as the lagged period k increases. For $k \geq 4$ the profit is actually

Table 4. Profits on return reversal portfolio strategies (different period lag (one period is five trading days)).

Horizon	$\bar{\pi}$	σ	t-value	$\pi_{\min}$	$\pi_{\max}$	$N_{R>0}/N_{\text{obs}}$	N_{obs}
Weights based on first 4-day-return of previous period, $k = 1$							
Five days	0.0114	0.0374	11.5121	−0.3885	0.3088	0.6478	1431
One month	0.0456	0.0896	9.5890	−0.4451	0.3469	0.7535	357
One quarter	0.1340	0.0910	15.9885	−0.0507	0.3746	0.9748	119
Half year	0.3077	0.1625	14.1720	0.0838	0.6086	1.0000	57
One year	0.6220	0.0868	37.2250	0.4725	0.8272	1.0000	28
Weights based on return two period ago, $k = 2$							
Five days	0.0042	0.0349	4.5021	−0.1960	0.2488	0.5538	1430
One month	0.0028	0.0866	0.6051	−0.2900	0.2115	0.5350	357
One quarter	0.0008	0.1204	0.0717	−0.3384	0.3047	0.4286	119
Half year	0.0444	0.1513	2.1953	−0.2410	0.4271	0.5965	57
One year	0.1153	0.1017	5.8884	−0.1095	0.3533	0.9286	28
Weights based on return three period ago, $k = 3$							
Five days	0.0030	0.0338	3.3527	−0.1472	0.2500	0.5416	1429
One month	0.0142	0.0814	3.3044	−0.2104	0.3234	0.5490	357
One quarter	0.1126	0.1300	9.4080	−0.1183	0.4266	0.7899	119
Half year	0.1217	0.1382	6.5867	−0.1114	0.3666	0.7719	57
One year	0.2135	0.1178	9.4228	−0.0399	0.4387	0.9643	28
Weights based on return four period ago, $k = 4$							
Five days	0.0008	0.0339	0.8361	−0.3635	0.2163	0.5175	1428
One month	0.0004	0.0811	0.0866	−0.1869	0.3098	0.4734	357
One quarter	−0.0087	0.1446	−0.6542	−0.2522	0.3315	0.4622	119
Half year	−0.0532	0.1452	−2.7423	−0.3803	0.1790	0.4035	57
One year	−0.0547	0.1098	−2.5876	−0.2457	0.0984	0.3629	28

negative. Again, the result indicated that the return reversal effect is most prominent at weekly intervals.

All the signs from Table 2 through Table 4 point to the direction that the market is not fully efficient if there is no trading cost. Clearly when considering a trading week as the base period and one lag length, $k = 1$, we can realize positive arbitrage profit over the entire 57 semiannual time segment and 28 annual ones without ever losing a penny. These results sharply reject the market efficiency hypothesis in the absence of market friction. However, as we have argued in Sec. 5.3, without proper consideration of trading cost, market efficiency can be falsely rejected. So we present the strategy's performance records with the presence of market friction in Table 5.

Table 5.   Profits on return reversal portfolio with transaction cost (weights based on first 4-day-return of previous 5-trading-day period).

Horizon	$\bar{\pi}$	σ	t-value	π_{min}	π_{max}	$N_{R>0}/N_{obs}$	N_{obs}
One-way transaction cost 0.10%							
Five days	0.0074	0.0374	7.4623	−0.3925	0.3048	0.5975	1431
One month	0.0296	0.0896	6.2211	−0.4611	0.3309	0.6667	357
One quarter	0.0860	0.0910	10.2599	−0.0987	0.3266	0.7815	119
Half year	0.2077	0.1625	9.5656	−0.0162	0.5086	0.9649	57
One year	0.4220	0.0868	25.2549	0.2725	0.6272	1.0000	28
One-way transaction cost 0.20%							
Five days	0.0034	0.0374	3.4126	−0.3965	0.3008	0.5353	1431
One month	0.0136	0.0896	2.8531	−0.4771	0.3149	0.5882	357
One quarter	0.0380	0.0910	4.5312	−0.1467	0.2786	0.6218	119
Half year	0.1077	0.1625	4.9592	−0.1162	0.4086	0.5614	57
One year	0.2220	0.0868	13.2848	0.0725	0.4272	1.0000	28
One-way transaction cost 0.30%							
Five days	−0.0006	0.0374	−0.6372	−0.4005	0.2968	0.4731	1431
One month	−0.0024	0.0896	−0.5149	−0.4931	0.2989	0.4594	357
One quarter	−0.0100	0.0910	−1.1975	−0.1947	0.2306	0.4286	119
Half year	0.0077	0.1625	0.3527	−0.2162	0.3086	0.4561	57
One year	0.0220	0.0868	1.3147	−0.1275	0.2272	0.5714	28
One-way transaction cost 0.50%							
Five days	−0.0086	0.0374	−8.7367	−0.4085	0.2888	0.3564	1431
One month	−0.0344	0.0896	−7.2508	−0.5251	0.2669	0.2969	357
One quarter	−0.1060	0.0910	−12.6548	−0.2907	0.1346	0.1261	119
Half year	−0.1923	0.1625	−8.8601	−0.4162	0.1086	0.2105	57
One year	−0.3780	0.0868	−22.6255	−0.5275	−0.1728	0.0000	28

It is not surprising that with the trading cost add-in, profitability is depressed, and semiannual return is not always positive if trading costs are higher than 0.1%. But still arbitrage profit exists, especially when we extend the time horizon to a year, and the return reversal strategy, on an average, yields a positive profit for one-way trading cost lower than 0.3%. And for trading cost lower than, or equal to, 0.2%, the strategy will earn without risk positive profit over all the 28 sample years.

It is interesting to see how much profit can be extracted from this strategy if the one-way trading cost is taken to be 0.2%. The daily capital turnover in this real estate market is $84 million. Suppose we can long and short 1% of the market without moving the price against us, then we can make an annual profit of

$$\pi_{\text{annual}} = 0.01\bar{\pi}M_c = 0.01 \times 0.2220 \times 84 \times 10^6 = \$186,480$$

for one portfolio. Moreover, if we can build five such portfolios without moving the price, that is, continuously building and unwinding a portfolio on each day of the trading week, then the total annual profit will grow to $\pi_{\text{total}} = 5 \times 186,480 = \$932,400$. From Table 5 we can also calculate that the worst year's profit is

$$\pi_{\text{total,w}} = \frac{\pi_{\min}}{\bar{\pi}}\pi_{\text{total}} = \frac{0.0725}{0.2220} \times 932,400 = \$304,500$$

and that of the best year is

$$\pi_{\text{total,b}} = \frac{\pi_{\max}}{\bar{\pi}}\pi_{\text{total}} = \frac{0.4272}{0.2220} \times 932,400 = \$1,794,240.$$

But in real transactions, the one-way trading cost, which for the most part is the implicit cost of bid–ask spread in our case, is likely to be greater than 0.2%, especially when taking into account the small capitalization of real estate stocks and low liquidity of such stocks. (Using the common bid–ask spread of \$0.125 (1/8) and the average real estate security price of \$9 at the end of 1990, further assuming that the market price is at the mid-point of the bid–ask prices, then the one-way implicit transaction cost is 0.125/2/9=0.69%. However, for those few very skillful traders who can get around the bid–ask spread and trade at the closing price, which is the price we use for the calculation, the transaction cost could be smaller.) For one-way trading cost over 0.5%, the strategy actually loses money all the time if a year is taken as the time horizon, So when the market friction is taken into account, the return reversal arbitrage strategy makes no abnormal returns for most traders. So the exchange-traded real estate security market is efficient in the sense that one cannot make arbitrage profits without committing capital or taking risk.

5.5 Conclusions

This chapter studies the return reversals of exchanged-traded real estate securities using an arbitrage portfolio approach. The approach is capable of calculating the arbitrage profits that could be earned by arbitrage traders if return reversals exist. Thus, it provides not only some statistical evidence of return reversals but also the economic significance of return reversals.

Using this approach, we find that there do exist some statistically significant return reversals in exchange-traded real estate securities. These return reversals could also lead to economically significant trading profits for arbitrage traders if trading cost could be ignored. However, in the current trading environment where traders have to bear relatively high cost of bid–ask spread due to the small capitalization of real estate securities, there are no trading profits left after taking into account the implicit cost of bid–ask spread and deducting the transaction cost. Thus, the real estate securities market is efficient in the sense that one can hardly profit from the return reversals.

Our results also provide some useful trading rules for long-term real estate security fund managers. Based on our weekly price reversal result, they can reduce the acquisition costs by buying a few days after a weekly rally and get higher prices by selling a fews days after a downturn. This trading rule does not guarantee investment savings or gains in each transaction, but over the long run, it should enhance portfolio performance.

References

Chen, K. C., P. H. Hendershott and A. Sanders, 1990, Risk and Return on Real Estate Evidence from Equity REITs, *AREUEA Journal* **18**(4), 431–452.

French, K. R. and R. Roll, 1986, Stocks Return and the Weekend Effect, *Journal of Financial Economics* **8**, 55–59.

Gau, G. W., 1984, Weak Form Tests of the Efficiency of Real Estate Investment Markets, *AREUEA* **19**(4), 301–320.

Gau, G. W., 1985, Public Information and Abnormal Returns in Real Estate Investment, *AREUEA* **13**(1), 15–31.

Gyourko, J. and D. Keim, 1992, What Does the Stock Market Tell Us about Real Estate Returns? *Journal of Real Estate Finance and Economics* (Forthcoming).

Hoag, J., 1980, Toward Indices of Real Estate Value and Return, *Journal of Finance* **35**, 568–580.

Lehman, B. N., 1990, Fads, Martingales, and Market Efficiency, *The Quarterly Journal of Economics* **105** (1), 1–28.

Liu, C. and J. P. Mei, 1992, Predictability of Returns on Equity REITs and Their Comovement with Other Assets, *Journal of Real Estate Finance and Economics* **5**, 401–418.

Liu, C. and J. P. Mei, 1994, An Analysis of Real Estate Risk Using the Present Value Model, *Journal of Real Estate Finance and Economics* **8**, 5–20.

Mei, J. P. and L. Ahyee, 1994, Is there a Real Estate Factor Premium? *Journal of Real Estate Finance and Economics* (Forthcoming).

CHAPTER 6

Bank Risk and Real Estate: An Asset Pricing Perspective

JIANPING (J.P.) MEI and ANTHONY SAUNDERS*

Leonard N. Stern School of Business, New York University,
900 Tisch Hall, New York, NY 10003

While a number of papers have investigated the time-series behavior of *ex post* bank stock returns and real estate returns, no study has comprehensively studied: (i) the relationship between *ex ante* risk premiums on both assets and (ii) the time-varying nature of such premiums in relationship to economic and real estate market conditions. In this study, we investigate how the changing nature of bank risk taking, especially in the real estate market, has affected the *ex ante* pricing of risk in the market for bank stocks. We find that the time variation in bank risk premiums are partly determined by interest rate and real estate market conditions. We also find that the real estate factor has been important for banks in the 1980s.

*Associate Professor of Finance and John M. Schiff Professor of Finance, Stern School of Business. Any comments can be sent to the authors at: 900 Tisch Hall, New York, NY 10003, Phone (212) 998-4183 and (212) (285)-6103, respectively. We thank john Campbell for letting us use his latent-variable model algorithm and Doug Herold, Wayne Ferson and Crocker Liu for providing data on real estate cap rates, REITs, and business condition variables. We are also grateful to Bin Gao for able research assistance. We have benefited from helpful discussion with Mitchell Berlin, Silverio Foresi, Crocker Liu. We acknowledge financial support from the Salomon Center at New York University.

6.1   Introduction

The 1980s have posed many loan management problems for large
U.S. banks. In the early 1980s, these banks faced growing problems
in both their LDC and oil and gas loan portfolios. In the mid-1980s,
farming and agricultural loans were added to this list, and more
recently, especially since 1987, commercial real estate has become a
new problem loan area. By contrast, the 1970s are often viewed as
a period of relative growth and prosperity for U.S. banking.

This unfolding of asset-exposure problems for major U.S. banks
raises an important empirical question: To what extent do investors
price such risks in the market? Previous studies of bank stock returns, such as Aharony *et al.* (1986), Flannery (1983), Flannery and
James (1984), and James (1989) have concentrated on explaining the
ex post behavior of bank stock returns, usually in an augmented two-
factor return-generating model with a market and interest rate risk
factor. However, no study has formally sought to identify whether
such factors are prices *ex ante*, in the sense of the APT, or whether
the influence of such factors changes over time as banks alter the
nature of their loan exposures. Perhaps the paper closest to ours is
by Sweeny and Warga (1986) who investigated the *ex ante* premiums in the pricing of public utility stocks in the presence of a market
and interest rate risk factors. However, their methodology was too
constraining in that their premiums were fixed (constant) through
time.

In this chapter we use data for 1970–1989 on large bank stock
returns to investigate the time-varying nature of three sources of
ex ante risk: (i) the market factor, (ii) an interest rate factor, and
(iii) a real estate factor. In the light of the problems of many large
banks in the real estate market, where at the end of 1990 ten major
banks had commercial real estate loan portfolios exceeding $3.5 bil-
lion each, and their problem commercial real estate loan-net worth
ratios exceeded 30%, considerable attention is given to the exposure
to and the pricing of real estate risk in bank stock returns. Moreover,
since banking is a regulated industry, we try to identify regulatory
induced impacts on these risk premiums. In particular, we seek to
identify whether changes in the Federal Reserve's monetary policy

regime (e.g., October 1979 to October 1982) affected the relative pricing of risk.

It is important for banks to understand the determinants of equity risk premium, because this premium affects not only their investment decision but also their financing decision. As is well known, the weighted average cost of capital (WACC) is a weighted average of the costs of debt and equity. The higher the equity risk premium, the higher the required rate of return on equity, and thus, the higher the WACC. The variation of risk premium is also of interest to regulators because it contains information about market perception of bank risk. Thus, if banks have increased their exposures to certain risks, regulators should consider actions, such as additional loss provisioning, additional capital infusion, as well as revising the required deposit insurance premium paid.

In Sec. 6.2 we outline the methodology of our study. In particular we employ a multi-factor latent-variable model on the lines of Campbell (1987), Campbell and Hamao (1991), and Ferson (1989) to derive time-varying *ex ante* (or expected) risk premiums. In Sec. 6.3 the estimation procedure is described. This is followed by a description of data in Sec. 6.4. Section 6.5 presents the empirical results and Sec. 6.6 is a summary and conclusion, in which we discuss our major findings: the time variation in bank risk premiums are predictably affected by a real estate market condition variable, and the real estate factor has been important in the 1980s for banks.

6.2 The Asset Pricing Framework

Following Campbell and Hamao (1991), Ferson (1989), and Liu and Mei (1992), we assume that asset returns are generated by the following K-factor model:

$$\tilde{r}_{i,t+1} = E_t[\tilde{r}_{i,t+1}] + \sum_{k=1}^{K} \beta_{ik}\tilde{f}_{k,t+1} + \tilde{\epsilon}_{i,t+1}, \tag{6.1}$$

where $\tilde{r}_{i,t+1}$ is the return on asset i, held from time t to time $t+1$, in excess of the risk-free (treasury bill) rate. $E_t[\tilde{r}_{i,t+1}]$ is the expected excess return on asset i, conditional on information known to investors at time t. The unexpected return on asset i equals the sum of K factor realizations $\tilde{f}_{k,t+1}$ times their betas or factor loadings β_{ik}, plus an idiosyncratic error term $\tilde{\epsilon}_{i,t+1}$. We assume also that $E_t[\tilde{f}_{k,t+1}] = 0$, $E_t[\tilde{\epsilon}_{i,t+1}] = 0$, and $E[\tilde{\epsilon}_{i,t+1}\tilde{f}_{k,t+1}] = 0$. Here the conditional expected excess return, $E_t[\tilde{r}_{i,t+1}]$, is allowed to vary over time, but the beta coefficients are assumed to be constant during the sample period.

Under certain regularity conditions, it is easy to derive that

$$E_t[\tilde{r}_{i,t+1}] = \sum_{k=1}^{K} \beta_{ik}\lambda_{kt}, \qquad (6.2)$$

where λ_{kt} is the "market price of risk" for the kth factor at time t. Equation (6.2) states that the conditional expected excess return, or *ex ante* risk premium on a stock, should be a weighted average of factor risk premiums, with the weights equal to the betas of the stock. Now suppose that the information set at time t consists of a vector of $L(L > K)$ economic or forecasting variables X_{pt}, $p = 1, \ldots, L$, and that conditional expectations are linear in those variables.[1] Then we can write λ_{kt} as

$$\lambda_{kt} = \sum_{p=1}^{L} \theta_{kp}X_{pt}, \qquad (6.3)$$

and substituting, we have

$$E_t[\tilde{r}_{i,t+1}] = \sum_{k=1}^{K} \beta_{ik} \sum_{p=1}^{L} \theta_{kp}X_{pt} = \sum_{p=1}^{L} \alpha_{ip}X_{pt}. \qquad (6.4)$$

Equation (6.4) suggests that expected excess returns are time varying and can be predicted by the economic variables, X_{pt}, in the information set. It is easy to see from Eq. (6.4) that the model puts some

---

[1]It is possible that the conditional expectation could be nonlinear in the forecasting variables. In that case, Eq. (6.3) could be thought of as a Taylor first-order approximation to the nonlinear relationship.

retrictions on the coefficients of Eq. (6.4). These are

$$\alpha = \begin{bmatrix} \alpha_{11} & \cdots & \alpha_{1L} \\ \vdots & \ddots & \vdots \\ \alpha_{N1} & \cdots & \alpha_{NL} \end{bmatrix}$$

$$= \begin{bmatrix} \beta_{11} & \cdots & \beta_{1k} \\ \vdots & \ddots & \vdots \\ \beta_{N1} & \cdots & \beta_{Nk} \end{bmatrix} \begin{bmatrix} \theta_{11} & \cdots & \theta_{1L} \\ \vdots & \ddots & \vdots \\ \theta_{k1} & \cdots & \theta_{kL} \end{bmatrix} = B^*\Theta \qquad (6.5)$$

where β_{ik} and θ_{kj} are free parameters.

The main differences between this model and that employed by Sweeny and Warga (1986) are that we allow for time-varying factor premiums as a result of a changing economic environment, and we do not assume that the factors in the model can be observed *a priori*. Instead, we let the data tell us whether certain factors, such as the market risk, interest rate risk, and real estate market risk are systematic factors that affect bank stock returns. This added flexibility allows us to use Eq. (6.4) to examine the degree to which economic (or "forecasting") variables, X_{pt} explain the *ex ante* time variation in expected excess returns on bank stocks. We can also use the model to examine the extent to which various economic risks drive the *ex post* movements in bank stock returns. As noted above, previous studies have concentrated on the *ex post* pricing of risk in bank stock returns, as opposed to the *ex ante* pricing of risk.

It is worth noting that part of Eq. (6.4) can be derived directly from linear projections *without* using the asset pricing framework of Eqs. (6.1)–(6.3). In other words, given that conditional expectations are linear in the forecasting variables, we will have

$$E_t[\tilde{r}_{i,t+1}] = \sum_{p=1}^{L} \alpha_{ip} X_{pt} \qquad (6.4')$$

This is an important observation, because it implies that the unconstrained conditional risk premium estimated using Eq. (6.4') does not depend on the assumption that beta coefficients are constant through time or the other restrictions imposed by the asset pricing model.

Thus, the sensitivities of bank stocks towards economic changes can vary over time, as long as the product of beta and factor premiums are linear in these economic variables.

6.3   The Estimation Procedure

A generalized method of moments (GMM) approach, similar to Campbell (1987), Campbell and Hamao (1991), and Ferson (1989) is employed to estimate Eq. (6.4') and to test the asset pricing restriction of (5). Equation (6.5) is a cross-equation restriction with unknown parameters; thus Eq. (6.4) must be estimated simultaneously across a number of assets to appropriately test the restriction. To ensure that the linear pricing condition holds for a wide range of assets, we use returns of five asset portfolios: the value-weighted index of NYSE and AMEX stock, a long-term U.S. government bond portfolio, an equally weighted index of real estate investment trust (REITs), a portfolio of money center banks, and a portfolio of non-money center banks. In other words, a wide range of asset portfolios are needed to test the asset pricing model restriction and study the risk premiums on stocks of money center banks and nonmoney center banks.

The forecasting variables chosen reflect those widely used in previous stock return studies (see Campbell (1987), Fama and French (1989), Keim and Stambaugh (1986), Ferson and Harvey (1989), Liu and Mei (1992), among others), and which can be expected to act as important variables in our study. These variables are a January dummy, the dividend yield on an equally weighted market portfolio, the level of interest rates, the spread between the yields on the long-term AAA corporate bonds and the 1-month treasury bill rate, and a proxy for the earnings–price ratio on a large, well-diversified portfolio of real estate assets (the capitalizatio rate).[2] Although all these variables have been found to be useful in explaining the time variation in expected returns on regular stocks, the last three variables may have particular relevance to the expected return on bank stocks.

---

[2]A constant is also included.

The treasury bill rate proxies for the level of interest rates. Changes in the level of interest rates will affect banks according to whether they mismatch the duration of their asset and liability portfolios and the direction of any such mismatch. Most studies of bank portfolios have concluded that on an average banks have longer-term asset durations than liability durations (see Bernanke (1990), for example).[3] As a result, given any positive duration gap, an expected rise in the level of rates, increases bank exposure to interest-rate risk. Thus in periods when interest rates are higher (or lower) than normal, we might expect a change in the interest-rate risk premium to be impounded in bank stock returns. In particular, we will expect a negative relationship when rates are high if the market expects interest rates to revert to some normal level.[4]

The spread between the yield on long-term AAA bonds and the treasury bill rate proxies for the default risk exposure of banks. A widening of the corporate bond–bill rate spread reflects investors' expectations of increased default risk in the corporate sector (see Friedman and Kuttner (1991), for example) and thus may be interpreted as reflecting increased default risk exposure on bank loans.

The capitalization rate (cap rate) on real estate assets seeks to capture changing expectations regarding future expected returns in the residential and commercial real estate markets.[5] The capitalization rate is equal to the earnings–price ratio on direct real estate investments. An increase in the risk of real estate investment, such as a glut of new commercial properties, will increase the required rate of return on real estate and thus lower the market value of real estate assets. This will result in an increase in the cap rate. The cap rate

---

[3] Although Flannery and James (1984) model the portfolio mismatch of banks using the repricing structure of assets and liabilities, their results are consistent with such a duration mismatch.

[4] See Campbell (1987), Keim and Stambaugh (1986) for mean reversion.

[5] Liu and Mei (1992) found that the cap rate is useful in explaining the time variation in real estate expected returns. Mei and Liu (1994) also found that the cap rate can be used in market timing of investment in real estate portfolios. Because of the large holdings of real estate loans in bank portfolios, it would be interesting to see how the cap rate would explain the risk premiums in bank stock returns.

is constructed as the ratio of net-stabilized earnings to the market value (market price) of a well-diversified property portfolio. The stabilized earnings factor adjusts actual earnings so that each holding in the property portfolio reflects a vacancy rate no higher than that which exists for other buildings in the same (local) market (see Liu and Mei (1992). These real estate data are reported by the Americal Council of Life Insurance (ACLI) publications (various issues).

6.4   Data

The forecasting (economic) variables discussed above were derived from a number of sources. Real estate capitalization rates were taken from the ACLI quarterly publication Investment Bulletin (various issues). Yields on 1-month bills and data for the AAA corporate bond–treasury bill spread were derived from the Federal Reserve Bulletin and Ibbotson and Associates (1989). The dividend yield variable, defined as the dividend paid during the last 12 months divided by current market price, was derived by using divided and price information on the CRSP file.

6.4.1   *Bank Stock Returns*

We used Compustat to identify the appropriate banks and bank-holding companies in our sample for the February 1971–April 1989 period. The bank group was divided into a money center bank (MCB) group and a nonmoney center bank (NMCB) group. This was done to examine whether there was any differential sensitivity to real estate (and other factors) between the largest banks and the more regionally specialized large nonmoney center banks. The money center bank group contained a total of 11 banks[6] while the nonmoney

---

[6]They are Bank of New York, Bankers Trust, Chase Manhattan, Chemical Bank, Citicorp, Manufacturers Hanover, J.P. Morgan, Republic New York, Bank of Boston, First Chicago, Continental Bank. The definition follows that of *Salomon Brothers Commercial Bank Stock Research* (various issues).

center group contained a total of 180 banks. We used all banking firms listed on Compustat over the period, not just those with a continuous trading histroy, so as to avoid a selection bias. As a result, approximately 90 banks are contained in the nonmoney center bank sample at any given time.

Based on the money center and nonmoney center classifications, 2-monthly return series on equally weighted bank stock portfolios are derived from the CRSP (daily) tapes.

6.4.2 *Other Portfolio Returns*

The market portfolio returns and the returns on long-term U.S. bonds were also derived from the CRSP tapes. The government bond return series was used below to reflect the degree to which bank stock returns (which are claims on underlying portfolios of fixed and variable rate, riskless, and risky bonds) mimicked the return behavior of bond assets rather than stocks. The government bond portfolio was formed from a portfolio of non-callable 20-year Treasury bonds. The (stock) market portfolio consisted of the value-weighted index of NYSE and AMEX stocks.

In addition to a money center, a nonmoney center, a stock return portfolio, and a bond return portfolio, we also analyze the comparative predictability of returns on a REIT portfolio. We construct an equally weighted equity REIT return series using all equity REITs on the CRSP from January 1971 to December 1989. All equity REITs are included, not just those having a continuous price history over the period in question to avoid the problem of survivorship bias. The REIT portfolio consists of 50 equity REITs on an average. A REIT is deemed to be an equity REIT if it is listed as such on at least two of the following three sources:

(i) *REIT Sourcebook* published by the National Association of Real Estate Investment Trusts, Inc.,
(ii) *The Realty Stock Review* published by Audit Investments, or
(iii) Moody's *Bank and Finance Manual, Volume 2.*

6.5 Empirical Results

Table 1 provides summary statistics for the variables used in this study. Panel A provides data on the monthly means, standard deviations (S.D.s) and first-order autocorrelations on five portfolios:

  (i) the market portfolio,
 (ii) the government bond portfolio,
(iii) the REIT portfolio,
 (iv) the nonmoney center bank (NMCB) portfolio, and
  (v) the money center bank (MCB) portfolio.

As can be seen, both MCBs and NMCBs had higher excess returns on their portfolios than both the market and the bond portfolio. However, their excess returns were lower than those for the portfolio of REITs. Interestingly, the excess mean return on the MCBs portfolio (0.381%) was lower than that for the NMCBs portfolio (0.401%) even though MCB banks had a higher standard deviation of returns (6.415% v.s. 4.783%). Bank stock returns in general also appeared to exhibit a higher degree of first-order autocorrelation than the nonbank portfolios (assets).

In Table 1, panel B, the sample is divided into three subsamples approximating to the three monetary policy regimes that existed over this period. Specifically, the mid subsample (October 1979–October 1982) is viewed as a period of relatively high interest rate volatility compared to the other two subsample periods. As can be seen, while the mean excess returns for NMCBs increase over three subperiods, those for MCBs were actually highest in October 1979–October 1982 even though the underlying volatility of returns was highest in November 1982–March 1989. Thus, the subperiod results suggest that MCB and NMCB stocks have diverged in their return performance during the 1980s, with the MCB stocks generating lower mean excess returns than NMCB stocks despite increasing relative return risk. Such evidence is consistent with the existence of implicit deposit insurance and safety net guarantees for large money center bank investors in the 1980s, which divorced the required returns on

Table 1.   A. Summary statistics for February 1971–April 1989.

	Mean (%)	S.D. (%)	ρ_1
Dependent variables			
Excess return on the market portfolio	0.282	4.822	0.055
Excess return on government bond portfolio	0.038	3.287	0.050
Excess return on REIT portfolio	0.679	4.887	0.115
Excess return on NMCBs portfolio	0.401	4.783	0.230
Excess return on MCBs portfolio	0.381	6.415	0.151

B. Summary statistics for subperiods.

	Mean (%)	S.D. (%)	Mean (%)	S.D. (%)	Mean (%)	S.D. (%)
Subperiods	Feb. 1971–Sep. 1979		Oct. 1979–Oct. 1982		Nov. 1982–Mar. 1989	
Market	0.018	4.627	0.043	5.373	0.748	4.831
Bonds	−0.088	1.953	−0.344	5.440	0.382	3.382
REITs	0.573	5.889	0.863	5.276	0.732	2.860
NMCBs	−0.052	4.616	0.469	5.137	0.974	4.827
MCBs	0.058	6.090	0.834	6.475	0.598	6.856

C. Correlations among excess returns of different assets.

	Market	Bonds	REITs	NMCBs	MCBs
Market	1.000	0.317	0.639	0.818	0.670
Bonds		1.000	0.186	0.345	0.355
REITs			1.000	0.734	0.606
NMCBs				1.000	0.845
MCBs					1.000

Notes: MCBs stands for money center banks, and NMCBs represents nonmoney center banks. The sample period for this table is February 1971–April 1989, with 219 observations. Units on excess returns are percentage points per month. Units on 1-month T-bill rate, term spread, dividend yield, and cap rate are percentage per annum ρ_1 is the first-order autocorrelation coefficient of the series.

bank stocks from the underlying riskiness of bank portfolios (see O'Hara and Shaw (1990)).

In Table 1, panel C, the correlation among excess returns of the market, bond, REIT, NMCBs, and MCBs portfolio are shown for the whole period. As can be seen, both NMCBs and MCBs are *more* highly correlated with the REIT portfolio than with the bond portfolio. This suggest that bank exposure to real estate risk may be

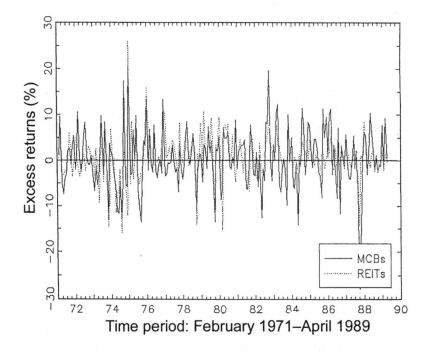

Fig. 1.   Excess returns on REITs and MCBs.

as important, if not more important, than their exposure to interest rate risk (as reflected in bond returns).[7]

The relationship between the excess returns on MCB stocks and REITs is also shown in Fig. 1. While MCB stock returns appear to be less volatile than REITs in the 1970s, they become more volatile in the 1980s. This is consistent with real estate factors having a relatively greater influence on bank stocks in the most recent decade as large banks expanded their loan portfolios in the real estate area.

Table 2 examines the extent to which the forecasting variables (the January dummy, the dividend yield, the treasury bill yield, the corporate–treasury bill spread, and the cap rate on real estate assets) explain the time variation in *ex ante* excess returns on our

---

[7]The positive correlation between bond returns and bank stock returns is consistent with a negative correlation between interest rates and bank stock returns. (See also, Flannery and James (1984)).

Table 2.   Difference between MCB and NMCB in unrestricted conditional risk premiums.

$$r_{i,t+1} = \text{Constant} + \beta_1 \text{Jandum} + \beta_2 \text{T-bill}_t + \beta_3 \text{Spread}_t + \beta_4 \text{DivYld}_t + \beta_5 \text{CapR}_t + \tilde{\epsilon}_i$$

Asset class	Constant	Jandum	T-bill	Spread	DivYld	CapR	$\bar{R}^2$	DW
Market	−7.408**	1.815	−0.597**	0.007	1.429**	0.724*	0.065	1.87
	(−2.41)	(1.56)	(−3.25)	(0.03)	(2.27)	(1.76)		
Equity	−9.335**	5.316**	−0.603**	−0.095	1.110*	1.040**	0.152	1.77
REITs	(−2.80)	(4.47)	(−3.40)	(−0.45)	(1.82)	(2.62)		
Gover-nment	−1.652	−0.747	0.077	0.362**	1.239**	−0.332	0.033	1.90
bonds	(−0.69)	(−0.92)	(0.61)	(2.41)	(2.84)	(−1.16)		
MCB	−9.494**	3.027*	−0.322	0.275	1.497*	0.649	0.030	1.67
stocks	(−2.03)	(1.92)	(−1.29)	(0.94)	(1.76)	(1.17)		
NMCB	−9.732**	3.690**	−0.402**	0.176	0.934	0.921**	0.082	1.54
stocks	(−2.86)	(3.23)	(−2.22)	(0.82)	(1.51)	(2.26)		
Small	−12.562**	5.604**	−0.841**	−0.104	2.014**	1.114**	0.133	1.76
stocks	(−2.58)	(3.42)	(−3.30)	(−0.34)	(2.38)	(2.00)		

Regression of the returns on each asset class at time $t+1$ on a January dummy, the yield on Treasury bills, the spread between the yield on AAA corporate bonds and the yield on T bills, the dividend yield for the overall stocks market, and the cap rate on real estate all at time t. Regression coefficients are given by the first line of each row, while the t-statistics are given in parenthesis in the second row. MCBs stands for money center banks and NMCBs represents nonmoney center banks.
* indicates significance level at 10%. ** indicates significance level at 5%.

five asset portfolios — and in particular, the *ex ante* excess returns on MCB and NMCB stocks. The t-statistic has been adjusted for heteroskedasticity and serial correlation in the regression using the GMM approach.

The most interesting finding here is the significant contribution (at 5% level) to the predictability of NMCB returns by the real estate variable (the cap rate). As we can see from the regression, the market will demand a high-risk premium (expected excess returns) when the real estate market cap rate is high, and a lower-risk premium will suffice if the cap rate is low. Since the cap rate is an indicator of real estate market condition, we can conclude that the risk premium on large nonmoney center banks is highly influenced by real estate market conditions. The interest rate variable also affects NMCB premiums in the expected direction.

To make sure that our results on NMCB are not driven by the small firm effect or the January effect, we here also provide the regression result for a small firm portfolio.[8] Although all coefficients are of same signs, it is worth noting that the January effect is much smaller for NMCB stocks while the same effect is much stronger in REIT. We can also see that short-term interest rates (T-bill) have a smaller effect on NMCB stocks compared to that on REIT and small stocks. The term spread has a positive (insignificant) effect on the two bank portfolios but a negative effect on REIT and small stocks.

Nevertheless, while interest rate and real estate variables have the expected signs, they are not statistically significant in the MCB regression. Overall, approximately 8.2% of the variation in monthly excess returns on NMCBs (compared to 3% on MCBs) is accounted for by our five forecasting variables after adjusting for degrees of freeedom. Thus, the simple unconstrained version of the latent-variable model implies greater interest rate and real estate exposure for large nonmoney center banks relative to money center banks.[9]

With respect to the other forecasting variables, the constant is significant for both bank stock return portfolios as is the January dummy (at the 10% level or better). The spread and dividend yield variables have the expected positive signs but are generally insignificant at the 10% level with one exception — the dividend yield variable in the MCB stocks regression.

The time-varying forecasting variables in Table 2 along with their estimated coefficients can be used to generate expected excess returns $E_t[\tilde{r}_{i,t+1}]$, or conditional risk premiums, for each portfolio. These can be compared to the actual excess returns, $\tilde{r}_{i,t+1}$, on each portfolio. Estimated expected excess returns relative to actual excess return for MCBs are shown in Fig. 2. As can be seen, the monthly predictable or forecastable risk premiums on MCBs can be as high as 6% for some months, while actual monthly excess returns vary from about −28% to 20%. Figure 3 plots the expected excess return (risk premiums) for MCBs relative to REITs over February 1971–April

---

[8]The small stock returns series are taken from Ibbotson and Associates' *Stocks, Bonds, Bills, and Inflation* (SBBI) series on CRSP.

[9]This result should not be surprising given the problems of regional banks (such as the Bank of New England) in the Northeast and California.

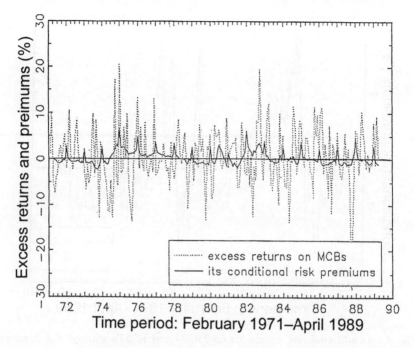

Fig. 2. Excess returns on money center banks and its conditional risk premiums.

1989.[10] Overall, both MCBs and REITs expected excess returns move closely in tandem with a high correlation coefficient of 0.868. The risk premium for the NMCB group exhibits an even closer co-movement with that of the REITs. Figure 3 also provides a supply side explanation to real estate market cycles in the last 20 years. As we can see from the figure, the gradual reduction of risk premium for banks and real estate certainly is consistent with the increase in real estate lending and real estate development in the late 1970s, while the high cost of leading in the recessions of 1980 and 1981–1982 also offer an explanation as to why larger numbers of U.S. banks adopted a relatively easy credit policy for real estate financing in the later 1980s.

---

[10]These results are *without* the January effects.

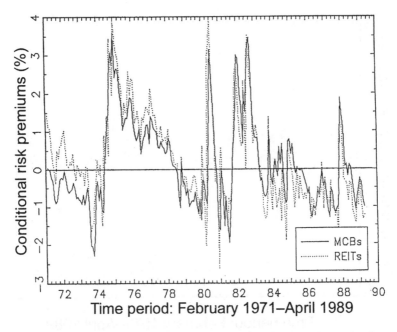

Fig. 3.   Conditional risk premiums on MCBs and REITs without the January
effects.

6.5.1   *Test of Asset Pricing Model*

The results in Table 2, such as the greater impact of interest rate
and real estate conditon on NMCB risk premium relative to that of
MCB, do not depend on the assumptions for the asset pricing model
of Eqs. (6.1)–(6.5) holding. All that is required is that the conditional
excess returns on each asset portfolio be a linear function of the
economic forecasting variables (X_{pt}). In order to obtain sensitivity
estimates of the market, interest rate, and real estate factors, *directly*
test the specification of the asset pricing model, and allow us to
examine the existence of pricing for MCB and NMCB stocks, we
estimated our Eq. (6.4) with the restriction of Eq. (6.5) imposed.
These results are reported in Table 3.

As is well known,[11] the number of factors are unknown *ex ante*
and the number has been found to be less than three in multi-factor

---

[11]See Campbell (1987), Ferson (1989, 1990), and Liu and Mei (1992).

models with time-varying risk premiums. Rather than assuming a fixed number of factors in our tests, we analyze our model for a number of different assumed systematic factors in Table 3. Specifically, a market factor (panel A). an interest rate factor, a real estate factor (panel B), and finally all three factors (market, interest rate, and real estate).

In Table 3, panel A, the asset pricing model is estimated under the assumption that there is only one systematic factor, $\tilde{f}_{k,t+1}$, in the economy (i.e. $K = 1$). With beta normalized to 1 for the market portfolio, the betas for both the MCBs and NMCBs are higher than

Table 3. Estimation of the latent variable model (6.4) with the rank restriction of Eq. (6.5) imposed.

$$E_t[\tilde{r}_{i,t+1}] = \sum_{k=1}^{K} \beta_{ik} \sum_{n=1}^{N} \theta_{k\nu} X_{\nu t} = \sum_{n=1}^{N} \alpha_{in} X_{nt} \qquad (6.4)$$

$$\alpha_{ij} = \sum_{k=1}^{K} \beta_{ik} \theta_{kj}. \qquad (6.5)$$

A. The number of systematic factors in the economy equals one ($K = 1$).

	β_{i1}	S.D.
Estimated beta coefficient for the following assets		
Excess return on the market portfolio	1.000*	—
Excess return on government bond portfolio	0.083	0.148
Excess return on REITs portfolio	1.525	0.318
Excess return on NMCBs portfolio	1.162	0.161
Excess return on MCBs portolio	1.068	0.167

χ^2-statistic of the rank restriction (6.5): 25.54 (DF = 20).
Significance level: $P = 0.181$.

B. The number of systematic factors in the economy equals two ($K = 2$).

	β_{i1}	S.D.	β_{i2}	S.D.
Estimated beta coefficient for the following assets				
Excess return on market portfolio	1.068	0.442	0.603	0.160
Excess return on government bond portfolio	1.000*	—	0.000*	—
Excess return on REITs portfolio	0.000*	—	1.000*	—
Excess return on NMCBs portfolio	0.323	0.243	0.732	0.089
Excess return on MCBs portfolio	0.734	0.464	0.665	0.141

χ^2-statistic of the rank restriction (6.5): 11.79 (DF = 12)
Significance level: $P = 0.462$.

Table 3.   *Continued.*

C. The number of systematic factors in the economy equals two ($K = 3$).

	β_{i1}	S.D.	β_{i2}	S.D.	β_{i3}	S.D.
Estimated beta coefficient for the following assets						
Excess return on market	1.000*	—	0.000*	—	0.000*	—
Excess return on government bond portfolio	0.000*	—	1.000*	—	0.000*	—
Excess return on REITs portfolio	0.000*	—	0.000*	—	1.000	—
Excess return on NMCBs portfolio	−0.461	0.649	0.832	0.624	1.006	0.400
Excess return on MCBs portfolio	−0.360	0.985	1.099	0.841	0.871	0.587

χ^2-statistic of the rank restriction (6.5): 3.16 (DF = 6).
Significance level: $P = 0.788$.

Notes: MCBs stands for money center banks and NMCBs for nonmoney center banks. S.D. stands for standard error for the corresponding parameter estimates. Asterisks indicate these numbers are normalized to be 1 or 0. The sample period for this table is February 1971–April 1989, with 219 observations. The standard errors reported here have been corrected for heteroskedasticity using the general method of moments (GMM) of Hansen (1982).

unity (1.068 and 1.162 respectively) but smaller than that for REITs ($\beta_{il} = 1.525$). As expected, the beta for the bond portfolio is low. Moreover, the chi-square test of the linear pricing restriction implied by Eq. (6.5) could not be rejected by the data at 18.1% level.

The model was then reestimated assuming $K = 2$ (panel B) and $K = 3$ (panel C). That is, we also estimate a two-factor and a three-factor model. To gain insights into the effects of the interest rate factor and the real estate factor on bank stock returns, we undertook a normalization procedure. Specifically, we normalize the bond portfolio to have a beta of 1 on the first factor and a beta of 0 on the second factor, and we normalize REITs to have a beta of 0 on the first factor and a beta of 1 on the second factor. Using this normalization procedure, the first factor in panel B of Table 3 can be called the bond or interest rate factor, and the second factor the real estate factor, because a given change in these factors will result in a corresponding change in the relevant portfolios' asset returns. From panel B, it can be seen that while the MCBs have a greater sensitivity to the interest rate factor than the NMCBs (0.734 v.s. 0323) over 1971–1989, they are slightly less sentivity to the real estate factor (0.665 v.s. 0.732). Nevertheless, in this model specification, the real-estate factor is strongly significant for both MCBs and NMCBs.

Further, the linear pricing restriction imposed by Eq. 5 on the two-factor model cannot be rejected by the data usng a Chi-square test ($p = 46.2\%$).

Finally in Table 3, panel C, we present the results of a three-factor model. As in the two-factor case, we normalize the betas on various asset portfolios. Specifically in the three-factor case, we normalize the betas on the stock market, bond, and REIT portfolios so that we have a stock factor, a bond factor, and a real estate factor. This allows us to identify the effects of these three factors on MCB and NMCB portfolio returns. As can be seen, the sensitivity of bank stocks to the stock factor is both negative and insignificantly different from zero. The exposure of bank stocks to the interest rate factor is again stronger for the MCBs, although the significance level is lower than in the two-factor model. The strongest factor, in terms of explanatory power, appears to be the real estate factor. This factor is positive for both portfolios of banks, but it is larger and more significant for the NMCB group.[12] These results appear to confirm our earlier findings in Table 2 with the unconstrained model, that the real estate factor is more important for NMCBs than for MCBs.

6.5.2 *Subsample Estimates*

As a test of robustness, we also split the sample into two subsamples: February 1971–September 1979 and 1979 October–April 1989. The latter period incorporates a more volatile interest rate environment as well as period in which many banks were expanding their real estate portfolios. By splitting the sample in this manner, we allow for structural changes in factor sensitivities.[13]

---

[12]It is worth noting that the three factors we choose may not be orthogonal. Thus, it is possible that some of the fundamental forces that move the stock factor also move the real estate factor. Therefore, it is not contradictory to see bank stocks having exposure to market risk in the one-factor model but little such exposure in a three-factor model, because some of the variations in stock returns originally explained by the stock factor are now explained by the real estate factor.

[13]The subperiod October 1979–October 1982 (the regime of nonborrowed reserve targets) was too short to include as a separate subperiod in these test.

For MCBs, the results in Table 4, panel A for the one-factor model suggest an increase in their sensitivity to the market factor in the more recent subperiod (0.975 vs. 0.394). The two-factor model (panel B) implies that while MCBs' interest rate sensitivity increased marginally in the more recent subperiod, their senstitivity to the real estate factor increased more dramatically. This probably reflects the fact that the market is increasingly aware of the real estate risk exposure of large U.S. banks. The results for the three-factor model (panel C) generally support the two-factor model conclusions regarding changes in MCBs' real estate factor sensitivity over the two periods. The results for NMCBs generally suggest an increase in sensitivity to all factors in the more recent subperiod.

These results are supported by recent changes in bank real estate holdings. According to *Standard and Poor's Industry Surveys* (*Industry Surveys, Banking Section 1991*), U.S. commercial banks has $285.7 billion of real estate loans in 1981. By 1990, the real estate loans almost tripled to $836.5 billion. In 1991, the ratio of real estate loans to all loans was 29%. By 1992, the same ratio became 40%!

Table 4.　Estimation of the latent variable model (6.4): Two subperiods.

$$E_t[\tilde{r}_{i,t+1}] = \sum_{k=1}^{K} \beta_{ik} \sum_{n=1}^{N} \theta_{k\nu} X_{\nu t} = \sum_{n=1}^{N} \alpha_{in} X_{nt} \qquad (6.4)$$

$$\alpha_{ij} = \sum_{k=1}^{K} \beta_{ik} \theta_{kj} . \qquad (6.5)$$

A. The number of systematic factors in the economy equals one ($K = 1$).

Estimated beta	β_{i1}	S.D.	β_{i1}	S.D.
	Feb. 1971–Sep. 1979		Oct. 1979–Mar. 1989	
Market	1.000*	—	1.000*	—
Bonds	0.123	0.120	0.158	0.207
REITs	0.729	0.362	0.151	0.182
NMCBs	0.848	0.144	0.998	0.142
MCBs	0.394	0.289	0.975	0.183

χ^2-statistic of the rank restriction (6.5): 19.40　　　χ^2-statistic of the rank restriction
(6.5): 25.42

Significance level:　　$P = 0.495$　　　　　Significance level:　　$P = 0.185$

Table 4. *Continued.*

B. The number of systematic factors in the economy equals two ($K = 2$).

	β_{i1}	S.D.	β_{i2}	S.D.	β_{i1}	S.D.	β_{i2}	S.D.
Estimated beta	Feb. 1971–Sep.1979				Oct. 1979–Mar. 1989			
Market	2.743	1.755	0.561	0.236	0.211	0.181	0.805	0.135
Bond	1.000*	—	0.000*	—	1.000*	—	0.000*	—
REITs	0.000*	—	1.000*	—	0.000*	—	1.000*	—
NMCBs	1.428	0.986	0.690	0.123	0.213	0.147	0.852	0.095
MCBs	0.637	1.088	0.390	0.187	0.737	0.313	0.931	0.177

χ^2-statistic of the rank restriction (6.5): 11.68

Significance level: $P = 0.471$

χ^2-statistic of the rank restriction (6.5): 11.25

Significance level: $P = 0.507$

C. The number of systematic factors in the economy equals two ($K = 3$).

	β_{i1}	S.D.	β_{i2}	S.D.	β_{i3}	S.D.
Estimated beta coefficient for the following assets						
Excess return on market	1.000*	—	0.000*	—	0.000*	—
Excess return on government bond portfolio	0.000*	—	1.000*	—	0.000*	—
Excess return on REITs portfolio	0.000*	—	0.000*	—	1.000*	—
Subperiod 1: February 1971–September 1979	χ^2-statistic 1.76 ($P = 0.940$)					
Excess return on NMCBs portfolio	−0.593	1.224	3.267	3.193	1.038	0.653
Excess return on MCBs portfolio	−0.714	1.234	2.931	3.029	0.813	0.631
Subpeirod 2: October 1979–March 1989	χ^2-statistic 1.58 ($P = 0.953$)					
Excess return on NMCBs portfolio	−0.514	0.583	0.378	0.310	1.218	0.519
Excess return on MCBs portfolio	−1.014	1.210	1.097	0.643	1.663	1.021

Notes: MCBs stands for money center banks and NMCBs for nonmoney center banks. S.D. stands for standard error for the corresponding parameter estimates. Asterisks indicate these numbers are normalized to be 1 or 0. The sample period for this table is February 1971–April 1989, with 219 obeservations. The standard errors reported here have been corrected for heteroskedasticity using the Generalized Method of Moments (GMM) of Hansen (1982).

6.6 Summary and Conclusions

This paper has sought to examine the *ex ante* pricing of risk implicit in money center and nonmoney center bank returns. Unlike previous studies that have concentrated on the *ex post* return generating processes of bank stock returns, or have assumed risk premiums to hold constant over time, we investigate an asset pricing model from which *ex ante* time-varying risk premiums can be derived.

We find that the time variation in bank risk premiums have been determined partly by interest rate and real estate market conditions.

We also find that the real estate factor, has been most important for large nonmoney center banks.[14] Moreover, we find that the time variation of risk premiums is consistent with changes in bank real estate lending during the sample period.

Acknowledgements

We thank John Campbell for letting us use his latest-variable model algorithm and Doug Herold, Wayne Ferson, and Crocker Liu for providing data on real estate cap rates, REITs, and business condition variables to us. We are also grateful to Bin Gao for able research assistance. We have benefited from helpful discussion with Mitchell Berlin, Silverio Foresi, and Crocker Liu. We acknowledge financial support from the Salomon Center at New York University.

Appendix

Name	Data begin	Date end	Value (in $1000)
Money center bank			
Bank of Boston Corp	710107	901231	0.469908E+06
Bank new York Inc	691204	901231	0.123442E+07
Bankers Trust NY Corp	690516	901231	0.350817E+07
Chase Manhattan Corp	650315	901231	0.134632E+07
Chemical Banking Corp	690305	901231	0.967274E+06
Chemical Banking Corp	870521	901231	0.337990E+05
Citicorp	681101	901231	0.419593E+07
First Chicago Corp	711230	901231	0.108930E+07

---

[14]To test the robustness of our results, we also conducted similar tests on excess returns for a portfolio of ten banks with the largest commercial real estate loans holdings (as defined by *Barrons* as of December 1990). The results are quite similar to those of MCBs.

Manufacturers Hanover

Corp	690428	901231	0.152318E+07
Mellon Bank Corp	810710	901231	0.104650E+07
Morgan JP & Co Inc	690401	901231	0.821710E+07
Republic New York Corp	720112	901231	0.171384E+07

Nonmoney center bank (NYSE & AMEX)

Amsouth Bancorporation	810520	901231	0.456554E+06
Arizona Commerce Bank Tucson	861223	900831	0.154250E+03
BBI Inc	620702	730508	0.989500E+03
BSD Bancorp Inc	851010	901231	0.242276E+05
Bache Group Inc	720531	810611	0.348742E+06
Baltimore Bancorp	880204	901231	0.541875E+05
Banc One Corp	830929	901231	0.439665E+07
Banctexas Group Inc	811023	901231	0.395719E+04
Bank New England Corp	880412	901231	0.478074E+05
Bank of San Francisco Hldg Co	880712	901231	0.107540E+05
Bankamerica Corp	760628	901231	0.565060E+07
Barnett Banks Inc	791217	901231	0.118465E+07
CVB Financial Corp	891214	901231	0.647932E+05
Chase Convertible Fd Boston Inc	720717	820319	0.717080E+05
Citizens & Southern Corp GA	890313	900831	0.129093E+07
Citizens First Bankcorp	781227	901231	0.504474E+05
City National Corp	900517	901231	0.388606E+06
Citytrust Bancorp Inc	880711	901231	0.796500E+04
Continential Bank Corp	730910	901231	0.440972E+06
Eldorado Bancorp CA	870924	901231	0.253036E+05
Equimark Corp	710720	901231	0.265770E+05
First of America Bank Corp	900629	901231	0.761685E+06
First Bank Systems Inc	840507	901231	0.100340E+07
First City Bancorporation TX Inc	880720	901231	0.845542E+05
First City Bancorporation TX	761201	880419	0.189433E+05
First Empire State Corp	880317	901231	0.361898E+06
First Fidelity Bancorporation NE	710517	901231	0.104589E+07
First Interstate Bancorp	620702	901231	0.145206E+07
First Interstate Bancorporation	880216	901231	0.149504E+05
First National Corp CA	871109	901231	0.416981E+05

First Pennsylvania Corp	720110	900305	0.585003E+06
First Union Corp	880801	901231	0.167834E+07
First Virginia Banks Inc	710419	901231	0.485440E+06
Firstar Corp New	710913	901231	0.657378E+06
Guarantee Bancorp Inc	791227	840117	0.364534E+05
Guardian Bancorporation LA	880209	901231	0.429944E+05
HUBCO Inc	840301	901231	0.219192E+05
Hibernia Corp	891026	901231	0.181803E+06
James Madison Ltd	861007	901231	0.973500E+04
Keycorp	830527	901231	0.983475E+06
LITCO Bancorporation NY Inc	780417	820609	0.957960E+05
La Jolla Bancorp	860604	900823	0.725355E+05
Landmark Bancshares Corp	841121	901231	0.390601E+05
MNC Financial Inc	890112	901231	0.280836E+06
NBD Bancorp Inc	730221	901231	0.240659E+07
National City Corp	881025	901231	0.189056E+07
Norwest Corp	621210	901231	0.209434E+07
PNC Financial Corp	871021	901231	0.205747E+07
Pacific Western Bancshares	890413	901231	0.983854E+05
Security Pacific Corp	790314	901231	0.251307E+07
Shawmut National Corp	881221	901231	0.373737E+06
Signet Banking Corp	710106	901231	0.275560E+06
Southeast Banking Corp	720807	901231	0.164244E+06
Southwest Bancorp	850716	891019	0.382326E+05
Southwest Bancshares Inc	760728	841010	0.373744E+06
Sovran Financial Corp	880913	900831	0.158348E+07
Sterling Bancorp	620702	901231	0.450514E+05
Suntrust Banks Inc	850701	901231	0.288424E+07
Texas American Bancshares Inc	820623	890725	0.138875E+04
UJB Financial Corp	701123	901231	0.319236E+06
Union Planters Corp	890207	901231	0.117205E+06
Wells Fargo & Co New	700209	901231	0.297744E+07
Westamerica Bancorporation	870108	901231	0.828516E+05
Worthen Banking Corp	830815	901231	0.125706E+06

Nonmoney center bank (NASDAQ)

Affiliated Bankshares Colo Inc	721214	901231	0.109897E+06

Ameritrust Corp	721214	901231	0.303639E+06
Amsouth Bancorporation	721214	810519	0.171887E+06
Arizona Commerce Bank Tuscon	861002	861222	0.152932E+05
Baltimore Bancorp	841025	880203	0.164866E+06
Banc One Corp	721214	830928	0.865059E+06
Banco Popular de PR	721214	901231	0.321568E+06
Bancorp Hawaii Inc	721214	901231	0.787539E+06
Banctexas Group Inc	770418	811022	0.603595E+05
Bank New England Corp	721214	880411	0.189932E+07
Bank of San Francisco Hldg Co	860627	880711	0.107278E+05
Bank south Corp	721214	901231	0.214331E+06
Bankamerica Corp	721214	760625	0.388828E+07
Banks Iowa Inc	721214	901231	0.205829E+06
Barnett Banks Inc	721214	791214	0.175601E+06
Baybanks Inc	721214	901231	0.204204E+06
Boatmens Bancshares Inc	721214	901231	0.110144E+07
CVB Financial Corp	830316	891213	0.127820E+06
Central Bancshares South Inc	721214	901231	0.295730E+06
Central Fidelity Banks Inc	721214	901231	0.379878E+06
Citizens & Southern Corp GA	721214	890310	0.164851E+07
City National Corp	721214	900516	0.676099E+06
Citytrust Bancorp Inc	721214	880708	0.200450E+06
Colorado National Bankshares Inc	721214	901231	0.104377E+06
Comerica Inc	721214	901231	0.702182E+06
Commerce Bancshares Inc	721214	901231	0.430171E+06
Corestates Financial Corp	721214	901231	0.172402E+07
Crestar Financial Corp	721214	901231	0.430512E+06
Cullen Frost Bankers Inc	770708	901231	0.565144E+05
Dauphin Deposit Corp	740405	901231	0.336757E+06
Deposit Guaranty Corp	721214	901231	0.156025E+06
Dominion Bankshares Corp	721214	901231	0.262508E+06
Eldorado Bancorp CA	810318	870923	0.229560E+05
Equitable Bancorporation	721214	900117	0.437543E+06
Fifth Third Bancorp	750423	901231	0.130119E+07
First Alabama Bancshares Inc	721214	901231	0.581685E+06
First Bancorporation Ohio Inc	820104	901231	0.301296E+06

First American Corp TN	721214	901231	0.148608E+06
First of American Bank Corp	780504	900628	0.841650E+06
First Bank Systems Inc	721214	840504	0.750868E+06
First City Bancorporation TX	721214	761130	0.297990E+06
First Commerce Corp New Orleans	721214	901231	0.161084E+06
First Empire State Corp	721214	880316	0.266084E+06
First Florida Banks Inc	721214	901231	0.141975E+06
First Hawaiian Inc	721214	901231	0.633560E+06
First Maryland Bancorp	721214	890321	0.703596E+06
First National Corp CA	821101	871106	0.236338E+05
First Security Corp DE	721214	901231	0.355113E+06
First Tennessee Natl Corp	721214	901231	0.355439E+06
First Union Corp	721214	880729	0.253192E+07
Florida National Banks FL Inc	721230	900126	0.675635E+06
Fourth Fianancial Corp	721214	901231	0.316931E+06
Guarantee Bancorp Inc	721214	791226	0.336034E+05
HUBCO Inc	721214	840229	0.181125E+05
Hibernia Corp	721214	891025	0.687808E+06
Huntington Bancshares Inc	721214	901231	0.651491E+06
INB Financial Corp	721214	901231	0.340879E+06
Integra Financial Corp	810115	901231	0.386272E+06
Keycorp	721214	830526	0.194985E+06
LITCO Bancorporation NY Inc	721214	780414	0.457710E+05
Landmark Bancshares Corp	760312	841120	0.338870E+05
MNC Financial Inc	721214	890111	0.129424E+07
Manufacturers National Corp	721214	901231	0.688882E+06
Marshall & Ilsley Corp	721214	901231	0.600012E+06
Mellon Bank Corp	721214	810709	0.753109E+06
Mercantile Bancorporation Inc	721214	901231	0.341397E+06
Mercantile Bankshares Corp	721214	901231	0.601708E+06
Merchants National Corp	730924	901231	0.216706E+06
Meridian Bancorp Inc	721214	901231	0.415884E+06
Michigan National Corp	721214	901231	0.244902E+06
Midlantic Corp	721214	901231	0.190470E+06
Multibank Financial Corp	800611	901231	0.355221E+05
NBD Bancorp Inc	721214	730220	0.292500E+06

National City Corp	730501	881024	0.134692E+07
Northeast Bancorp Inc	721214	901231	0.375660E+05
Northern Trust Corp	721214	901231	0.100111E+07
Old Kent Fiancial Corp	770802	901231	0.615426E+06
PNC Financial Corp	721214	871020	0.255371E+07
Pacific Western Bancshares	831102	890412	0.818235E+05
Premier Bancorp Inc	850111	901231	0.676858E+05
Puget Sound Bancorp	780705	901231	0.299763E+06
Riggs National Corp Wash DC	721214	901231	0.120549E+06
Security Pacific Corp	721214	790313	0.761228E+06
Shawmut National Corp	721214	881220	0.169942E+07
Society Corp	721214	901231	0.105680E+07
South Carolina National Corp	721214	901231	0.354126E+06
Southwest Bancorp	780802	850715	0.114538E+05
Southwest Bancshares Inc	721214	760727	0.150975E+06
Sovran Financial Corp	721214	880912	0.194216E+07
Star Banc Corp	721214	901231	0.483874E+06
State Street Boston Corp	721214	901231	0.127465E+07
Sunwest Financial Service Inc	770803	901231	0.127562E+06
Texas American Bancshares Inc	721214	820622	0.257430E+06
Trustcorp Inc	730131	900105	0.428558E+06
Trustmark Corp	721214	901231	0.171938E+06
Union Planters Corp	721214	890206	0.197398E+06
United Banks Colorado Inc	721214	901231	0.350532E+06
United Missouri Bancshares Inc	721214	901231	0.338229E+06
United State Bancorp OR	721214	901231	0.122172E+07
United State Trust Corp	721214	901231	0.283309E+06
Valley National Corp AZ	721214	901231	0.215553E+06
West One Bancorp	741028	901231	0.306672E+06
Westamerica Bancorporation	761015	870107	0.147537E+06
Zions Bancorp	721214	901231	0.190310E+06

REIT (NYSE & AMEX)

American Fletcher Mtg Invs	701106	771202	0.152100E+04
American Health Pptys Inc	870212	901231	0.365804E+06
American Realty Trust Inc	691002	901231	0.116490E+05
Americana Hotels & Realty Corp	830113	901231	0.153750E+05

Angles Mortgage Investment Tr	880104	901231	0.292530E+05
Angles Participating Mtg Trust	891115	901231	0.289800E+05
Arizona Land Income Corp	880607	901231	0.966000E+04
Asset Investors Corp	861219	901231	0.111160E+06
Associated Mortgage Investors	700303	731026	0.740675E+04
BB Real Estate Invt Corp	851025	890717	0.200375E+05
BRT Realty Trust	730523	901231	0.174491E+05
BRE Properties Inc	800814	901231	0.182479E+06
BT Mortgage Investors	710318	820618	0.343850E+04
Boddies Noell Restaurnt	870519	901231	0.270750E+05
Bradley Real Estate Trust	891005	901231	0.208835E+05
Burnham Pacific Properties Inc	870604	901231	0.686250E+05
CRI Insured Mtg Invs II Inc	860630	891127	0.106700E+06
CRI Insured Mortgage Assn Inc	891207	901231	0.135972E+06
CRI Liquidating REIT Inc	891207	901231	0.368915E+06
CV REIT Inc	730321	901231	0.216810E+05
California Real Estate Invt Tr	801229	901231	0.215840E+05
Capital Housing Mtg Partners Inc	890609	901231	0.305148E+05
Capstead Mortgage Corp	850905	901231	0.121800E+06
Citizens Mortgage Investment Tr	710817	760120	0.248675E+04
Columbia Real Estate Invts Inc	860221	901231	0.367579E+05
Continental Mortgage Investors	650614	750723	0.234428E+05
Copley Property Inc	850719	901231	0.345395E+05
Countrywide Mortgage Invts Inc	850909	901231	0.614025E+05
Delaware Valley Finl Corp	820714	901231	0.777600E+04
Derwood Investment Trust	700128	860115	0.132559E+05
Dial REIT Inc	900518	901231	0.565356E+05
Duke Realty Investments Inc	860317	880815	0.611000E+04
Duke Realty Investments Inc	880831	901231	0.247078E+05
EQK Realty Investors 1	850305	901231	0.189725E+05
Eastgroup Properties	730117	901231	0.306862E+05
Equitable Life Mtg & Rlty Invs	710122	830105	0.838058E+05
FGI Investors	710430	831208	0.102878E+05
Federal Realty investment Trust	750609	901231	0.240249E+06

First Union Real Est Eq &			
Mg Inv	700521	901231	0.128598E+06
General Growth Pptys	730305	850925	0.712598E+05
Guild Mortgage			
Investments Inc	860624	880629	0.189875E+05
HMG Courtland			
Properties Ltd	720926	901231	0.562400E+04
HRE Properties	700518	901231	0.586850E+05
Harris Teeter Pptys Inc	860808	871230	0.219188E+05
Health Care Ppty Invs Inc	850523	901231	0.380341E+06
Healthvest	860529	901231	0.188528E+05
Health & Rehabilitation			
Pptys Tr	861217	901231	0.133983E+06
Health Care REIT Inc	840223	901231	0.824836E+05
Health Equity Properties Inc	861021	901231	0.204960E+05
Highlands National Inc	731128	750609	0.382362E+04
Homeplex Mortgage			
Investments	880721	901231	0.423281E+05
Hotel Investors Trust	720503	901231	0.136485E+05
Hotel Properties Inc	840106	860915	0.758400E+05
ICM Properties Inc	850125	901231	0.216630E+05
IDS Realty Trust	730521	761216	0.451688E+04
IRT Property Co	711011	901231	0.912102E+05
International Income			
Ppty Inc	840607	900626	0.309983E+06
Kavanau Real Est Tr	620702	760521	0.145622E+04
Koger equity Inc	880818	901231	0.112620E+06
Landsing Pacific Fund	881213	901231	0.475462E+05
Lincoln North carol Rlty			
Fd Inc	851216	901231	0.104895E+05
Linpro Specified Pptys	860723	901231	0.104400E+04
MGI Properties Inc	720302	901231	0.693029E+05
MIP Properties Inc	850701	901231	0.146575E+05
MSA Realty Corp	841001	901231	0.291836E+05
Massmutual Mortgage &			
Rlty Invs	710113	850625	0.121420E+06
Medical Properties Inc	870310	901231	0.112528E+05

Meditrust	870623	901231	0.388482E+06
Metropolitan Realty Corp	881117	901231	0.186945E+05
Mortgage & Realty Trust	710503	901231	0.263055E+05
Nationwide Health Properties Inc	851219	901231	0.195912E+06
New Plan Rlty Tr	790307	901231	0.601961E+06
North American Mortgage Invs	690905	810519	0.163899E+05
Northwestern Mutual Lf Mtg & Rlty	710722	821115	0.654225E+05
Nova Corp	731031	750930	0.241600E+04
Novus Properties Co	720428	740418	0.176675E+05
One Liberty Properties Inc	861008	901231	0.887088E+04
Pacific Realty Trust	721219	830215	0.382500E+05
Pennsylvania Real Est Invt Tr	700610	901231	0.124373E+06
Pittsburgh & West Virginia RR	620702	901231	0.887125E+04
Plaza Realty Invs	730524	760616	0.153175E+04
Presidential Realty Corp New	620702	901231	0.197588E+04
Presidential Realty Corp New	620702	901231	0.856800E+04
Property Capital Trust	720906	901231	0.627491E+05
Property Trust Amer	890627	901231	0.354970E+05
Prudential Realty Trust	851001	901231	0.173984E+04
REIT America Inc	710416	841213	0.923449E+05
RPS Realty Tr	881228	901231	0.154096E+06
Rampac	800417	840123	0.118184E+06
Real Estate Investment Tr Amer	620702	831004	0.640952E+05
Real Estate Investment Trust CA	870819	901231	0.923625E+05
Realty Refund Tr	721121	901231	0.134006E+05
Residential Resources Mg Invt Cp	880624	890316	0.279938E+04
Residential Mortgage Invt Inc	860616	901231	0.896750E+04
Resort Income Invs Inc	881025	901231	0.327285E+05
Rockefeller Center Pptys Inc	850912	901231	0.712690E+06
Rymac Mortgage Investment Corp	880916	901231	0.360456E+05
Saul BF Real Estate Invt Tr	730710	880817	0.147436E+06
Sierra Capital Realty Trust VIII	900727	901231	0.102064E+05
Sizeler Property Investors Inc	870130	901231	0.290568E+05

Storage Properties Inc	901001	901231	0.185006E+05
Storage Equities Inc	821001	901231	0.760351E+05
Strategic Mortgage Invts Inc	841212	891106	0.696788E+05
TIS Mortgage Investment Co	880819	901231	0.546750E+05
Trammell Crow Real Estate Invs	851121	901231	0.226875E+05
Transcontinental Realty Invstrs	860910	901231	0.122760E+05
Transamerica Realty Investors	710719	860930	0.383952E+05
TRI South Investors Inc	720530	850415	0.369380E+05
Turner Equity Invs Inc	850719	881221	0.304020E+05
USP Real Estate Investmt Trust	880810	901231	0.111550E+05
United Dominion Realty Tr Inc	900507	901231	0.173041E+06
United Realty Investors Inc	720619	831026	0.543300E+05
United States Realty Invts	680226	821223	0.344158E+05
Universal Health Rlty Incm Tr	870120	901231	0.766361E+05
Wachovia Realty Investments	710128	820318	0.250125E+05
Washington Real Est Invt Tr	710507	901231	0.259340E+06
Weingarten Realty Investors	850816	901231	0.408202E+06
Wedgestone Financial	851001	901231	0.362188E+04
Wells Fargo Mortgage & Equity Tr	720425	891222	0.925925E+04
Western Investment Real Est Tr	840613	901231	0.233320E+06
Wincorp Realty Invts	771004	841207	0.581030E+05
REIT NASDAQ			
API Trust SBI	721214	830414	0.417000E+04
American Equity Invt Tr	740524	840913	0.596159E+05
Americana Hotels & Realty Corp	821104	830112	0.123714E+06
Arlington Realty Investors	721214	880503	0.998000E+03
Bradley Real Estate Trust	850517	891004	0.382200E+05
Burnham Pacific Properties Inc	870105	870603	0.238560E+05
CPL Real Estate Investment Tr	851220	880205	0.123761E+05
CV REIT Inc	721214	730320	0.000000E+00
Cedar Income Fund Ltd	861217	901231	0.104805E+05
Cedar Income Fund 2 Ltd	881021	890929	0.623700E+04
Central Realty Investors Inc	721214	901231	0.341031E+03
Centrevest Corp	861107	880715	0.433838E+04
Chicago Dock and Canal Trust	861021	901231	0.650700E+05

Citizens Growth Pptys	721214	901231	0.259875E+04
Clevetrust Realty Investors	721214	901231	0.394600E+04
Commonwealth Fin Gp Rl Es Inv Tr	721214	901231	0.535594E+03
Commonwealth Realty Tr	740313	880311	0.227540E+05
Continental Mortgage & Equity Tr	821018	901231	0.164558E+05
Cousins Properties Inc	721214	901231	0.173370E+06
Delaware Valley Finl Corp	730209	820713	0.203712E+05
Denver Real Estate Invt Assn	721214	801222	0.401865E+05
Dial REIT Inc	861219	900517	0.771690E+05
Dominion Mortgage & Realty Trust	721214	860213	0.197635E+05
Eastover Corp	730302	901231	0.629200E+04
First Fidelity Investment Trust	721214	781109	0.941775E+04
Flatley Realty Investors	810615	810902	0.962500E+04
Florida Gulf Rlty Tr	730504	851210	0.600064E+05
General Real Estate Shs	721214	901231	0.423438E+02
Grubb & Ellis Rlty Income Tr	850419	901231	0.116000E+05
Health Care REIT Inc	780217	840222	0.257118E+05
Highlands National Inc	721214	860430	0.120478E+05
Hotel Properties Inc	760430	840105	0.148046E+05
Independence Mortgage Trust	721214	770808	0.703125E+03
International Income Ppty Inc	791218	840606	0.859275E+05
JMB Realty Trust	801128	900928	0.711500E+04
Landsing Institutional Ppts Tr V	850422	881125	0.121560E+05
Lincoln Investors	721214	820308	0.228312E+04
MYM Liquidating Trust	901204	901231	0.259326E+05
Maxxus Inc	731218	850116	0.100462E+05
Meditrust	851009	870622	0.217100E+06
Mellon Part Mtg Tr Coml Pptys	850213	901231	0.389025E+05
Merry Land & Investment Co Inc	810706	901231	0.358554E+05
Miller Henry S Rlty Tr	721214	821223	0.140000E+05
Monetary Realty Trust	721214	821130	0.780000E+03
Monmouth Real Estate Invt Corp	721214	901231	0.898625E+04

Murray Mortgage Investors	730621	840608	0.100600E+04
Nationwide Real			
Estate Investors	721214	810220	0.168829E+05
Nooney Realty Trust Inc	851015	901231	0.780300E+04
Nova Corp	721214	830630	0.137918E+05
Novus Properties Co	770628	861103	0.457875E+05
One Liberty Properties Inc	830425	861007	0.243971E+05
Pacific Southern			
Mortgage Trust	730409	820701	0.735000E+04
Plaza Realty Invs	771104	840918	0.922281E+04
Property Trust Amer	721214	890626	0.512426E+05
Rainier Realty Investors	850412	8707156	0.320975E+05
Real Estate Investment			
Trust CA	840823	870818	0.116960E+06
Resources Pension Shs 3	850606	881227	0.546411E+05
Resources Pension Shs 1	821126	881227	0.435705E+05
Resources Pension Shs 2 Tr	831223	881227	0.593060E+05
Riverside Properties IL	721214	901231	0.547250E+03
Saul BF Real Estate Invt Tr	721214	730709	0.000000E+00
Sierra Real Estate Equity Tr 84	850513	901231	0.103849E+05
Storage Equities Inc	801118	820930	0.294548E+05
Terrydale Realty Trust	730403	820111	0.185288E+04
Towermare	721214	841031	0.110775E+05
Travelers Real Estate Invt Tr	840426	890330	0.207359E+05
Travelers Realty Income Invs	850321	890330	0.237185E+05
USP Real Estate Investmt Trust	780425	901231	0.000000E+00
Unicorp Realty Investors Inc	721214	811102	0.750375E+04
United Dominion Realty Tr Inc	800211	900504	0.179816E+06
United States Equity & Mtg Tr	721214	770404	0.571050E+04
United States Mutual Finl Corp	800307	860821	0.146231E+04
Vanguard Real Estate Fund II	900807	901231	0.416250E+05
Vinland Property Trust	760611	901231	0.745750E+03
Virginia Real Estate Invt Tr	721214	810202	0.215680E+05
WMI Equity Invs	721214	811013	0.414150E+04
Wedgestone Financial	821013	850930	0.162049E+05
Wespace Investors Trust II	831212	880622	0.170888E+04
Wespace Investors Trust III	851003	880412	0.545912E+04

References

Aharony, J, A. Saunders and I. Swary, 1986, The Effects of a Shift in Monetary Policy Regime on the Profitably and Risk of Commercial Banks." *Journal of Monetary Economics* **17**, 493–506.

Bernanke, B.S., 1990, On the Predictive Power of Interest Rates and Interest Rate Spreads, *New England Economic Review* November, December, 51–68.

Campbell, J.Y., 1987. Stock Returns and the Term Structure, *Journal of Financial Economics* **18**, 373–399.

Campbell, J.Y. and Y. Hamao, 1991, Predictable Stock Returns in the United States and Japan: A Study of Long-Term Capital Market Integration, Working Paper, Princeton University.

Chan, K.C., P. Hendershott and A. Sanders, 1990. Risk and Return on Real Estate: Evidence from Equity REITs, *AREUEA Journal* **18**, 431–452.

Fama, E. and K. French, 1988, Dividend Yields and Expected Stock Returns, *Journal of Financial Economics* **22**, 3–25.

Fama, E. and K. French, 1989, Business Conditions and Expected Return on Stocks and Bonds, *Journal of Financial Economics* **25**, 23–49.

Ferson, W., 1989, Changes in Expected Security Returns, Risk and Level of Interest Rates, *Journal of Finance* **44**, 1191–1217.

Ferson, W., 1990, Are the Latent Variables in Time-Varying Expected Returns Compensation for Consumption Risk? *Journal of Finance* **45**, 397–430.

Ferson, W. and C. Harvey, 1991, The Variation of Economic Risk Premia, *Journal of Political Economy* **99** (2), 385–416.

Ferson, W., S. Kandel and R. Stambaugh, 1987, Test of Asset Pricing with Time-Varying Expected Risk Premia and Market Betas, *Journal of Finance* **42**, 201–219.

Flannery, M.J., 1983, Interest Rates and Bank Profitability: Additional Evidence, *Journal of Money, Credit and Banking* **15**, 355–362.

Flannery, M.J. and C.M. James, 1984, The Effect of Interest Rate Changes on the Common Stock Returns of Financial Institutions, *Journal of Finance* **39**, 1141–1153.

Friedman, B.M. and K. Kuttner, 1991, Why Does the Paper-Bill Spread Predict Real Economic Activity? Working Paper, Federal Reserve Bank of Chicago.

Hansen, L. P., 1982, Large Sample Properties of Generalized Method of Moments Estimators, *Econometrica* **50** (4), 1029–1054.

Harvey, C.R., 1989, Time-Varying Conditional Covariances in Tests of Asset Pricing Models, *Journal of Financial Economics* **24**, 289–317.

James, C., 1989, "Empirical Evidence on Implicit Government of Bank Foreign Loan Exposure," Carnegie-Rochester Conference on Public Policy, **30**, 129–162.

Keim, D. and R. Stambaugh, 1986, Predicting Returns in the Stock and Bond Markets, *Journal of Financial Economics* **17**, 357–390.

Liu, C. and J.P. Mei, 1992, Predictability of Returns on Equity REITs and Their Co-movement with Other Assets, *Journal of Real Estate Finance and Economics* **5**, 401–418.

Mei, J. P. and C. Liu, 1994, Predictability of Real Estate Returns and Market Timing, *Journal of Real Estate Finance and Economics*, Forthcoming.

Mei, J.P. and A. Lee, 1994, Is There a Real Estate Factor Premium? *Journal of Real Estate Finance and Economics* **9**, 113–126.

Miles, M., B. Webb and D. Guilkey, 1991, On the Nature of Systematic Risk in Commercial Real Estate, Graduate School of Business, Indiana University, Working Paper #467.

Nourse, H.O., 1987, The "Cap Rate" 1966–1984: A Test of the Impact of Income Tax Changes on Income Property," *Land Economics* **63**, 147–152.

O'Hara, M. and W. Shaw, 1990, "Deposit Insurance and Wealth Effects: The Value of Being "Too Big to Fail," *Journal of Finance* **45**, 1587–1600.

Roll, R. and S.A. Ross, 1980, An Empirical Investigation of the Arbitrage Pricing Theory, *Journal of Finance* **35**, 1073–1103.

Ross, S., 1976, The Arbitrage Theory of Capital Asset Pricing, *Journal of Economic Theory* **13**, 341–360.

Saunders, A. and T. Urich, 1988, The Effect of Shifts in Monetary Policy and Reserve Management Behavior in the Federal Funds Market, *Journal of Banking and Finance* **12**, 523–535.

Sweeny, R. and A. Warga, 1986, "The Pricing of Interest Rate Risk: Evidence from the Stock Market," *Journal of Finance* **41**, 393–410.

White, H., 1980, A Heteroskedasticity-Consistent Covariance Matrix Estimator and a Direct Test for Heteroskedasticity, *Econometrica* **48**, 817–838.

CHAPTER 7

Assessing the "Santa Claus" Approach to Asset Allocation: Implications for Commercial Real Estate Investment

JIANPING (J.P.) MEI*

*Associate Professor of Finance, Department of Finance,
Stern School of Business, New York University,
44 West 4th Street, New York, NY 10012-1126.*

Casual observation suggests the prevalence of a "Santa Claus" approach to fund allocation, that is, giving more money to fund managers whose performance has been "nice" (good) in the recent past and less to those whose performance has been "naughty" (poor). We show that this backward-looking "Santa Claus" approach to asset allocation is not consistent with optimal portfolio management and that this may have contributed to the poor performance of financial institutions' real estate portfolios. We also discuss the role of loan-to-value ratio analysis and point out how this standard bank loan underwriting procedure may have affected commercial banks' "Santa Claus" strategy. We propose that this backward-looking strategy be replaced by either a simple buy-and-hold strategy or a contrarian investment strategy of increasing real estate exposure after a market downturn and reducing exposure after a market rally.

7.1 Research Background and Objective

The allocation of investment funds among different classes of assets, such as stocks, bonds, and real estates, is probably the most important decision for financial institutions. Casual observation suggests

*A Research Sponsored by The Real Estate Research Institute. Phone (212) 998 0354, Fax: 212-998-4233, E-mail: jmei@rnd.stern.nyu.edu

the prevalence of a "Santa Claus" approach to fund allocation, that is, giving more money to fund managers whose performance has been "nice" (good) in the recent past and less to those whose performance has been "naughty" (poor). Although this may be a sensible approach in solving the asset allocation problem in a quite political corporate environment, few studies have asked the question whether the approach is consistent with rational portfolio management.

In this chapter we use asset allocation data from 1973 to 1989 for commercial banks to address the issue. These institutions report on a regular and homogeneous basis, for example, in bank call report and other statistical releases, their positions in real estate assets and other assets. As such they present a unique laboratory to analyze investment behavior over time and the rationality of such behavior in the light of asset pricing theories. Our major objective is to show that the backward-looking "Santa Claus" approach to asset allocation is not consistent with optimal portfolio management and that this may have contributed to the poor performance of U.S. commercial banks' real estate portfolios.

The chapter is organized as follows: Section 7.2 outlines a framework for real estate market timing test. In particular, we employ the nonparametric market timing test developed by Henriksson and Merton (1981). The nonparametric test is used to evaluate investors' market timing performance that requires only the observation of excess return and the prediction of forecasters. This is followed by a description of data in Sec. 7.3. Section 7.4 presents the empirical results in which we discuss our major findings:

(i) U.S. commercial banks' real estate investments have been driven largely by past real estate excess returns over the sample years;

(ii) real estate investments increase at times when future excess returns on real estate may be below their mean levels and decline at times when their future returns may be above their mean levels;

(iii) the "Santa Claus" strategy offers one explanation for the poor real estate investment performance of U.S. commercial banks.

We also discuss the role of loan-to-value ratio analysis and how this may have contributed to the commercial banks' poor investment timing. Section 7.5 is a summary and conclusion.

7.2 Description of Methodology

The methodology used in this chapter is a combination of the non-parametric market timing test developed by Henriksson and Merton (1981) and the portfolio performance test developed by Mei and Saunders (1995). The nonparametric test is used to evaluate investors' market timing performance that requires only the observation of excess returns and the prediction of forecasters. It does not depend on knowledge of the distribution of excess returns or any particular model of security valuation. Given that the prediction of forecasters is generally unobservable, later studies have tried to use *ex post* portfolio excess return to proxy for the unobservable *ex ante* predictions. In this chapter, we propose to use an alternative proxy, the percentage increase in investments, to evaluate the market timing performance of various investment strategies.

The intuition behind this proxy is that, in a frictionless market where commercial banks are engaged in profit maximizing and where real estate loans depend only on the banks' forecasts of future real estate excess returns, the banks will increase their positions in stocks if they forecast next period real estate excess return as positive and reduce or close their position in real estate if they forecast next period real estate excess return as negative. Thus, there is a one-to-one correspondence between real estate loan increase and commercial banks' predictions of next period real estate excess returns.

Following Henriksson (1984), we first define Z_t as the one-period return on the real estate portfolio and r_t as the one-period return on riskless securities. We also define γ_t as investment decision (forecast) variable where $\gamma_t = 0$ if commercial banks decide to increase their position (relative to their mean increase) during time, and $\gamma_t = 0$ if commercial banks decide to reduce their position during time $t - 1$. The two probabilities of interest for γ_t conditional on the realized return on the market are

$$p_{1t} = \text{prob}[\gamma_t = 0 | Z_t \leq r_t] \quad \text{and},$$

$$p_{2t} = \text{prob}[\gamma_t = 1 | Z_t > r_t].$$

Thus, p_{1t} is the conditional probability of a correct forecast, given that $Z_t \leq r_t$, and p_{2t} is the conditional probability of a correct forecast, given that $Z_t > r_t$. Merton (1981) showed that a necessary and sufficient condition for a forecaster's predictions to have no value is that $p_{1t} + p_{2t} = 1$. The existence of forecasting ability will result in $p_{1t} + p_{2t} > 1$.[1]

Based on the above theoretical results, Henriksson and Merton (1981) proposed the following test statistic to test the null hypothesis of $p_{1t} + p_{2t} = 1$:

$$S = \frac{n_1}{N_1} + \frac{N_2 - n_2}{N_2} - 1 \qquad (7.1')$$

where n_1 is the number of correct forecasts, given $Z_t \leq r_t$; n_2 is the number of times forecast that $Z_t \leq r_t$ subtracting n_1; N_2 is the number of observatins where $Z_t > r_t$; and N_1 is the total number of observations subtracting N_2. They have provided asymptotic standard errors for the statistic; thus a simple t-test of the null hypothesis could be formed.

7.3 Data

In this chapter, we use security market-based data to construct real estate returns.[2] Specifically, we construct two real estate stock return-based series: an equally weighted return index of equity real estate investment trusts (EREITs) and an equally weighted return index of mortgage real estate investment trusts (Mortgage). These series consist of all available REITs liste on NYSE, AMEX, and NASDAQ over the sample period. Based on the above classifications, 2-monthly real estate return series are derived from the CRSP (daily) tape.

---

[1]For a more thorough presentation of this framework, see Merton (1981) and Henriksson and Merton (1981).

[2]We also performed our study using the Russell-NCREIF appraisal-based return data in addition to real estate equity data, but the series is too short for rigorous statistical analysis.

To measure asset allocation by the nation's commercial banks, we use the seasonally adjusted monthly percentage changes in various assets (total assets and real estate loans) of the banks. These data are obtained from the Citibase data files.

7.4 Empirical Results

7.4.1 *A Simple Model for Real Estate Expected Excess Returns*

To construct proxies for *ex ante* real estate expected returns, we follow previous studies such as Campbell (1987) and Fama and French (1988), by assuming that the conditional expectations for asset excess returns are linear in several prespecified economic forecasting variables:

$$E_t[e_{i,t+1}] = \sum_{p=1}^{L} \alpha_{ip} X_{pt}, \qquad (7.2)$$

where $e_{i,t+1}$ is the continuously compounded real estate return on asset i, held from time t to time $t+1$, in excess of the risk-free rate. $E_t[e_{i,t+1}]$ is the expected excess return on asset i for time period $t+1$, conditional on information set I_t being known to market participants at end of time t. Equation (7.2) implies that expected excess returns are time varying and can be predicted by economic variables, X_{pt}, in the information set. This allows us to use Eq. (7.2) to examine the degree to which economic (or "forecasting") variables, X_{pt}, explain the *ex ante* time variation in expected excess returns on various real estate assets. We note here that Eq. (7.2) can be derived formally from a multi-factor arbitrage pricing model and we can also verify that the expected return given by (7.2) is consistent with equilibrium asset pricing (see Mei and Saunders (1996)).

The economic or forecasting variables (X_{pt}) chosen to estimate Eq. (7.2) include those widely used in previous asset pricing studies (see Campbell (1987), Fama and French (1988), Keim and Stambaugh (1986), and Ferson and Harvey (1991), among others). The variables included are the excess returns on the value-weighted market portfolio, the difference between the 1-month T-bill rate and inflation, the 1-month T-bill rate relative to its past 12-month moving average, and the dividend yield (on an equally weighted market portfolio).[3] While each of these variables has been found to be useful in explaining the time variation in expected returns on regular stocks, the second and third variables may have particular relevance to the expected excess returns on real estate assets.

The difference between the 1-month T-bill rate and the inflation rate proxies for the level of real interest rates. Changes in the level of real interest rates can be expected to impact real estate assets in a number of ways. First, the real cost of funds for real estate development finance will increase as real rates rise. Secondly, changes in real rates impact the discounted present value of cash flows on such investments. Previous studies of real estate portfolios have concluded that higher real interest rates are associated with lower expected real estate excess returns (see Liu and Mei (1993) and Mei and Saunders (1995) for example). Thus, in periods when real interest rates are higher (or lower) than "normal" we might expect a real estate return that is below (above) its historical levels.

The 1-month t-bill rate relative to its past 12-month moving average (the relative bill rate) proxies for *changes* in nominal interest rates in the economy. A high relative bill rate is consistent with a sudden increase in the short-term interest rates in the economy and increased inflationary expectations, which could adversely impact the payoff on financial institutions' commercial real estate assets — especially those assets with relatively fixed nominal rental incomes (see Miles *et al.* (1991)). Campbell (1987) and Campbell and Ammer (1993) use the relative bill rate in their models to forecast future real and excess returns on bonds and stocks.

The forecasting (economic) variables were derived from a number of sources. Yields on 1-month bills were derived from the Federal Reserve Bulletin and Ibbotson and Associates (1990). The dividend yield variable, defined as the dividend paid during the last 12 months divided by the current market price, was derived using dividend and price information on the CRSP file.

---

[3] A constant is also included. A number of other specifications were also examined as robustness checks.

Table 1. Regression of excess returns on each asset class at time $t + 1$ on the excess return on the value-weighted market portfolio, the real interest rate, the relative bill rate (rrel), the dividend yield at time t. Regression coefficients are given by the first line of each row, while the t-statistics are given in paranthesis in the second row. The sample period is February 1973–December 1989.

$r_{i,t+1} = \text{Constant} + \alpha_1 \text{VW ret}_t + \alpha_2 \text{real} - \text{rate}_t + \alpha_3 \text{rrel}_t + \alpha_4 \text{DivYld}_t + \tilde{\varepsilon}_i$

Asset class	Constant	VWret	real rate	rrel	DivYld	$\bar{R}^2$
Equity REITs	−2.669	0.151	0.046	−0.454	0.862	0.054
Mortgage REITs	−3.153	0.066	0.172	−0.667	0.792	0.044

Note: Units on the 1-month real interest rates, the relative bill rate, and the dividend yield are percentage per annum.

Table 1 examines the extent to which the forecasting variables, the excess return on the value-weighted market portfolio, the real interest rate, the relative bill rate, and the dividend yield, explain the time variation in *ex ante* excess returns on real estate assets. (The t-statistics have been adjusted for herteroskedasticity.)

The results in Table 1 show a degree of predictability of real estate returns, with the lagged market returns, interest rate variable, the relative bill rate, and the dividend yield, exhibiting their expected signs. Specifically, approximately 5.4% of the variation in monthly excess returns on EREITs is accounted for by the four forecasting variables, after adjusting for degrees of freedom. Similar degrees of predictability are exhibited for the mortgage REIT portfolios. It is worth noting that the predictability reported in Table 1 is consistent with other studies using similar variables to forecast future expected excess returns on stock and bond portfolios for different smaple perios.[4]

7.4.2 What has Driven Financial Institutions' Real Estate Investment Decisions?

To find out what has driven commercial' real estate investment decisions at the aggregate level, we regress the monthly percentage change in real estate investments of banks (in excess of their sample

---

[4]See Campbell (1988), Fama and French (1988), Liu and Mei (1993), Mei and Saunders (1995, 1996).

means), I_t, on their past investment changes (I_{t-1}), lagged real estate unexpected excess returns, and lagged interest rates. To determine how many lags we should use in these regressions, we began by using a fairly long lag length and then performed t-tests to eliminate those lagged variables that were statistically insignificant. The final results are presented in Table 2. The top panel of Table 2 shows the regression results for commercial banks' real estate investment behavior. The first line shows the regression equation using EREITs as the real estate return proxy. The second shows the regression equations using the mortgage REIT portfolio returns as the real estate return proxies.

As can be seen from the top panel of Table 2, banks' current real estate investments (I_t) are positively and significantly related to their one period lagged real estate investments (I_{t-1}), and positively and significantly related to the two lagged real estate unexpected excess returns $(v_{e,t-1}$ and $v_{e,t-2})$. The goodness of fit $(\bar{R}^2)$ for the investment equation is approxmately 68% for commercial banks after adjusting for degrees of freedom. Similar results hold if we use mortgage REITs as real estate return proxy. In short, we find evidence that commercial banks were increasing real estate investment after a

Table 2.   A. Regression of bank real estate loans on lagged loans and past unexpected excess returns.

	Constant	I_{t-1}	$v_{e,t-1}$	$v_{e,t-2}$	Tbill$_{t-1}$	F-test	$\bar{R}^2$
EREITs	4.107**	0.760**	0.077*	0.103**	−0.166**	0.00	0.677
Mortgage	4.001**	0.776**	0.051	0.060*	−0.174**	0.00	0.671

B. Regression of bank real estate loans on total loans and past unexpected excess returns

	Constant	Total Loan$_t$	$v_{e,t-1}$	$v_{e,t-2}$	F-test	$\bar{R}^2$
EREITs	7.96**	0.44**	0.10	0.15**	0.00	0.218
Mortgage	7.74**	0.47**	0.02	0.05	0.00	0.193

Note: Real estate investments (I_t) by various financial institutions are measured by: the monthly (%) changes in real estate laons made by all commercial banks. The lagged uxpected return, $v_{e,t}$, is defined as $e_{i,t} - E_{t-1}(e_{i,t})$. All variables are seasonally adjusted and obtained from the CITI-base. * indicates significance level at 10% while ** indicates significance level at 5%. The sample period covers January 1973–December 1989.

good real estate market performance and lowering investment after a bad real estate market performance during the sample period — a backward-looking "Santa Claus" investment strategy.

To test the possibility that commercial banks' real estate investments were just passively responding to increases and decreases in overall financial institutions' investments, we also regressed the percentage changes in commercial banks' real estate investment against percentage changes in total investments and past real estate returns for each class of real estate assets. The results are reported in panel B. We find that real estate returns are only partly responsive to total investment changes. For example, a 1% increase in total bank investments leads to a 0.44% increase in banks' real estate investments. Moreover, past real estate returns still had a significant effect in determining real estate investments after controlling for total investment changes.

To test further the robustness of our results, we also performed regression using the Russell-NCREIF appraisal-based return index instead of real estate equity returns. We found similar positive relationships between *lagged* unexpected returns and current investments as shown in Table 2.[5] These results are the same as those reported in Mei and Saunders (1996).

7.4.3 *Market Timing Test*

Obviously, this positive relationship between *past* real estate returns and current commercial bank investments represents a "Santa Claus" investment strategy for many bank managers. This strategy appears to involve increasing real estate investments *after* the returns have gone up and reducing them after the returns have gone down. The interesting question is whether this "Santa Claus" approach to fund allocation, that is, giving more money to fund managers whose performance has been "nice" (good) in the recent past and less to those whose performance has been "naughty" (poor), represents good real estate market timing. That is, whether this strategy will lead to an increase in real estate loans when future excess returns on real

---

[5]These results are available on request.

estate are high and a decrease in real estate loans when future excess returns are low.

Table 3 presents the results of the market timing test of Henriksson and Merton (1981). We find that although there is some evidence of banks' real estate loans having good market timing in the short run on equity real estate (less than a year), there is strong evidence that they have quite poor market timing on mortgage real estate, which is statistically significant for 3-, 24-, 36-, and 48-month holding periods. They also appear to have quite poor market timing on equity real estate for the longer holding periods of 24, 36, and 48 months. In other words, U.S. banks at the aggregate level appear to have increased real estate investments at times when future excess returns on real estate were decreasing and to have reduced real estate investments at times when future real estate returns were increasing. Since U.S. banks have been adopting this apparent investment strategy based on past returns for most of the 1970s and 1980s, it is perhaps no surprise that they have exhibited mediocre or bad performance on their real estate investment portfolios. Our results here confirm that a poor investment strategy, that is, a belief that high past excess returns imply high future excess returns, has

Table 3.   A. Market timing test of Henriksson and Merton (1981).

	Equity REITs			Mortgage REITs		
	$p_1 + p_2$	S.D.	t-test	$p_1 + p_2$	S.D.	t-test
3-Month	1.091	0.052	1.743	0.874	0.051	−2.418
6-Month	1.099	0.054	1.808	0.981	0.053	−0.355
12-Month	1.103	0.057	1.815	1.040	0.054	0.736
24-Month	0.974	0.055	−0.453	0.836	0.064	−2.538
36-Month	0.904	0.059	−1.631	0.624	0.071	−5.256
48-Month	0.969	0.063	−0.477	0.776	0.087	−2.553

Note: p_1 is the conditional probability of a correct forecast, given that $Z_t \leq r_t$, and p_2 is the conditional probability of a correct forecast, given that $Z_t > r_t$. The t-test gives the t-statistic to test the null hypothesis of $p_1 + p_2 = 1$.

resulted in poor investment performance.[6] As a matter of fact, Mei and Saunders (1996) have shown that past excess returns often imply low future excess returns, because real estate returns tend to be mean-reverting. As we all know in elementary finance, consistently gambling with bad odds will sooner or later lead to financial loss.[7]

7.4.4 *Comparison between the performances of the "Santa Claus" versus the buy-and-hold strategies*

To further gauge the economic significance of the "Santa Claus" strategy of banks, we formed two real estate portfolios based on out-of-sample excess return forecasts and specific investment strategies assumed for bank managers. The out-of-sample excess return forecasts are formed using 10-year rolling regressions with the forecasting variables listed in Table 2. For any time period t, we estimate Eq. (7.2) using data from $t - 1$ to $t - 120$. This regression is then used to form an excess return forecast, $E_t[e_{i,t+1}]$, using X_{pt}. The excess return forecasts (expected excess returns) are calculated for the time period of February 1981–December 1989. Based on the return forecast, we form a passive buy-and-hold portfolio and two active portfolios: a Long (−) portfolio and a Long (+) portfolio.

Specifically, the buy-and-hold portfolio is formed by holding onto real estate assets over the full February 1981–December 1989 period. The Long (−) portfolio is formed by taking a long position in the real estate asset whenever the excess return forecast is negative (it generally happens after good real estate market performance), closing the position and putting the proceeds in treasury bills whenever the excess return forecast is positive. The Long (+) portfolio is formed by taking a long position in real estate assets whenever the excess return forecast is positive (it generally happens after poor real estate

---

[6]Owing to the lack of long time-series data, we could not study the relationship between investment and appraisal-based real estate returns.

[7]As a robustness check, we also computed all the correlations in Table 5 using real estate-specific returns. We find that similar results hold for real estate-specific return as well.

performance), while closing the position and putting the proceeds in treasury bills whenever the excess return forecast is negative.

Table 4 reports the mean excess returns for the passive buy-and-hold portfolio and the two active portfolio strategies using three different proxies for real estate asset returns. It is interesting to see that not only is the Long (-) portfolio easily beaten by the buy-and-hold portfolio but that it also generates negative excess returns during the holding period. By contrast, the Long (+) portfolio beats the buy-and-hold portfolio by a significant margin. Although most banks cannot adjust their real estate loan portfolios as easily as buying and seling real estate investment trusts (as well as "shorting" real estate), the results tentatively suggest that a financial institution manager could do *better* by following a simple buy-and-hold strategy instead of using the "Santa Claus" strategy of increasing his real estate investments when past excess returns are positive (expected excess returns

Table 4.   Annulized mean portfolio excess returns based on out-of-sample predictions.

Strategy	Long (-)	Buy and hold	Long (+)	50% Buy and hold, 50% T-bill
EREITs	−0.948	6.600	7.548	3.444
	(20.1)	(36.1)	(30.9)	(18.4)
	[−0.48]	[1.84]*	[2.56]**	[1.84]
Mortgage	−4.704	4.128	8.844	2.064
	(28.2)	(48.7)	(38.5)	(24.3)
	[−1.72]*	[0.87]	[2.36]**	[0.87]

Note: The out-of-sample excess return forecast is based on a 10-year rolling regression using the forecasting variables listed in Table 2. The numbers in the parentheses are the standard deviations of the excess returns of the portfolios. The numbers in the square brackets are the t-statistic for the test of mean excess return being zero. * indicates significance level at 10% while ** indicates significance level at 5%. The Long (-) portfolio is formed by taking a long position in the real estate asset whenever the excess return forecast is negative, closing the position and putting the proceeds in treasury bills whenever the excess return forecast is positive. The buy-and-hold portfolio is formed by holding the real estate portfolio. The Long (+) portfolio is formed by taking a long position in the real estate asset whenever the excess return forecast is positive, closing the position and putting the proceeds in treasury bills whenever the excess return forecast is negative. The portfolios are formed over the period of February 1982–December 1989.

are negative) and decreasing positions when past excess returns are negative (expected excess returns are positive).[8]

7.4.5 *Loan-to-Value Ratio and the "Santa Claus" Strategy*

One partial explanation for the "Santa Claus" strategy of commercial banks could be their loan approval procedures. In general banks approve loans with a low loan-to-value ratio, that is, given a fixed loan amount, a loan is more likely to be approved if its underlying real estate has a high market value. In other words, they are less likely to decline real estate loans if the underlying real estate has a high appraisal value. In such a world, a run-up in real estate prices may lead to high appraisal value of real estate assets and high collateral value, which lead to easy access to real estate credits. On the other hand, a fall in real estate prices may lead to enhanced perceptions among loan officers that the underlying collateral position of the loan is weak and lead to a rejection of real estate loans. This means relatively easy credit availability (increased real estate investments) during and after a real estate market boom and a possible credit crunch (decreased real estate investments) during and after a market fall.

If this is a fair characterization of the loan approval process, then the loan-to-value ratio analysis may be partly to blame for contributing to the "Santa Claus" behavior of bank loan officers. Further, it might be that the more strict the loan-to-value standard, the more powerful the "Santa Claus" strategies of commercial banks.

The fundamental flaw of the loan-to-value analysis is that it implicitly assumes that real estate value will either remain unchanged over time or past performance will persist over time. Unfortunately,

---

[8]It is worth noting that although the buy-and-hold strategy offers higher excess returns over the Long (-) strategy (e.g., 6.600% v.s. −0.948% *per annum* for EREITs), it might be argued that it is also more risky (e.g., 36.1% v.s. 20.1% *per annum* for EREITs). However, a simple "asset allocation" approach of investing 50% in real estate (via buy-and-hold) and 50% in risk-free asset (T-bills) will cut the portfolio risk by half and still allow the investor to enjoy significant positive excess returns. This result is shown in the last column of Table 4. These results are the same as those reported in Mei and Saunders (1996).

as we have shown, real estate returns do change over time. Moreover, high returns today often imply low returns tomorrow. Thus, a sensible contrarian investment strategy will be to relax loan-to-value standards after a market downturn and tighten the standards after a market rally.

7.5 Summary and Conclusions

In this chapter, we used commercial banks' real estate investment data to address the issue of whether their poor performance in recent years has been consistent with a poor investment strategy. We first used a simple linear pricing model to derive the time-varying *ex ante* (or expected) excess returns on various real estate investment portfolios. We find the expected returns on real estate are time varying, and they generally increase after a real estate market rally and fall after a market downturn. We then document the evidence that commercial banks have been using the "Santa Claus" approach in determining the allocation of investment funds among different classes of assets. We found that their real estate investments have been driven largely by past real estate performances, that is, they were increasing real estate investment after a bad real estate market performance and lowering investment after a good real estate market performance during the sample period. This "Santa Claus" strategy ignored the potential negative correlation between current and past real estate returns and their future expected values. Indeed, using the Henriksson and Merton (1981) test, we show empirically that such a negative correlation is supported by available data.

Our further analysis shows that either a simple buy-and-hold strategy or a contrarian strategy can easily beat the "Santa Claus" strategy. We then argue that the standard loan-to-value ratio analysis used in bank loan underwriting process may have contributed to this "Santa Claus" behavior. To avoid repeating the costly mistakes of the recent real estate debacle, we propose that the backward-looking "Santa Claus" strategy be replaced by either a simple buy-and-hold strategy or a contrarian investment strategy of increasing real estate exposure after a market downturn and reducing real estate exposure after a market rally.

References

Campbell, J.Y., 1987, Stock Returns and the Term Structure, *Journal of Financial Economics* **18**, 373–399.

Campbell, J.Y. and J. Ammer, 1993, What Moves the Stock and Bond Markets? A Variance Decomposition for Long-Term Asset Returns, *Journal of Finance* **48**, 3–37.

DeBondt, W. and R. Thaler, 1988, Further Evidence of Investor Overreaction and Stock Market Seasonality, *Journal of Finance* **42**, 557–581.

Fama, E. and K. French, 1988, Dividend Yields and Expected Stock Returns, *Journal of Financial Economics* **22**, 3–25.

Ferson, W. and C. Harvey, 1991, The Variation of Economic Risk Premia, *Journal of Political Economy* **99**, 385–415.

Fisher, J.D., R,B. Webb and D. Geltner, 1991, Historical Value Indices of Commercial Real Estate, Working Paper, University of Indiana.

Geltner, D. and J.P. Mei, 1995, The Present Value Model with Time-Varying Discount Rates: Implications for Commercial Property Valuation and Investment Decisions, *Journal of Real Estate Finance and Economics* (Forthcoming).

Gyourko, J. and D. Keim, 1992, What Does the Stock Market Tell Us about Real Estate Return?, *AREUEA Journal* **20**, 457–485.

Henriksson, R.D., 1984, Market Timing and Mutual Fund Performance: An Empirical Investigation, *Journal of Business* **57**, 73–96.

Henriksson, R.D. and R.C. Merton, 1981, On Market Timing and Investment Performance II: Statistical Procedures for Evaluating Forecasting Skills, *Journal of Business* **54**, 513–533.

Keim, D. and R. Stambaugh, 1986, Predicting Returns in the Stock and Bond Markets, *Journal of Financial Economics* **17**, 357–390.

Liu, C. and J.P. Mei, 1993, Predictability of Returns on Equity REITs and Their Co-movement with Other Assets, *Journal of Real Estate Finance and Economics* **5**, 401–418.

Merton, R.C., 1981, On Market Timing and Investment Performance. I: An Equilibrium Theory of Value for Market Forecasts, *Journal of Business* **54**, 363–406.

Mei, J.P. and A. Lee, 1994, Is there a Real Estate Factor Premium? *Journal of Real Estate Finance and Economics* **9**, 113–126.

Mei, J.P. and C. Liu, 1994, Predictability of Real Estate Returns and Market Timing, *Journal of Real Estate Finance and Economics* **8**, 115–135.

Mei, J.P. and A. Saunders, 1995, Bank Risk and Real Estate: An Asset Pricing Perspective, *Journal of Real Estate Finance and Economics* (Forthcoming).

Mei, J.P. and A. Saunders, 1996, Have U.S. Financial Institutions' Real Estate Investments Exhibited "Trend-Chasing" Behavior?, *Review of Economics and Statistics* (Forthcoming).

Miles, M., B. Webb and D. Guilkey, 1991, On the Nature of Systematic Risk in Commercial Real Estate, Graduate School of Business, Indiana University, Working Paper #467.

CHAPTER 8

The Time-variation of Risk for Life Insurance Companies

JIANPING (J.P.) MEI and ANTHONY SAUNDERS*

*Leonard N. Stern School of Business,
New York University*

In this chapter we study the *ex ante* risk premiums on life insurance stocks and the time-varying nature of such premiums in relation to changes in economic environment, especially in the real estate market. We find that a premium for real estate risk is increasingly apparent in the market for life insurance stocks, presumably reflecting their growing exposures in this area. We also find some preliminary evidence that factor risks are underpriced for life insurance stocks. This underpricing is consistent with the presence of government safety net subsidies for the nation's public life insurance companies.

*Associate Professor of Finance and John M. Schiff Professor of Finance. Stern School of Business. Any comments can be sent to the authors at: 900 Tisch Hall, New York, NY 10003. Phone (212) 998-4183 and (212) 285-6103, respectively. We thank John Campbell for allowing us to use his latent-variable model algorithm and Doug Herold, Wayne Ferson and Crocker Liu for providing data on real estate cap rates, REITs and business condition variables. We are also grateful to Bin Gao for able research assistance. We have benefited from helpful discussion with Crocker Liu. We acknowledge financial support from the Salomon Center at New York University.

8.1   Introduction

This chapter studies the economic environment that determines the risk premium on life insurance stocks. Using the life insurance stock index and some financial and real estate variables, we address the following issues: First, do economic conditions, especially the real estate market condition, affect the risk premium on life insurance stocks and other assets? Second, does the life insurance regulatory process have an impact on the determination of the life insurance risk premium? Third, how closely are variations in expected returns on life insurance stocks and real estate related to each other?

This study uses a multi-factor, latent-variable model that allows us to address these issues. This methodology is appropriate for our purpose because it allows for time-varying risk premiums, which are designed to capture the time variation in *expected* excess returns due to changing economic environments. It gives us a concise framework to study the co-movement of life insurance stocks and real estate market simultaneously so that we can measure the impact of changing real estate market on life insurance stocks. It requires only a few assumptions associated with Hansen's (1982) Generalized Method of Moments (GMM) for the estimation procedure.

Our study finds that variation in excess return on life insurance stocks are predictable. This predictability for life insurance stocks is due in a significant part to movements in the cap rate, a real estate business condition variable. We also find that the expected return on life insurance stocks and equity real estate investment trusts (REITs) are very closely related. We have some preliminary evidence that there is a seemingly undercompensation for risk for life insurance companies, which reflects the recognition of the existence of state and federal safety net by the market place. The safety net reduces the risk of bankruptcy of large insurance companies; therefore, the risk premium paid on these stocks should be lower than what would be without such government intervention. There is fairly strong evidence that life insurance companies have generally increased their risk exposure in the 1980s, especially real estate risks.

The chapter is organized as follows: Section 8.2 outlines the asset pricing framework and estimation procedure. A description of our data set is given in Sec. 8.3. This is followed by an empirical study of the time variation in risk premium on life insurance stocks in Sec. 8.4. Section 8.6 summarizes the results.

8.2 The Asset Pricing Framework

Using the multi-factor, latent-variable model of Campbell (1987), Campbell and Hamao (1991), and Ferson (1989), we begin by assuming that asset returns are generated by the following K-factor model:

$$\tilde{r}_{i,t+1} = E_t[\tilde{r}_{i,t+1}] + \sum_{k=1}^{K} \beta_{ik} \tilde{f}_{k,t+1} + \tilde{\varepsilon}_{i,t+1}, \qquad (8.1)$$

where $\tilde{r}_{i,t+1}$ is the return on asset i held from time t to time $t+1$, in excess of the treasury bill rate. $E_t[\tilde{r}_{i,t+1}]$ is the expected excess return on asset i, conditional on information known to investors at the end of time period t. The unexpected return on asset i equals the sum of K-factor realizations $\tilde{f}_{k,t+1}$ times their betas or factor loadings β_{ik}, plus an idiosyncratic error $\tilde{\varepsilon}_{i,t+1}$. We assume that $E_t[\tilde{f}_{k,t+1}] = 0$, $E_t[\tilde{\varepsilon}_{i,t+1}] = 0$ and $E[\tilde{\varepsilon}_{i,t+1}|\tilde{f}_{k,t+1}] = 0$. Here, the conditional expected excess return $E_t[\tilde{r}_{i,t+1}]$, is allowed to vary over time but the beta coefficients are assumed to be constant through time.

Thus, given that the market is perfect and frictionless, we should have:[1]

$$E_t[\tilde{r}_{i,t+1}] = \sum_{k=1}^{K} \beta_{ik} \lambda_{kt}, \qquad (8.2)$$

where λ_{kt} is the "market price of risk" for the kth factor at time t. Equation (8.2) states that the conditional expected excess return should be weighted average of factor risk premiums, with the weights equal to the betas of each asset. Now suppose that the information set at time t consists of a vector of $L(L > K)$ forecasting variables

---

[1] This type of linear pricing relationship can be generated by a number of intertemporal asset pricing models, under either a no arbitrage opportunity condition or through a general equilibrium framework.

$X_{pt}, p = 1, \ldots, L$, and that conditional expectations is linear in these variables. Then we can write λ_{kt} as

$$\lambda_{kt} = \sum_{p=t}^{L} \theta_{kp} X_{pt} \,, \tag{8.3}$$

and we have

$$E_t[\tilde{r}_{i,t+1}] = \sum_{k=1}^{K} \beta_{ik} \sum_{p=1}^{L} \theta_{kp} X_{pt} = \sum_{p=1}^{L} \alpha_{ip} X_{pt} \,. \tag{8.4}$$

Equations (8.4) suggests that expected excess returns are time varying and can be predicted by the forecasting variables, X_{pt}, in the information set. It is easy to see from Eq. (8.4) that the model puts some restrictions on the coefficients of Eq. (8.4), which is that

$$\alpha \;=\; \begin{bmatrix} \alpha_{11} & \cdots & \alpha_{1L} \\ \vdots & \ddots & \vdots \\ \alpha_{N1} & \cdots & \alpha_{NL} \end{bmatrix}$$

$$= \begin{bmatrix} \beta_{11} & \cdots & \beta_{1k} \\ \vdots & \ddots & \vdots \\ \beta_{N1} & \cdots & \beta_{Nk} \end{bmatrix} \begin{bmatrix} \theta_{11} & \cdots & \theta_{1L} \\ \vdots & \ddots & \vdots \\ \theta_{k1} & \cdots & \theta_{kL} \end{bmatrix} = B * \Theta \,, \tag{8.5}$$

where β_{ik} and θ_{kj} are free parameters. It is easy to see from the above equation that

$$\mathrm{rank}(\alpha) \leq \min(\mathrm{rank}(\tilde{\beta}), \mathrm{rank}(\Theta)) \leq \min(K, L) = K \,.$$

The objectives of the chapter are to use the regression system in Eq. (8.4) to see to what extent the economic conditions affect the *ex ante* conditional risk premium $E_t[\tilde{r}_{i,t+1}]$ and to test the equilibrium asset pricing restriction of Eq. (8.5).

It is worth noting that part of Eq. (8.4) can be derived directly from linear projection *without* using the asset pricing framework of Eqs. (8.1)–(8.3). In other words, given that conditional expectations are linear in the forecasting variables, we will have

$$E_t[\tilde{r}_{i,t+1}] = \sum_{p=1}^{L} \alpha_{ip} X_{pt} \, . \tag{8.4$'$}$$

This is a non-trivial result because it implies that the conditional risk premium estimated using Eq. (8.4') does not depend on the assumption of beta coefficients being constant through time and other restrictions imposed by the asset pricing model. Thus, even the sensitivities of life insurance stocks towards economic changes vary over time, and assumptions about model (8.1) do not hold; as long as the product of beta and factor premiums in Eq. (8.2) are linear in forecasting variables, Eq. (8.4') will still be valid and useful in describing the time variation in expected returns. For simplicity, we will call the conditional risk premium estimated by Eq. (8.4') "unconstrained risk premium" and risk premium estimated with Eq. (8.5) and other restrictions imposed "constrained risk premium".

The methodology adopted here has several distinct advantages. First, the model allows for time-varying risk premiums. This is a significant improvement over previous studies on life insurance stocks, such as Sweeny and Warga (1986), which generally assume constant risk premiums. This assumption is in contrast to a large body of evidence on time-varying risk premiums, which has been documented extensively by Campbell (1987), Fama (1990), Fama and French (1989), Ferson *et al.* (1987), Kandel and Stambaugh (1990), among others. Secondly, the estimation procedure is robust to the existence of heteroskedasticity and contemporaneous correlation among idiosyncratic shocks across securities and requires no other distributional assumptions on the error terms except those required by GMM.

8.2.1   *The Estimation Procedure*

A GMM approach similar to those of Campbell (1987), Campbell and Hamao (1991), Ferson (1989), Ferson and Harvey (1990) is used to estimate Eq. (8.4') and test the rank restriction of (8.6). In our study we chose the forecasting variables to be a constant, a January

Dummy, the yield on 1-month treasury bill, the spread between the yields on long-term AAA corporate bonds and the 1-month treasury bill, the dividend yields on the equally weighted market portfolio, and the cap rate on real estate. The yield variable shows the level of the current interest rate. The spread variable gives us the slope of the term structure of interest rates. The dividend yield variable conveys information about future cash flows and required returns on stocks in general. These variables have been used extensively by previous studies and have been found to carry important information on changing risk premiums on various assets.[2]

To capture the ever-changing real estate market condition and study the issue of whether movements in real estate market affect life insurance stock return, we also include the cap rate on real estate assets which contains information about the underlying real estate market.[3] The cap rate represents a weighted average cost of capital for income property with an adjustment for equity buildup and an adjustment for anticipated increases or decreases in property value. The cap rate is defined as "the ratio of net-stabilized earnings to the transaction price (or market value) of a property. Net-stabilized earnings means that the income figure used in the numerator of the ratio assumes that full leaseup of the building has occurred such that the building's vacancy is equal to or less than the vacancy of the market."[4] Although both the cap rate and dividend yield are similar in the sense that they are both measures of income-to-value, one is for the equity market and the other is for the real estate market. Moreover, the cash flows of buildings are not identical to the cash flows of firms. Thus, we include the cap rate as an extra forecasting variable, because we hypothesize that its movements may contain important information about the real estate market that is not captured by the dividend yield. The cap rate can be thought of as the equivalent of the earnings–price ratio on direct real estate

---

[2]Campbell (1987), Campbell and Hamao (1991). Fama and French (1988, 1989). Ferson (1989), Ferson and Harvey (1990), Keim and Stambaugh (1986), Liu and Mei (1992), among others.

[3]See Nourse (1987).

[4]See Liu and Mei (1992).

investment. The data is taken from the American Council of Life Insurance publication *Investment Bulletin: Mortgage Commitments on Multifamily and Nonresidential Properties Reported by 20 Life Insurance Companies.*

The yield on the 1-month Treasury bill, the spread between the yields on long-term AAA corporate bonds and the 1-month Treasury bill are obtained from Federal Reserve Bulletin and Ibbotson and Associates (1989). The divided yields are defined as the dividend paid during the last 12-month dividend by the current price constructed by using the dividend and price information from CRSP.

Figure 1 plots the movements of the yield on T-bills, the spread, the dividend yield, and the cap rate. It is easy to see that the dividend yield generally increases between the peak and trough of a business cycle, which reflects the usual price drop on stocks due to higher economic risk during a recession. The yield on the T-bill generally rises sharply before the peak of a cycle, reflecting a rise in

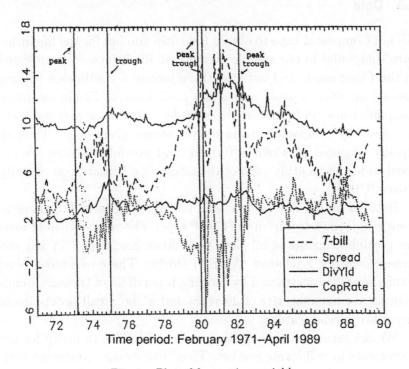

Fig. 1.   Plot of forecasting variables.

interest rates. It also seems that the yield spread between long-term corporate bond and the short-term treasury bill narrows before the peak of a cycle but increases between the peak and trough of a cycle. The cap rate on real estate assets also tends to rise right before or during the peak and trough of a business cycle, reflecting capital loss on real estate assets investment due to changing market conditions.

It is worth pointing out that our results are robust to omitted information. In other words, we do not assume that we have included all relevant variables that can forecast factor premiums. In any case, we can interpret our study as evidence of time variation in factor premium captured by the information variables, X_{pt}. Moreover, we also need to point out that the rank condition is independent of the choice of the information variables. A detailed discussion of this later point is provided in Appendix A.

8.3   Data

We use Compustat tape to obtain the cusip number for the life insurance companies in our sample. We use all life insurance firms listed in the Compustat, and not just those having a continuous trading history, in order to avoid a selection bias. Overall, 52 life insurance companies are contained in the sample, and on an average there are about 25 companies in the sample at any given time. Then an equally weighted portfolio is formed, and portfolio returns are derived from the monthly tape of the Center for Research on Security Prices (CRSP).

Returns on the market portfolio and the long-term U.S. government bonds are taken from the CRSP tape. The value-weighted market portfolio consists of all New York Stock Exchange (NYSE) and American Stock Exchange (AMEX) stocks. The government bond return series is constructed by forming a portfolio of treasury bonds with an average maturity of 20 years and without call provisions or any other special features.

We use return on the equally weighted EREITs to proxy for the movements in real estate market. These real estate investment trust are close-end mutual funds traded on national stock exchanges, which specialize in investment of real estate properties across the country. The REITs portfolio consists of 50 REITs on an average. For a detailed account on the construction of REITs portfolio and the definition of REITs, see Liu and Mei (1992).

8.4 Empirical Results

Table 1 provides summary statistics on the behavior of monthly excess returns for life insurance stocks over the 1-month Treasury bill rate in comparison with other assets. We report the mean, standard deviation, and the first-order autocorrelation coefficient of excess returns. Table 1 reveals that life insurance stocks have higher excess returns relative to the market portfolios and government bonds, but lower returns than REITs. The excess returns on all assets display positive first-order autocorrelation. What is interesting is the fairly high first-order autocorrelation coefficients for life insurance stocks (0.136), suggesting that 1.85% of its excess return variation can be explained by a regression of the excess return of its first lag.

In Table 1, we also report the mean, the standard deviation of excess returns on various assets for three subperiods, based on three different interest rate regimes. The first subperiod covers February 1972–September 1979, when the interest rates are relatively low. The second subperiod covers October 1979–October 1982, when the interest rates are extremely high and volatile. The third subperiod covers November 1982–April 1989, when the interest rates have stabilized. In general, excess return on life insurance stocks seems to be more volatile than other assets but they also command higher mean excess returns.

Table 1 also reports the correlations of returns among four asset classes. The excess returns on life insurance stocks are highly correlated with REITs. But among all the stocks, life insurance stocks have the highest correlation with bonds in excess returns, which is due to its heavy exposure to interest risks. The correlation between excess returns of life insurance stocks and bonds being positive is due to the fact that an increase (decrease) in interest rates will have a similar negative (positive) impact on both assets.

Table 1.   A. Summary statistics for February 1971–April 1989.

	Mean (%)	S.D.(%)	ρ_1
Dependent variables			
Excess return on the market portfolio	0.282	4.822	0.055
Excess return on government bond portfolio	0.038	3.287	0.050
Excess return on REITs portfolio	0.679	4.887	0.115
Excess return on LIFEs portfolio	0.570	5.884	0.136

B. Summary statistics for sub-periods.

	Mean (%)	S.D. (%)	Mean (%)	S.D. (%)	Mean (%)	S.D. (%)
Subperiods	Feb. 1971–Sep. 1979		Oct. 1979–Oct. 1982		Nov. 1982–Mar. 1989	
Market	0.018	4.627	0.043	5.373	0.748	4.831
Bonds	−0.088	1.953	−0.334	5.440	0.382	3.382
REITs	0.573	5.889	0.863	5.276	0.732	2.860
LIFEs	0.523	6.347	−0.009	6.473	0.908	4.924

C. Correlations among excess returns of different assets.

	Market	Bonds	REITs	LIFEs
Market	1.000	0.317	0.639	0.812
Bonds		1.000	0.186	0.348
REITs			1.000	0.654
LIFEs				1.000

D. Summary statistics for forecasting variables.

	Mean (%)	S.D. (%)	ρ_1
Forecasting variables			
Yield on 1-month T-bill (TB)	7.373	2.800	0.918
Yield spread between AAA bond and T-bill (SP)	2.373	1.818	0.750
Dividend yield on equal-weighted portfolio (DY)	3.055	0.628	0.940
Capitalization rate on equity REITs (CAPR)	10.44	1.141	0.958

Note: LIFE stands for a portfolio of life insurance company stocks. The sample period for this table is February 1971–April 1989, with 219 observations. Units on excess returns are percentage point per month. Units on one-month T-bill rate, term spread, dividend yield, and cap rate are percentage per annum. ρ_1 is the first-order autocorrelation coefficient of the series.

Figure 2 plots the movements of excess return of life insurance stocks in comparison of REITs. As we can see from the figure, excess returns on the two assets move closely together, which reflects to some extent the exposure of life insurance companies to real estate market risk. This confirms the correlation results given in Table 1.

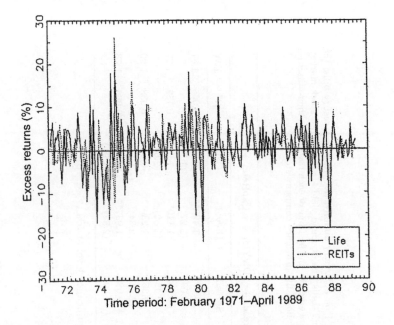

Fig. 2.   Excess returns on life insurance stock and REITs.

Table 2 reports the results of regressing excess returns on a constant term, a January dummy, yield on 1-month treasury bills, the yield spread, the dividend yield on the equally weighted market portfolio, and the cap rate on REITs. The first four variables have been used in previous studies for forecasting U.S. stock returns.

The most interesting finding here is that a fairly large component of the excess return on life insurance stocks is predictable and the significant contribution to this predictability is by the real estate variable — the cap rate. To be more specific, approximately 6.4% of the variation in monthly excess returns on life insurance companies is accounted for by our five forecasting variables after adjustment for degrees of freedom. The returns on REITs and the market stocks also post a fairly large predictability component (6.5% and 15.2%, respectively). The capability of the real estate variable to predict asset returns, especially life insurance stock returns and REITs, reflects the fact that changing real estate market conditions affect the risk premiums paid to life insurance stocks and REITs due to their real estate holdings.

Table 2.   Regression of the returns on each asset class at time $t+1$ on a January dummy, the yield on treasury bills, the spread between the yield on AAA corporate bonds and the yield on T-Bills, the dividend yield for the overall stock market, and the cap rate on real estate all at time t. Regression coefficients are given by the first line of each row, while the t-statistics are given in parenthesis in the second row. LIFE stands for a portfolio of life insurance company stocks.

$$r_{i,t+1} = \text{Cons.} + \gamma_1 \text{Jandum} + \gamma_2 T\text{-Bill} + \gamma_3 \text{Spread}_t + \gamma_r \text{DivYld}_t + \gamma_5 \text{CapRate}_t + \bar{\varepsilon}_i$$

Asset class	Constant	Jandum	T-bill	Spread	Divyld	CapR	$\bar{R}^2$	DW
Market	-7.408**	1.815	-0.597**	0.007	1.429**	0.724	0.065	1.87
	(-2.41)	(1.56)	(-3.25)	(0.03)	(2.27)	(1.76)		
EREITs	-9.335**	5.316**	-0.603**	-0.095	1.110*	1.040**	0.152	1.77
	(-2.80)	(4.47)	(-3.40)	(-0.45)	(1.82)	(2.62)		
Government bonds	-1.652	-0.747	0.077	0.362**	1.239**	-0.332	0.033	1.90
	(-0.69)	(-0.92)	(0.61)	(2.41)	(2.84)	(-1.16)		
LIFE stocks	-10.260**	1.903	-0.706**	-0.024	1.937**	0.960*	0.064	1.73
	(-2.43)	(1.34)	(-3.15)	(-0.09)	(2.52)	(1.91)		

Note: *indicates significance level at 10% while **indicates significance level at 5%.

From Table 2, we can also see that a high cap rate and a dividend yield predict a high future expected return. This means current high cap rates (or dividend yields) are associated with high expected future return. From Fig. 1, it is easy to see that the cap rate tends to rise right before or during the peak and trough of a business cycle, reflecting a price drop due to changing market conditions. Thus, our results suggest that investors demand a high expected rate of return on their investment during times of economic difficulty. Prior studies suggest that the major movement in the dividend yield series is related to long-term business conditions. When business conditions are weak and turbulent, the dividend yield forecasts high future expected returns while low returns are predicted when conditions are strong. And the high future expected returns represent compensation for holding risky assets during times of uncertainty and economic recession.

The T-bill variable is also significant for life insurance stocks. This negative relationship suggests that life insurance stocks exhibit "perverse" inflation behavior. The yield spread variable which tracks in part a maturity premium in expected returns is highly significant for bonds, but it is not significant for other assets, including life insurance stocks. The addition of a dummy variable to capture the January seasonality impact has an important positive effect on RE-ITs, but this January effect is not evident for stocks or bonds.

A visual presentation of the results in Table 2 is given in Fig. 3. This figure plots the actual excess returns on life insurance companies $(\tilde{r}_{i,t+1})$ and its conditional expected excess return $[E_t(\tilde{r}_{i,t+1})]$ using a dotted line and a solid line, respectively. Figure 3 shows that the expected excess return, which is assumed to be constant in prior life insurance studies, does vary over time. In fact, the sign of $[E_t(\tilde{r}_{i,t+1})]$ changes over time, taking on negative values in some time periods and positive values in other periods. Figure 3 also shows that the monthly predictable risk premiums on the life insurance stocks can be as high as 8% (January 1975). Although the predictability in the expected excess return does not necessarily imply that the market is inefficient but rather reflects rational pricing in an efficient market under different business conditions, the huge variation in expected excess returns or the risk premiums is astonishing and suggests the

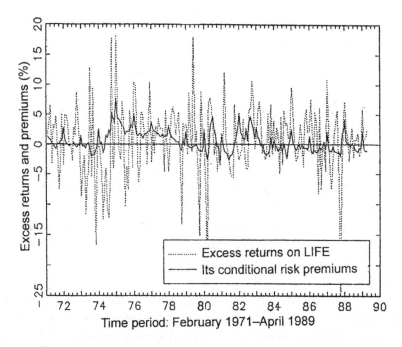

Fig. 3.   Excess returns on life insurance stock and its conditional risk premiums.

existence of bargain opportunities for investors with good risk tolerance. Another interesting result is that the risk premium on life insurance stocks remained relatively low during the second half of the last decade despite its huge real estate holdings. As a matter of fact, the conditional risk premium was mostly negative after 1983. As we shall see later, this negative premium could be the result of the existence of government safety net.

Figure 4 plots the expected excess return (risk premiums) for life insurance stocks relative to REITs over the February 1971–April 1989 period.[5] Overall, both life insurance stocks and REITs expected excess return move closely in tandem with a correlation coefficient of 0.868.

---

[5]These results are *without* the January effects.

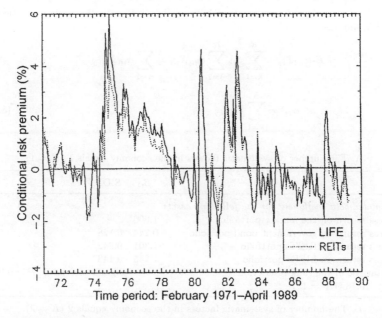

Fig. 4. Conditional risk premium on REIT and life insurance without the January effects.

8.5 Test of Asset Pricing Models

Before we proceed to test the asset pricing model, it is worth pointing out that the above results do not depend on the assumptions required for asset pricing model of Eqs. (8.1)–(8.5), such as constant betas and linear factor structure. All that is needed is that the conditional expected return is a linear function of economic state variables, X_{pt}.

To test the asset pricing model, we report our estimates of Eq. (8.4') with the restriction of (8.5) imposed in Table 3. In panel A, we estimate the regression system under the assumption that there is only one systematic factor, $\tilde{f}_{1,t+1}$, in the economy $(K = 1)$. With beta normalized to be 1 for value-weighted stocks, we observe that the beta for life insurance stocks is higher than those for value-weighted stocks but smaller than that of REITs. Bonds have the lowest beta of all asset classes. The chi-square test in Table 3 indicates that a one-factor model is not rejected by the data $(p = 0.205)$.

The model is then estimated assuming $K = 2$ (panel B). We normalize the bonds to have a beta of 1 on the first factor, and a beta

Table 3.   Estimation of the latent variable model (8.4) with the rank restriction of Eq. (8.5) imposed:

$$E_t[\tilde{r}_{i,t+1}] = \sum_{k=1}^{K} \beta_{ik} \sum_{n=1}^{N} \theta_{kn} X_{nt} = \sum_{n=1}^{N} \alpha_{in} X_{nt}, \tag{8.4}$$

$$\alpha_{ij}{}^i = \sum_{k=1}^{K} \beta_{ik} \theta_{kj}. \tag{8.5}$$

A. The number of systematic factors in the economy equals 1 ($K = 1$).

	β_{i1}	S.D.
Estimated beta coefficient for the following assets		
Excess return on the market portfolio	1.000*	–
Excess return on government bond portfolio	0.244	0.128
Excess return on REITs portfolio	1.301	0.242
Excess return on LIFEs portfolio	1.245	0.143
χ^2-statistic of the rank restriction (8.5): 19.18 (DF = 15)	Significance level: $P = 0.205$	

B. The number of systematic factors in the economy equals 2 ($K = 2$).

	β_{i1}	S.D.	β_{i2}	S.D.
Estimated beta coefficient for the following assets				
Excess return on the market portfolio	0.794	0.379	0.580	0.136
Excess return on government bond portfolio	1.000*	–	0.000*	–
Excess return on REITs portfolio	0.000*	–	1.000*	–
Excess return on LIFEs portfolio	1.077	0.403	0.697	0.128
χ^2-statistic of the rank restriction (8.5): 6.822 (DF = 8)	Significance level: $P = 0.555$			

Note: LIFE stands for a portfolio of life insurance company stocks. S.D. stands for standard error for the corresponding parameter estimates. (*) indicates these numbers are normalized to be 1 or zero.

of zero on the second factor, and we normalize REITs to have a beta of zero on the first factor and a beta of 1 on the second factor. Under the normalization, we can call the first factor the "bond factor" and the second factor the "real estate factor", because changes in these factors will lead to a same change in their corresponding asset returns. From panel B, if the market is largely driven by a interest rate factor and a real estate factor, we can see that life insurance stocks are more sensitive that the market portfolio to both pervasive forces that affect bond returns and real estate returns. The test of restriction (8.5) suggests that the "two-factor" model is not rejected

Table 4. Estimation of the latent variable model (8.4): Two subperiods.

$$E_t[\tilde{r}_{i,t+1}] = \sum_{k=1}^{K} \beta_{ik} \sum_{n=1}^{N} \theta_{kn} X_{nt} = \sum_{n=1}^{N} \alpha_{in} X_{nt} \qquad (8.4)$$

$$\alpha_{ij} = \sum_{k=1}^{K} \beta_{ik} \theta_{kj}. \qquad (8.5)$$

A. The number of systematic factors in the economy equals 1 ($K = 1$).

	β_{i1}	S.D.	β_{i1}	S.D.
Estimated beta	Feb. 1971–Sep. 1979		Oct. 1979–Mar. 1989	
Market	1.000*	–	1.000*	–
Bonds	0.126	0.098	0.021	0.228
REITs	0.979	0.301	1.220	0.183
LIFEs	0.646	0.284	1.094	0.172

χ^2-statistic of the rank restriction (8.5): 14.91

Significance level: $P = 0.457$

χ^2-statistic of the rank restriction (8.5): 19.74

Significance level: $P = 0.181$

B. The number of systematic factors in the economy equals 2 ($K = 2$).

	β_{i1}	S.D.	β_{i2}	S.D.	β_{i1}	S.D.	β_{i2}	S.D.
Estimated beta	Feb. 1971–Sep. 1979				Oct. 1979–Mar. 1989			
Market	2.283	1.180	0.584	0.174	0.248	0.187	0.825	0.139
Bond	1.000*	–	0.000*	–	1.000*	–	0.000*	–
REITs	0.000*	–	1.000*	–	0.000*	–	1.000*	–
LIFEs	4.534	1.513	0.608	0.223	0.267	0.180	0.905	0.113

χ^2-statistic of the rank restriction (8.5): 6.37

Significance level: $P = 0.606$

χ^2-statistic of the rank restriction (8.5): 7.15

Significance level: $P = 0.519$

Note: LIFE stands for a portfolio of life insurance company stocks. S.D. stands for standard error for the corresponding parameter estimates. *indicates these numbers are normalized to be 1 or zero.

by data.

Although the latent-variable model in general is not rejected by the data, it might be informative to have a measure of goodness of fit on the risk premium by the asset pricing model. Thus, we define the pricing error of the model to be the difference in the unrestricted and the restricted values of $E_t(\tilde{r}_{i,t+1})$. The unrestricted value of $E_t(\tilde{r}_{i,t+1})$ is estimated by Eq. (8.4'), while the restricted value is estimated by Eq. (8.4') with restriction (8.5) imposed. If the model is

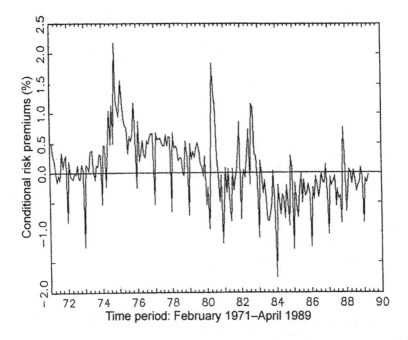

Fig. 5.   Pricing error on life insurance stocks.

correctly specified and there is no mispricing in the market then the pricing error should be zero, independent of the choice of the forecasting variables. Figure 5 shows the pricing error for life insurance companies for the whole sample period. It is easy to see that the pricing error varies over time. What is interesting is the negative pricing errors during most of the time period after 1981. This result is consistent with the negative risk premiums during the same period discovered in Fig. 4. The average pricing errors during the period of April 1984–February 1989 is −0.284% per month, with a standard error of 0.340%.[6] Although a simple t-test suggest that we cannot say that these pricing errors are significantly different from zero due

---

[6]The standard error is calculated by treating it as a nonlinear function of the parameters in Eq. (8.4') estimated with and without restriction (8.5). A GMM procedure is applied to obtain the joint estimates. Define the parameter estimates as I and its covariance matrix V, then the standard error, which is a nonlinear function $f(l)$, can be calculated as $\sqrt{f_\lambda(\lambda)'V f_\lambda(\lambda)}$.

to the large standard error, the persistence of these negative pricing errors demands a further study.[7]

To reduce the possibility of spurious mispricing due to a misspecification problem associated with the assumption of constant beta in the latent-variable model, we split the sample period into two subperiods: February 1971–September 1979 and October 1979–February 1989 and then estimate the model for the two subperiods. The results are presented in Table 4. Here, we do find some evidence of time-varing betas. For example, the sensitivity towards "market factor", β_{i1}, for life insurance companies has significantly increased from 0.646 to 1.094 in the one-factor model. The sensitivity towards "bond factor" has decreased from 4.534 to 0.267, while the sensitivity towards "real estate factor" has increased from 0.608 to 0.905 in the two-factor model. This decrease in sensitivity towards "bond factor" and increase in sensitivity towards "real estate factor" suggest that life insurance companies have generally increased their risk exposure in real estate risks during the second sample period.

Figure 6 shows the pricing error for life insurance companies for the subperiod of October 1979–February 1989. It is easy to see that the pricing errors during most of the period after 1984 are still negative, with an average pricing error of -0.279% per month. During the same period, the averaging pricing errors for the market, bond, and REITs portfolios are 0.007%, 0.050%, and 0.523%, respectively. Although the averaging pricing errors here are estimated with large measurement errors, the persistency of negative pricing errors on life insurance companies displayed in Fig. 5 suggest that we at least have some preliminary evidence of undercompensation for risk on life insurance companies during the 1980s.

We believe that this undercompensation is not a market anomaly but rather reflects the recognition of the existence of government safety net by the market place. The insurance reduces the downside risk of bankruptcy of large life insurance companies; therefore, the risk premium paid on these life insurance companies should be lower than what would be if there is no such government intervention.

---

[7]The average pricing error is highly significant, if we ignore the measurement error in the parameter estimates.

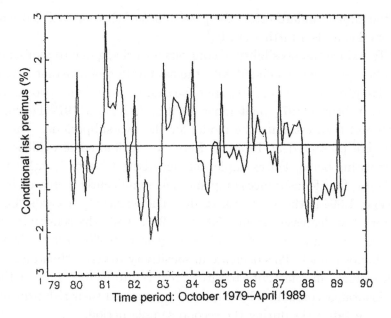

Fig. 6.   Pricing error on life insurance stocks.

8.6   Summary and Conclusions

In this chapter, we study the relationship between the financial strengths of real estate market and life insurance companies. Our main finding is that the expected excess returns on life insurance stocks are predictable, partly by movements in real estate market conditions. We also find that the risk premiums paid on life insurance stocks vary substantially over time. We have some preliminary evidence that there is a seemingly undercompensation for risk for life insurance companies, which could reflect the recognition of the existence of government safety net by the market place. The safety net reduces the risk of bankruptcy of large life insurance companies; therefore, the risk premium paid on these life insurance companies should be lower than what they would be without such regulatory subsidy. There is fairly strong evidence that life insurance companies have generally increased their risk exposure in the 1980s, especially real estate risks. Another finding of the study is that these results are consistent with the view that the time variation in expected asset returns could be explained by the changing price of risk of one or two systematic factors.

Appendix A

To estimate Eq. (8.4') under restriction (8.5), we first renormalized the model by setting the factor loadings of the first K assets as follows: $\beta_{ij} = 1$ (if $j = i$) and $\beta_{ij} = 0$ (if $j = i$) for $1 \leq i \leq K$. Next, we partition the excess return matrix $R = (R_1, R_2)$, where R_1 is a $T \times K$ matrix of excess returns of the first K assets and R_2 is a $T \times (N - K)$ matrix of excess returns on the rest of the assets. Using Eqs. (8.4') and (8.5), we can derive the following regression system:

$$
\begin{aligned}
R_1 &= X\Theta + \mu_1, \\
R_2 &= X\alpha + \mu_2
\end{aligned}
\tag{A.1}
$$

where X is a $T \times L$ matrix of the forecasting variables, Θ a matrix of θ_{ij} and α a matrix of α_{ij}. If the linear pricing relationship in Eq. (8.2) holds, the rank restriction implies that the data should not be able to reject the null hypothesis H_0: $\alpha = \Theta B$, where B is a matrix of β_{ij} elements.

The regression system of Eq. (A.1) given the restriction in Eq. (8.5) can be estimated and tested using Hansen's (1982) GMM, which allows for conditional heteroskedasticity and serial correlation in the error terms of excess returns. It is easy to see from Eq. (8.4') that the error term in system (A.1) has conditional mean zero given the instruments X_{pt}. This implies an orthogonality condition $E(U'X) = 0$. Following Hansen, we first construct an $N \times L$ sample mean matrix: $G_T = U'X/T$. Next, we stack the column vector on top of each other to obtain an $NL \times 1$ vector of g_T. A two-step algorithm is then used to find an optimal solution for the quadratic form. $g_T'W^{-1}g_T$, by minimizing over the parameter space of (Θ, α). In the first step, the identity matrix is used as the weighting matrix W. After obtaining the initial solution of Θ_0 and α_0, we next calculate the residuals μ_1 and μ_2 from the system of equations in (A.1) and construct the following weighting matrix:

$$W = \frac{1}{T} \sum_t (u_t u_t') \otimes (Z_t Z_t'),$$ (A.2)

where $\otimes$ is the Kronecker product. In the second step, we use the weighting matrix as given by (A.2) to resolve the optimization problem of minimizing $g_T' W^{-1} g_T$ over the choice of (Θ, α). Hansen proved that under the null hypothesis (i.e., when the model is correctly specified). T times the weighted sum of squares of the residuals, $g_T' W^{-1} g_T$, is asymptotically chi-square distributed, with the degrees of freedom equal to the difference between the number of orthogonality conditions and the number of parameters estimated: $(N - K)$ $(L - K)$, where N is the number of assets studied, K the number of factor loadings, and L the number of forecasting variables.

After obtaining the weighted sum of squared residuals, we can perform a chi-square test to determine if the data rejects the restricted regression system (A.1). If it does not, then we can use (A.1) to study the issue of how much of the variation in asset returns can be predicted by these forecasting variables. Since these forecasting variables are closely related to financial and real estate market conditions, we can also interpret the regression results as to what extent these economic conditions affect conditional factor risk premiums.

By taking conditional expectations of Eq. (8.2), it is straightforward to show that the rank restrictions hold in the same form when a subset of the relevant information is used. Thus, if the coefficients in Eq. (8.4') are subject to the restrictions in Eq. (8.5) under the true information vector used by the market, they will be subject to the same form of restrictions in Eq. (8.5) if a subset of this vector is included in the information set. Similarly, if the test using the full set of the market's information does not reject the K-factor model, then the test using a subset of the market's information should not reject the model either. A more detailed elaboration of this robustness issue is discussed in Campbell (1987) and Ferson (1989).

References

Campbell, J.Y., 1987, Stock Returns and the Term structure, *Journal of Financial Economics* **18**, 373–399.

Campbell, J.Y. and Y. Hamao, 1992, Predictable Stock Returns in the United States and Japan: A Study of Long-Term Capital Market Integration, *Journal of Finance* **47** (1), 43–70.

Chan, K.C., P. Hendershott and A. Sanders, 1990, Risk and Return on Real Estate: Evidence from Equity REITs, *AREUEA Journal* **18**, 431–452.

Fama, E. and K. French, 1988, Dividend Yields and Expected Stock Returns, *Journal of Financial Economics* **22**, 3–25.

Fama, E. and K. French, 1989, Business Conditions and Expected Return on Stocks and Bonds, *Journal of Financial Economics* **25**, 23–49.

Fama, E. and G.W. Schwert, 1977, Asset Returns and Inflation, *Journal of Financial Economics* **5**, 115–146.

Ferson, W., 1989, Changes in Expected Security Returns, Risk, and Level of Interest Rates, *Journal of Finance* **44**, 1191–1217.

Ferson, W., 1990, Are the Latent Variables in Time-Varying Expected Returns Compensation for Consumption Risk? *Journal of Finance* **45**, 397–430.

Ferson, W. and C. Harvey, 1991, The Variation of Economic Risk Premiums, *Journal of Political Economy* **99** (2), 385–416.

Ferson, W., S. Kandel and R. Stambaugh, 1987, Test of Asset Pricing with Time-Varying Expected Risk Premiums and Market Betas, *Journal of Finance* **42**, 201–219.

Gilberto, S.M., 1990, Equity Real Estate Investment Trust and Real Estate Returns, *Journal of Real Estate Research* **5**, 259–263.

Hansen, L. P., 1982, Large Sample Properties of Generalized Method of Moments Estimators, *Econometrica* **50** (4), 1029–1054.

Harvey, C.R., 1989, Time-Varying Conditional Covariances in Tests of Asset Pricing Models, *Journal of Financial Economics* **24**, 289–317.

Harrington, S.E., 1983, The Relationship Between Risk and Return: Evidence For Life Insurance Stock, *JRI* **50**(4), 587–610.

Keim, D.B., 1983, Size Related Anomalies and Stock Return Seasonality: Empirical Evidence, *Journal of Financial Economics* **12**, 13–32.

Keim, D. and R. Stambaugh, 1986, Predicting Returns in the Stock and Bond Markets, *Journal of Financial Economics* **17**, 357–390.

Nourse, H.O., 1987, The "Cap Rate," 1966–1984: A Test of the Impact of Income Tax Changes on Income Property, *Land Economics* **63**, 147–152.

Sirmans, C.F. and J.R. Webb., 1980, Expected Equity Returns On Real Estate Financed With Life Insurance Company Loans: 1967–1977, *AREUEA*, **8**(2), 218–228.

Sweeny, R. and A. Warga, 1986, The Pricing of Interest Rate Risk: Evidence from the Stock Market, *Journal of Finance* **41**, 393–410.

Webb, J.R., 1984, Real Estate Investment Acquisition Rules For Life Insurance Companies And Pension Funds: A Survey, *AREUEA* **12**(4), 495–520.

White, H., 1980, A Heteroskedasticity-Consistent Covariance Matrix Estimator and a Direct Test for Heteroskedasticity, *Econometrica* **48**, 817–838.

CHAPTER 9

The Return Distributions of Property Shares in Emerging Markets

KEVIN WENLI LU*

*Corporate Finance Division, Global Risk Advisors,
845 Third Avenue, 20 Floor, New York, NY 10022*

JIANPING (J.P.) MEI†

*Stern School of Business
44 West 4th Street, 7-69, New York, NY 10012*

Previous studies have characterized emerging market equities as having higher returns, higher volatility, and higher predictability compared with developed markets returns. The recent Asian crisis has once again drawn attention to the return and risk feature of emerging market properties. Increasingly, conventional wisdom about emerging markets has been questioned because of the abysmal performance of these markets in times of adversity. Do real estate investment in emerging markets still offer attractive returns to U.S. investors? Do correlations across different markets increase in down markets so that the much desired diversifications may not be present when they are needed the most? Are real estate securities markets predictable in emerging markets? To answer these questions, we examine the behavior of the property indices' returns in 10 emerging markets.

---

*Investment Banking Associate. Available at Phone/Fax: (201) 420-4473,
 E-mail: WL11@STERN.NYU.EDU

†Associate Professor of Finance and International Business. Available at
Phone: (212) 998-0354, Fax: (212) 995-4221, E-mail: JMEI@STERN.NYU.EDU

9.1 Data Source

We use quarterly dollar-denominated returns on property indices for 10 emerging market countries: Argentina, China, Hong Kong, Indonesia, Malaysia, Peru, Philippines, Singapore, Thailand, and Turkey. As performance benchmarks, we studied 10 broad market indices as well as the S&P500 and the NAREIT index. Except for some historical data on exchange rates, which come from the Federal Reserve Bank's data releases, all index data have been extracted from *Datastream*.

Table 1 outlines the descriptive characteristics of the property indices. The indices vary greatly in number of constituents, duration, and size. The indices of Argentina, China, and Turkey are composed of only one property stock each, while the Hong Kong index consists of 34 stocks. The indices with the longest history, those of Hong Kong and Singapore, data back to 1973. Some of the newer indices contain only five years of data, such as in the case of China, Peru, Philippines, and Argentina. The disparity in size is even more pronounced. As of July 1997, the largest index, the Hong Kong index, has a market capitalization of $43.6 billion. This is comparable to the size of *Datastream*'s U.S. property index, which is valued at $66.3 billion. Taking the recent sharp decline of the Hong Kong real estate market into consideration, it is safe to assume that until recently the Hong Kong index has been bigger than the U.S. index. In sharp contrast, the Peruvian index has a capitalization of $29 million. However, it is worth noting that the index values may not always accurately reflect the true magnitude of the underlying local markets, because the indices may not be exhaustive of all the property stocks. On a similar note, the measurement for trading volume used here is the volume for a single quarter instead of the average quarterly volume for a long period; therefore it can only serve as a proxy measurement of the markets' turnover level.

Table 1 also provides the price-to-earnings ratio and dividend yield for the indices. Again the indices indicate drastically different levels of market valuation. Interestingly, the Hong Kong index, the largest index and probably the mostly actively traded index as well, also has the lowest P/E ratio and the second highest dividend yield.

Table 1.   Data summary.

Index	Number of firms in sample	First quarter in sample	Market capitalization (US$ million)	Quarterly trading volume (million)	P/E ratio	Dividend yield
Argentina property index	1	Q3 93	715	9	20.1	2.97
China property index	1	Q3 94	618	35	28.2	0.65
Hong Kong property index	34	Q4 73	43618	9535	4.6	8.96
Indonesia property index	7	Q4 91	265	191	9.5	7.07
Malaysia property index	9	Q4 86	1022	262	9.3	6.54
Philippines property index	9	Q4 89	4366	2549	12.7	1.03
Peru property index	3	Q1 94	29	16	N/A	8.8
Singapore property index	15	Q4 73	5974	945	8.5	3.63
Thailand property index	3	Q4 90	86	5	7.4	11.1
Turkey property index	1	Q2 89	746	2632	31.4	2.2

Notes: The market capitalization is calculated based on the data of 7/31/98. The quarterly trading volume is the trading volume for the second quarter of 98.

This is of course the direct result of last year's crisis (the current Hong Kong index price is only 28.5% of last year's price level).

9.2   Return and Risk

In Table 2, we provide the following data for the property indices of the 10 countries: the geometric mean of quarterly returns in U.S. dollar; the arithmetic mean of quarterly returns in U.S. dollar; the geometric mean of the quarterly returns in local currency; and the standard deviation of the quarterly returns. The dollar data for Argentina and market index return for Peru are not available.

Using the geometric means to compare property returns and market returns, we find that neither of them overwhelmingly performs better in all nine countries. (Peru is excluded owing to lack of market index data.) For Indonesia, Malaysia, Philippines, and Thailand, the market indices far outperform the respective property indices. For Argentina, China, Turkey, Hong Kong, and Singapore, property indices do better than the market indices. The arithmetic returns display a similar picture for all countries except China. China's geometric return of property index is greater than that of the market index, but its arithmetic return of property index is smaller than that of its market index. This is because China's property index experiences a much smaller volatility than its market index. As to volatility, in all countries except China, property indices have a higher volatility than market indices. As a result, in four of the nine countries, the property indices dominate the market indices. It seems that we have two initial observations. Firstly, neither property index nor market index in emerging markets overwhelmingly outperforms the other in average return. The p-value of the paired t-test is 23%, which shows that the difference between the two types of indices is not statistically significant, even at the 10% level. Secondly, in emerging markets, property indices are mostly more volatile than market indices. The difference between the volatilities is statistically significant at 5% level.

We include the data from U.S. equity market (1973–1998) to further our analysis. As we can see from Table 2, the NAREIT index

Table 2. Quarterly return summary (in U.S.$ terms) for market and property indices.

Index	Geometric return[1]	Arithmetic return[2]	Standard deviation[3]	Local return[4]
Argentina (local)				
PI	1.46	3.11	19.24	1.46
MI	1.04	2.19	16.09	1.04
China				
PI	6.25	11.12	39.21	5.95
MI	1.93	14.50	66.08	10.08
Hong Kong				
PI	3.51	6.20	23.40	3.98
MI	3.33	4.99	17.92	3.78
Indonesia				
PI	−13.15	−5.79	37.84	−6.19
MI	−1.86	1.45	22.80	3.67
Malaysia				
PI	−0.98	2.60	26.24	−0.21
MI	1.95	3.59	17.27	2.74
Philippines				
PI	−3.18	0.26	26.30	−1.29
MI	0.42	2.27	19.13	2.32
Peru				
PI	1.47	2.46	14.99	3.23
Singapore				
PI	2.45	5.07	24.81	1.87
MI	2.08	3.40	16.00	1.49
Thailand				
PI	−10.93	−1.99	44.42	−9.40
MI	−1.03	0.95	19.69	0.42
Turkey				
PI	5.30	14.12	45.19	20.44
MI	3.52	8.93	35.87	22.69
U.S.				
NAREIT	3.37	3.64	7.47	3.37
S&P500	2.13	2.45	7.95	2.13

Notes:

(1) PI — Property index. MI — market index. All data in U.S. dollar terms except for Argentina. There is no market index data for Peru.
(2) A paired *t*-test is performed to examine the difference between the geometric returns of property indices and market indices. The *t*-value is −1.3, which is not statistically significant at 10% level.
(3) A paired *t*-test is also performed to examine the difference between the standard deviations of the two types of indices. The *t*-value is 2.9, which is significant at 5% level, indicating property indices are more volatile.

outperforms all but three emerging market counterparts (China, Hong Kong and Turkey). The most noticeable point is that NAREIT index has exceptionally low quarterly return volatility. The implication of this is that NAREIT easily dominates seven out of 10 emerging market property indices in our sample, and that NAREIT is far less risky than any of the emerging market property indices. Compared to S&P500 index, NAREIT index also has a much higher average quarterly return and a smaller volatility over the past 25 years.

Figure 1 displays the monthly P/E ratios and the 12-month moving volatility of the 11 property indices. The relationships between these two data series are different in two groups of countries within our sample. For U.S., Turkey, China, Argentina, and Peru, P/E ratios and volatility of the returns are positively correlated. For the other group including all six East Asian markets, P/E ratios and volatility mostly behave in a similar fashion as the first group only before the crisis, and higher P/E corresponds with higher volatility. However, in the second post-crisis period, starting from early and mid-1997 for Malaysia, Indonesia, Philippines, Singapore, Thailand, and early 1996 for Hong Kong, P/E series and moving volatility series deviate. During this period, the market volatility increased significantly while the P/E ratios went down significantly. This clearly appears to reflect the impact of the Asian financial crisis: the prices were going down mostly with big fluctuation. Owing to flight-to-quality, investors were no longer willing to take risks. Graphically, we see that MV series went up substantially as the P/E series went down.

Taking exchange rates into consideration, we produce Fig. 2 to show the correlation between the percentage change in exchange rate and the local property index return. Without exception, all the correlation coefficients are negative, implying the existence of a "double squeeze" in emerging market property indices, that is, a negative return in a certain property index tends to be accompanied by a depreciation of the local currency. Therefore, when there is a negative return in a property index, the U.S. dollar return tends to be double squeezed both by the negative local return and the currency depreciation.

9.3 Normality, Skewness and Kurtosis

Figure 3 consists of the normality plots for the 11 property market return series in our sample. We can see the theoretical normal distribution return curves and the actual returns histograms.

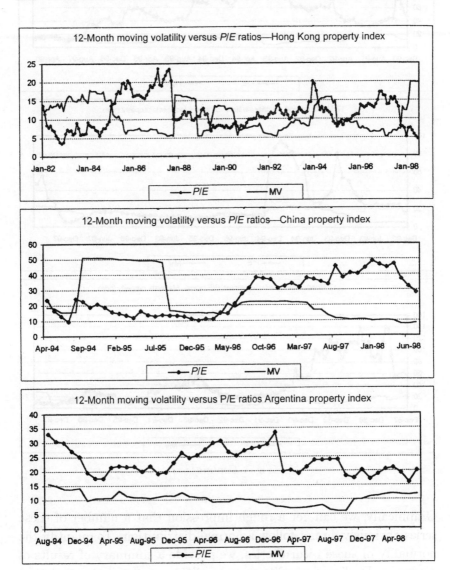

Fig. 1.   Property markets monthly P/E ratios and 12-month moving volatility.

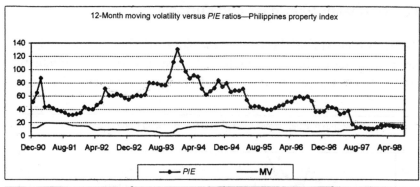

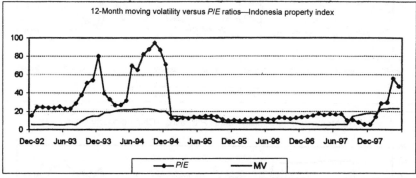

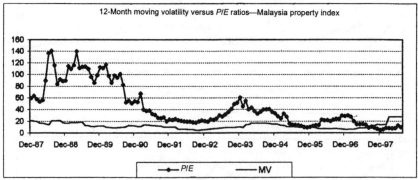

Fig. 1 *Continued.*

Graphically, we can get a rough impression that a number of these series obviously do not follow a normal distribution. To quantify the normality of these return series, we provide a summary of results of Anderson–Darling normality tests to all 11 series and the statistical inference we made from the tests in Table 3.

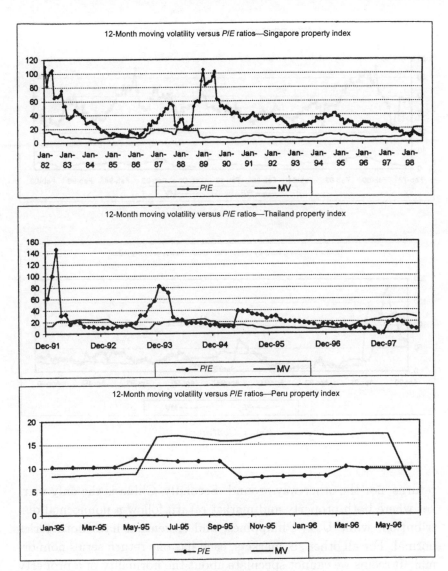

Fig. 1 *Continued.*

Several observations can be drawn from the normality tests of both property indices and the broad market indices. Firstly, there are four property index return series, which clearly do not follow a theoretical normal distribution. Generally, property index returns do not deviate from a normal distribution more than market index

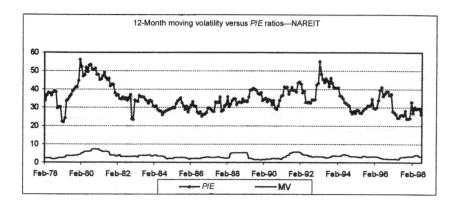

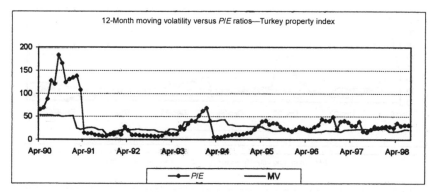

Fig. 1 *Continued.*

returns, nor the other way around. Secondly, China is the only market where both property and market return follow a nonnormal distribution, while U.S., Philippines, and Argentina have both series normal. For all other six markets, each has one return series nonnormal. It seems we cannot speculate about the normality of a property return series from the corresponding market index, nor vice versa.

To further describe the return and risk characteristics of the emerging market, we examine skewness and kurtosis, which are also presented in Table 3. A positive (negative) skewness signals a higher(lower)-than-normal-distribution chance of higher(lower)-than-mean returns. Kurtosis captures the degree of "fat tail" in returns, namely the excess probability of abnormal returns in both

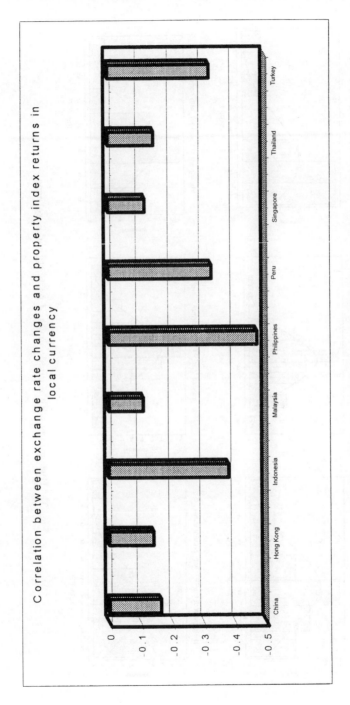

Fig. 2. Exchange rate and local property index returns.

206   *Asset Pricing*

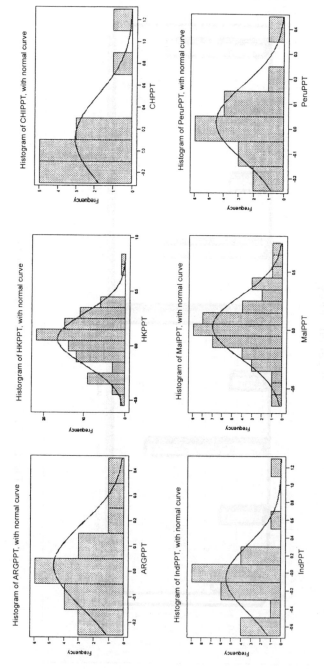

Fig. 3.   Histograms with normal curves of property index returns.

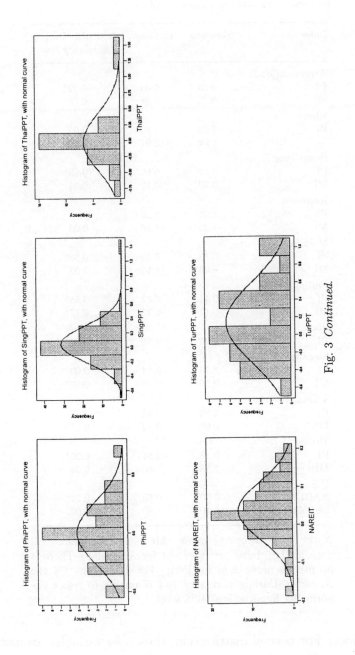

Fig. 3 *Continued.*

Table 3.   Additional distributional characteristics and normality tests for market and property indices

Index	Skewness	Kurtosis	Anderson–Darling normality test
Argentina(local)			
PI	0.63	0.04	0.52*
MI	0.72	1.58	0.73*
China			
PI	2.02	3.80	0.00
MI	1.94	3.27	0.00
Hong Kong			
PI	0.12	0.62	0.23*
MI	−0.39	0.17	0.04
Indonesia			
PI	1.06	3.20	0.01
MI	−1.20	1.79	0.09
Malaysia			
PI	0.13	0.45	0.50*
MI	−0.93	1.15	0.02
Philippines			
PI	0.41	0.82	0.68*
MI	−0.12	0.13	0.77*
Peru			
PI	0.87	1.32	0.67*
Singapore			
PI	1.76	9.14	0.00
MI	−0.29	0.80	0.36*
Thailand			
PI	1.83	5.32	0.00
MI	0.00	0.42	0.15*
Turkey			
PI	0.48	−0.51	0.26*
MI	1.13	1.86	0.02
U.S.			
NAREIT	−0.20	0.53	0.27*
S&P500	−0.70	1.89	0.09

Notes: PI — Property index. MI — market index. All data in U.S. dollar terms except for Argentina. There is no market index data for Peru. For data with "*", the Anderson–Darling normality test is unable to reject the normality hypothesis at 10% level.

directions. For normal distribution, these two variables are not significantly different from zero.

An examination of Table 3 shows several patterns which warrant our attention. First of all, all emerging market property returns displayed a positive skewness, that is, for all emerging market property indices, the chance of getting an excess return is unusually high. Among them, China, Singapore, and Thailand are the most heavily positively skewed. Secondly, as opposed to the property index, six out of nine market index returns displayed a negative skewness, which means there is an unusually higher chance of collecting lower-than-average returns in the market indices. This also shows that a higher-than-mean return is not a feature of emerging markets but a characteristic of property indices. Thirdly, the two benchmark U.S. indices all exhibited modest negative skewness.

Fat tails are common in security return processes, and our sample is no exception. All indices in our sample, except Turkey property index, reasonably display fat tails and have a positive kurtosis. But the heterogeneity in kurtosis is also apparent. Singapore property index return has a 9.14 kurtosis, while several other series, Argentina property, Hong Kong, and Philippines market indices, display kurtosis close to zero. Interestingly, the S&P500 index, which is considered to be normal, also has a 1.89 kurtosis, showing some kind of sign of abnormal returns in either direction. Another point we noticed is that seven out of 10 emerging market property indices display a kurtosis higher than that of NAREIT.

Comparing the quarterly kurtosis data with monthly data, we found that only three out of 21 series have significantly higher kurtosis in quarterly data than in monthly data (Hu and Mei, 2000). An overwhelming majority of these series displayed larger kurtosis in monthly data than in quarterly data. The implication from this is useful and clear: the unusual jumps in these return series, either jumping up or down, mostly did not last more than three months. Therefore when the data is quarterly aggregated, because not all three monthly jumps within a quarter are equally abnormal, they tend to cancel each other out or mask the most abnormal one. As a result, the aggregate magnitude of the quarterly jumps is smaller than that of monthly jumps, thus creating less abnormal quarterly returns, in either direction. If data with more intervals are collected and analyzed we may know more about how long these jumps which constitute the fat tails actually last and what is the relationship between the duration of a jump and its magnitude. But these questions go beyond the scope of this chapter.

Several important implications and insights can be drawn based on the analyses in this and the preceding parts. Firstly, the average return provided by the emerging market property indices is generally similar to that provided by the market indices in emerging markets. Within emerging market investment vehicles, property indices do not systematically outperform or underperform the market indices. At the same time, within emerging markets, property indices are much more volatile than market indices. Secondly, compared to the U.S. investments, the risk premium provided by investments in the emerging market property indices is not sufficiently high. Thirdly, emerging market property index investments have more short-term positive jumps than their market indices as well as the U.S. counterpart. Therefore despite the lackluster performance of the property markets, there were opportunities to make abnormal positive returns. Fourthly, the magnitude of this abnormality in short-term returns is significantly greater in monthly data than quarterly data, which implies that the duration of a jump is mostly shorter than three months.

9.4   Predictability

Under the efficient market hypothesis, a security price series follows a martingale process and its return would be a white noise series that has no predictability. Markets in developed countries like U.S. are deemed highly efficient, and the information set at time t would reflect all available information and the increment between t and $t+1$ would be unpredictable and mimic a white noise. Emerging markets have been deemed comparatively inefficient and therefore have higher predictability.

A key and the simplest starting point regarding the predictability of a return series is its autoregressive feature. We will limit our discussion of predictability to the autoregression of the series. In

Table 4. Autocorrelation (Run's test) for market and property indices

		Observed number of runs versus Expected number of runs	P-value	Statistical inference
Argentina (local)	PI	24/30	0.11	Not autocorrelated
	MI	26/29	0.34	Not autocorrelated
China	PI	31/30	0.77	Not autocorrelated
	MI	26/25	0.66	Not autocorrelated
Hong Kong	PI	97/105	0.24	Not autocorrelated
	MI	146/148	0.78	Not autocorrelated
Indonesia	PI	25/40	0.00***	Positively autocorrelated
	MI	41/50	0.05*	Positively autocorrelated
Malaysia	PI	68/69	0.73	Not autocorrelated
	MI	57/70	0.02**	Positively autocorrelated
Philippines	PI	39/51	0.01***	Positively autocorrelated
	MI	44/52	0.09*	Positively autocorrelated
Peru	PI	30/25	0.20	Not autocorrelated
Singapore	PI	92/105	0.06*	Positively autocorrelated
	MI	129/154	0.00***	Positively autocorrelated
Thailand	PI	45/46	0.86	Not autocorrelated
	MI	42/46	0.31	Not autocorrelated
Turkey	PI	50/54	0.36	Not autocorrelated
	MI	49/54	0.20	Not autocorrelated
U.S	PI	145/157	0.15	Not autocorrelated
	MI	151/154	0.70	Not autocorrelated

Notes: ***significant at 1% level; **5% level; *10% level. The statistical inference is made on 10% level.

other words, in predicting Y_{t+1}, we will limit our information set to Y_t, Y_{t+1}, etc., without considering other variables like regulatory changes, monetary policy, exposure to political risk, and so on. Given the context of limited numbers of data points for some countries, we did not nonparametric Run's test to try to explore the autoregressive features in all the 21 series we have in our sample. Table 4 shows the result. The implications of these results are interpreted as follows.

Firstly, the autoregressive feature seems to be country-specific rather than sector-specific. In other words, property indices did not generally display different autoregressive features from market indices but the autoregressive features of indices of both property and market indices did differ from one country to another. From Table 4, we can see that in the cases of Indonesia, Philippines, and Singapore, both property indices and market indices are autocorrelated and thus have higher predictability. For seven other countries, including the U.S., neither of the indices was autocorrelated. Only Malaysia's two series did not resonate each other's autoregressive nature. Secondly, for the seven indices that are autocorrelated, all of them are positively autocorrelated. None of them has a negative autocorrelation. a higher-than-mean return of this period tends to bring another higher-than-mean return. Therefore for these seven series, there are less actual runs than their respective standard runs. For the other 14 series, the hypothesis that there is no autocorreltion was not rejected at 90% confidence level. Thirdly, U.S. property index and market index seemed to conform to the efficient market hypothesis and did not appear to have strong autoregression. Fourthly, contrary to our previous belief, a majority of the emerging market return series did not seem to display a clear autoregressive nature, and as a result these series did not have the predictability we previously assumed they had.

A positive autocorrelation would give rise to the possible success of a trading strategy based on momentum. To investigate whether this is true, we used our sample to compare the performance of two trading strategies for all 11 property markets. Trading strategy one (TS1) is a straight forward buy-and-hold strategy. Trading strategy two (TS2) is a momentum-based strategy: the investor buys one share at month $t + 1$ if the return in month t is positive, and vice versa. Table 5 shows the result of the performance comparison, which include the monthly geometric returns, monthly standard deviations, and Sharpe ratios for the two strategies. We found that in six markets, the momentum-based trading strategy did better than the buy-and-hold strategy. Another finding is that for more volatile markets (Indonesia, Philippines, Thailand, Turkey, and Malaysia), the momentum-based strategy did a much better job and had much better Sharpe ratios. For markets with a lower volatility (Argentina, Peru, and Singapore), the buy-and-hold strategy performed better. The reason why the momentum-based trading strategy performs better in markets with higher volatility certainly warrants more research.

Table 5. Comparison of risk and returns of two trading strategies

Property index	Buy and Hold geometric return	Momentum geometric return	Buy and Hold standard deviation	Momentum standard deviation	Buy and Hold sharpe ratio	Momentum sharpe ratio
Argentina	0.9	−0.33	11.45	11.55	0.27	−0.10
China	−0.72	−1.11	26.27	26.32	−0.09	−0.15
Hong Kong	0.65	1.51*	11.73	11.71	0.19	0.45**
Indonesia	−4.60	6.57*	16.59	15.50	−0.96	1.47**
Malaysia	−3.84	1.75*	14.58	14.49	−0.91	0.42**
Philippines	−1.06	3.57*	12.20	11.67	−0.30	1.06**
Peru	4.16	−3.51	10.02	9.41	1.44	−1.29
Singapore	4.51	1.80	11.17	11.08	1.40	0.56
Thailand	−3.78	1.83*	19.89	19.88	−0.66	0.32**
Turkey	2.47	4.59*	29.77	30.01	0.29	0.53**
NAREIT	1.09	0.47	3.92	4.07	0.96	0.40

Notes: The average returns presented are geometric returns. The momentum-based strategy buys one share in month $t + 1$ if the return in month t is positive, and shorts one share in month $t + 1$ if the return in the previous month is negative. * and ** indicate a higher return and a higher Sharpe ratio respectively under momentum trading strategy.

9.5   Portfolio Diversification

The main rationale for investment in emerging markets is that such a portfolio can be diversified and the portfolio risk minimized. Recent studies, however, show that the correlation between developed countries and emerging countries have significantly increased. It is also documented by recent studies that the correlations between the U.S. market and emerging markets tend to be asymmetrical between better time and worse time (Erb *et al.*, 1998), so that "when you need diversification, you don't have it, and you get it when you don't need it" (Patel and Sarkar, 1998). Is this also true for property market investment?

Table 6.A is the correlation matrix for the U.S. indices and the emerging markets property indices using quarterly data for the past four years. Generally, investing in the emerging property markets will generate certain diversification benefits, because the correlation between NAREIT and the property indices in question is much lower than that between NAREIT and S&P500. For four countries, the correlation coefficients are even negative.

We sorted the 16 quarters by the returns for the NAREIT index. Table 6.B shows the three different types of correlation coefficients between NAREIT and emerging market property indices:

- The overall correlation for the entire past four years.
- The correlation for the eight better-performing quarters.
- The correlation for the eight worse-performing quarters.

From Table 6.B, we can clearly see the following.

First, for a majority number of the emerging markets (seven out of 10), the correlation coefficients with NAREIT in the worse period are actually higher than those in the better. This mimics the asymmetry for the general equity markets found in other studies in terms of diversification. ("You get it when you don't need it.")

Second, for markets such as Hong Kong, Indonesia, Philippines, and Singapore, linkages between their respective property indices with the NAREIT are significantly higher in worse quarters than in better quarters. For several markets, a negative correlation in the

Table 6. A. Correlation matrix for the U.S. indices and the emerging markets property indices

	SP500	NAREIT	ARG	CHI	HK	INDO	MAL	PHI	PER	SIN	THA
NAREIT	0.977										
ARG	0.698	0.771									
CHI	0.847	0.870	0.739								
HK	0.471	0.472	0.574	0.644							
INDO	-0.587	-0.525	-0.144	-0.216	0.334						
MAL	-0.696	-0.681	-0.397	-0.359	0.200	0.888					
PHI	0.174	0.105	0.045	0.353	0.679	0.497	0.479				
PER	0.725	0.647	0.195	0.474	0.272	-0.528	-0.578	0.260			
SIN	-0.169	-0.219	-0.151	-0.015	0.595	0.708	0.674	0.862	-0.041		
THA	-0.941	-0.972	-0.774	-0.879	-0.544	0.429	0.607	-0.172	-0.605	0.124	
TUR	0.972	0.989	0.728	0.867	0.416	-0.577	-0.725	0.054	0.639	-0.272	-0.963

B. Correlation coefficients between the U.S. NAREIT index and the emerging markets property indices

	Past four years overall correlation (QI/94–QI/98)	Correlation in the better-performing eight quarters for NAREIT	Correlation in the worse-performing eight quarters for NAREIT
SP500	0.977	0.986	0.951
ARG	0.771	0.872	0.515
CHI	0.870	0.780	0.892
HK	0.472	0.359	0.948
INDO	-0.525	-0.519	0.618
MAL	-0.681	-0.698	0.260
PHI	0.105	-0.417	0.810
PER	0.647	0.747	0.384
SIN	-0.219	-0.598	0.671
THA	-0.972	-0.980	-0.930
TUR	0.989	0.986	0.983

better quarters turns to a very positive correlation in th worse quarters. This indicates that U.S. investors in NAREIT may not find that investing in these emerging markets provides strong diversification benefits, especially when the NAREIT itself does not do well.

9.6   Conclusion

We empirically examined the return process of the emerging equity markets and that of property indices in particular. We found that the emerging market property indices are more volatile than both the respective market indices and the U.S. equity indices. We found a substantial negative risk premium for the East Asian property markets during the Asian crisis. The emerging market property indices also move against exchange rates, thus creating a double squeeze in negative periods. In terms of predictability, contrary to traditional wisdom, we did not find overwhelming evidence for autocorrelation in most of these indices. We found certain diversification benefits in investing in the emerging market property indices, but we also found unfavorable asymmetry in the correlation between emerging property indices and the U.S. NAREIT index.

References

Bekaert, G., C.B. Erb, C.R. Harvey and T.E. Viskanta, 1998, Distributional Characteristics of Emerging Market Returns and Asset Allocation, *Journal of Portfolio Management* **24**(2), 102–116.

Erb, C.B., C.R. Harvey and T.E. Viskanta, 1998, Contagion and Risk, *Emerging Markets Quarterly* (Summer 1998) 46–64.

Harvey, C.R., 1995, Predictable Risk and Returns in Emerging Markets, *Review of Financial Studies* **8**(3), 773–816.

Hu, J. and J.P. Mei, 2000, Conditional Risk Premium in Asian Real Estate Properties, *Journal of Real Estate Finance and Economics* **3**, 295–311.

Patel, S. and A. Sarkar, Stock Market Crises in Developed and Emerging Markets, *Financial Analysts Journal* (Forthcoming).

Patel, S., 1998, Cross-Sectional Variation in Emerging Market Equity Returns January 1988–March 1997, *Emerging Market Quarterly* (Spring 1998) 1–14.

CHAPTER 10

Conditional Risk Premiums of Asian Real Estate Stocks **

JIANPING (J.P.) MEI* and JIAWEI HU†

Stern School of Business, New York University

This paper uses a multi-factor, latent-variable model to examine the time variation of expected returns on Asian property stocks. Using data from 1990 to 1997, we found strong evidence of time-varying risk premium, suggesting that property development based on constant discount rate may underestimate the cost of capital. A further study using a multi-country model suggests that conditional excess returns of many crisis-stricken economies appear to move quite closely with each other. This supports the hypothesis that the risk premiums in these Asian markets move closely over time. As a result, they provide a partial explanation of market contagion in the region

10.1 Introduction

The Asian financial crisis in 1997 caught may economists, investors, and regulators by surprise. While the crisis could be attributed to a

*Associate Professor of Finance. Any comments can be sent to Jianping Mei at Department of Finance, New York University, 44 West 4th Street, New York, NY 10003, Phone (212) 998-0354.

†Graduate Student.

** We thank John Campbell for letting us use his latent-variable model algorithm. We have also benefited from helpful discussion with Burton Malkiel and Enrico Peroti.

confluence of many factors, excessive real estate speculation, which undermined the countries' banking system, has been identified as one important factor (see Krugman (1998) and Malkiel and Mei (1998)).

There was a common perception in Asia before the crisis that real estate investment, including real estate stocks, is low risk because real estate represents tangible assets. This paper develops a framework for measuring volatility and conditional risk premiums in real estate stocks. This methodology allows us to relate movements in required risk premiums to currency, interest rates and real estate market conditions. We conclude that real estate investment is actually quite risky in Asia. Moreover, conditional risk premiums vary substantially over time. As a result, better financial planning is required because many viable projects planned in the past can fail if market conditions and risk premiums change.

This chapter also tries to shed light on the issue of contagion in Asian real estate markets. Why do those real estate companies that develop properties in different markets and that are traded on different markets and that are traded on different stock exchanges tend to rise and collapse together? Using an integrated capital markets model, we show that one possible explanation is that the conditional risk premiums of these markets are driven by a similar set of world market variables. As a result, the conditional equity premiums tend to rise and fall together, which help contribute to market contagion.

The chapter is organized as follows: Section 10.2 describes the asset pricing framework. Section 10.3 analyzes the conditional excess returns under the assumption that the world's equity markets are segmented by national markets. Section 10.4 examines the conditional excess returns on property shares under the assumption that the world real estate securities markets are integrated. Section 10.5 concludes the study.

10.2   The Asset Pricing Framework

The asset pricing framework used in this study assumes that the equity markets are perfectly competitive and frictionless with investors believing that asset returns are generated by the following K-factor model:

$$\tilde{r}_{i,t+1} = \mathrm{E}_t[\tilde{r}_{i,t+1}] + \sum_{k=1}^{K} \beta_{i,k}\tilde{f}_{k,t+1} + \tilde{\varepsilon}_{i,t+1}. \qquad (10.1)$$

Here $\tilde{r}_{i,t+1}$ is the excess return on asset i held from time t to time $t+1$ and represents the difference between return on asset i and the risk-free rate of interest. $\mathrm{E}_t[\tilde{r}_{i,t+1}]$ is the expected excess return on asset i, conditional on information known to market participants at the end of time period t. $\tilde{f}_{k,t+1}$ is one of the K pricing factors and $\tilde{\varepsilon}_{i,t+1}$ is the error term. We assume that $\mathrm{E}_t[\tilde{f}_{k,t+1}] = 0$ and that $\mathrm{E}_t[\tilde{\varepsilon}_{i,t+1}] = 0$. The conditional expected excess return is allowed to vary through time in the current model, but the beta coefficients are first assumed to be constant through time.

This ability of $\mathrm{E}_t[\tilde{r}_{i,t+1}]$ to vary through time is absent in prior real estate investment trust (REIT) studies. However, if $\mathrm{E}_t[\tilde{r}_{i,t+1}]$ is not restricted to be constant, then we need to look at both the similarities in beta(s) and the co-movement of $\mathrm{E}_t[\tilde{r}_{i,t+1}]$ through time when analyzing the co-movement of excess returns on two or more assets. In other words, it is possible for the risk premiums and excess returns of two assets to move independently even though they have similar betas. However, this problem will not occur if the following linear pricing relationship holds:

$$\mathrm{E}_t[\tilde{r}_{i,t+1}] = \sum_{k=1}^{K} \beta_{ik}\lambda_{kt}. \qquad (10.2)$$

where λ_{kt} is the "market price of risk" for the kth factor at time t.[1]

Now suppose that the information set at time t consists of a vector of L forecasting variables X_{nt}, $n = 1, \ldots, L$ (where X_{lt} is a constant), and that conditional expectations are a linear function of

---

[1]Equation (10.2) states that the conditional expected rate of return should be a linear function of factor risk premiums, with the coefficients equal to the betas of each asset. This type of linear pricing relationship can be generated by a number of intertemporal asset pricing models, under either a no arbitrage opportunity condition or through a general equilibrium framework. See for example Ross (1976) and Campbell (1993).

these variables. We can then write λ_{kt} as

$$\lambda_{kt} = \sum_{n=1}^{L} \Theta_{kn} X_{nt}.$$ (10.3)

and therefore Eq. (10.2) becomes

$$E_t[\tilde{r}_{i,t+1}] = \sum_{k=1}^{K} \beta_{ik} \sum_{n=1}^{L} \theta_{kn} X_{nt} = \sum_{n=1}^{L} \alpha_{in} X_{nt}.$$ (10.4)

α_{in} is the risk premium for the forecasting variable X_{nt}. Equations (10.1) and (10.4) combined are sometimes called a multi-factor, latent-variable model.[2] The model implies that expected excess returns are time varying and can be predicted by the forecasting variables in the information set. From Eqs. (10.3) and (10.4), we can see that the model places the following restrictions on the coefficients of Eq. (10.4):

$$\alpha_{ij} = \sum_{k=1}^{K} \beta_{ik} \theta_{kn}.$$ (10.5)

Here, β_{ik} and θ_{kn} are free parameters. Normally, the (α_{ij}) matrix should have a rank of P, where P is defined as $P = \min(N, L)$ and N denotes the number of assets. Equation (10.5) restricts the rank of the (α_{ij}) matrix to be K, which is smaller than than P. To test the restriction in Eq. (10.5), we first normalize the model by setting the factor loadings of the first K assets as follows: $\beta_{ij} = 1$ (if $j = 1$) and $\beta_{ij} = 0$ (if $j \neq i$) for $k = 1, \ldots, K$. Next, we partition the excess return matrix $R = (R_1, R_2)$. Define T as a $1 \times K$ matrix, then R_1 is a $T \times K$ matrix of excess returns of the first K assets and R_2 is a $T \times (N - K)$ matrix of excess returns on the rest of the assets. Using Eqs. (10.4) and (10.5), we can derive the following regression system

$$\begin{aligned} R_1 &= X\Theta + \mu_1, \\ R_2 &= X\alpha + \mu_2, \end{aligned}$$ (10.6)

---

[2]For more details on this model, see Hansen and Hodrick (1980), Gibbons and Ferson (1985), Campbell (1987), and Ferson and Harvey (1993).

where X is a $T \times L$ matrix of the forecasting variables, Θ is a matrix of θ_{ij} and α is a matrix of α_{ij}. If the linear pricing relationship in Eq. (10.2) holds, the rank restriction implies that the data should not be able to reject the null hypothesis $H_0 : \alpha = \Theta B$, where B is a matrix of β_{ij} elements. The objective of the paper is to use the regression system in Eq. (10.6) to see to what extent the forecasting variables, X, explain the conditional excess returns under the asset pricing constraint (10.4).

It is worth noting that while Eq. (10.4) has derived the conditional excess returns $E_t[r_{i,t+1}]$ with the pricing restrictions (10.5), one can also obtain *unrestricted* conditional excess returns directly from linear projections *without* using the asset pricing framework of Eqs. (10.1)–(10.5). In other words, given that conditional expectations are linear in the forecasting variables, we can simply project the excess returns on the forecasting variables:

$$ E_t[r_{i,t+1}] = \sum_{n=1}^{L} \mu_{in} X_{nt}. \qquad (10.4') $$

Since (10.4') is derived directly from linear projection, μ_{in}, the risk premium for X_{nt} does not have to be the same as α_{in} in Eq. (10.4). In what follows we call estimates of conditional excess returns, using Eq. (10.4'), unrestricted conditional excess returns, and those estimates derived using Eqs. (10.4) and (10.5) together, restricted conditional excess returns.

10.3 The Single-Country Model

We assume that financial markets are segmented internationally but are frictionless domestically.[3] This implies that the market price of each macro risk factor is the same across all asset markets, including stocks, bonds, and real estate (see Ling and Naranjo (1999) for evidence to support this assumption). As a result, we can use the

---

[3]Several recent studies suggest that emerging equity markets are segmented. See Bekaert and Harvey (1995).

latent-variable model to estimate the conditional premiums for real estate portfolios. It also allows us to estimate the sensitivities of real estate stocks to domestic factors. To ensure that the pricing model holds for a wide range of assets, we use returns on six equity portfolios for each economy: a value-weighted market index, a value-weighted banking portfolio index, a value-weighted property portfolio index plus three other industry indices. In other words, a wide range of asset portfolios is used to test the asset pricing model restriction and to estimate the required risk premiums for property stocks. A generalized method of moments (GMM) approach, similar to Campbell and Hamao (1992) and Ferson (1989), is used to estimate the unrestricted model of Eq. (10.4') and the restricted model of Eqs. (10.4) and (10.5). Equation (10.5) is a cross-equation restriction with unknown parameters. Thus, Eq. (10.4) must be estimated simultaneously across a number of assets to appropriately test the restriction imposed by Eq. (10.5). We also need to adjust for possible heteroskedasticity and serial correlation in regression (10.4).

The forecasting variables chosen to estimate the unrestricted and the restricted model (Eqs. (10.4') and (10.4)) reflect those widely used in previous studies of conditional risk premiums on stocks in general (see Bekaert and Harvey (1995), Ferson (1989), and Bessler and Booth (1994)), which can be expected, a priori, to act as important variables in determining the conditional risk premiums on real estate stocks. The local variables included are constant, short-term interest rates, the spread between long- and short-term rates,[4] changes in the dollar exchange rates, the dividend yield on the

---

[4]The short-term interest rates used for each economy are: 1-month deposit rate for Hong Kong, 1-month deposit rate for Singapore, 91-day deposit rate for South Korea (closest available), 1-month money rate for Taiwan, 1-month deposit rate for Indonesia, 1-month deposit rate for Malaysia, 91-day Treasury bill rate for the Philippines (closest available), and 1-month deposit rate for Thailand. The long-term interest rates used for each economy are: 1-year deposit rate for Hong Kong, 1-year deposit rate for Singapore, 1-year bond invest trust rate for South Korea, 6-month money rate for Taiwan, 1-year deposit rate for Indonesia, 1-year deposit rate for Malaysia, 1-year Treasury bill rate for the Philippines, and 6-month deposit rate for Thailand. These data are obtained from Datastream, Central Bank of China, and Bank of Malaysia.

market portfolio, and the proportion of property company market capitalization in the total market capitalization. This last variable is a proxy for real estate market speculation. Owing to its illiquidity, real estate market prices are hard to obtain, and so we use the proportion of properties in the total market capitalization as a proxy. Generally, a real estate market boom tends to make the property index outperform the market index, thus raising the proportion of property stocks in the total market capitalization.

To estimate the asset pricing model (10.4), we use six industry portfolios for each economy. We choose six portfolios rather than three (market, banking, property or building) portfolios to ensure that the pricing model is estimated across a wide range of industries so that factor pricing is not biased by one single industry.[5] The model is estimated separately for each economy, because there is significant evidence of market segmentation (see Bekaert and Harvey (1995)). In essence, we are assuming that different economies are driven by different latent systematic factors. The returns are computed in local currencies, and they include both dividends and capital gains. The excess returns are computed over the short-term local interest rates.

Table 1 provides summary statistics for the sample period covered, the monthly means, and the standard deviations (SD's) of two portfolios: (i) the market portfolio, (ii) the real estate stock portfolio for each economy. One can see that those economies that were severely hit by the 1997 Asian crisis had negative market and property returns during the sample period. These include Indonesia, Malaysia, the Philippines, and Thailand. The monthly volatility

---

[5]The other three industrial portfolios chosen for each economy are: utilities, textiles, and general industry for Hong Kong; consumer goods, services, and general industry for Singapore; consumer goods, services, and steel for Taiwan; consumer goods, general industry, and plantation for Indonesia; consumer goods, services, and oil industry for Malaysia; consumer goods, general industry, and utilities for the Philippines; consumer goods, services, and oil industry for Malaysia; consumer goods, general industry, and electronics for Thailand. These data are obtained from Datastream, the Hong Kong Stock Exchange, and the Taiwan Securities Exchange.

Table 1.   Monthly excess returns in local currency for the market and real estate company portfolios for each country during the sample periods.

Country	Time period	Mean (market)	S.D. (market)	Mean (real state)	S.D. (real state)
Hong Kong	86.1–97.12	1.46	8.64	1.74	10.57
Singapore	87.1–97.12	0.43	6.52	0.91	9.42
Indonesia	91.9–97.12	−0.21	7.70	−1.37	16.04
Malaysia	91.1–97.12	−0.03	6.55	−0.59	9.49
Philippines	90.1–97.12	−0.03	8.99	−0.94	11.22
Thailand	92.1–97.12	−1.08	10.42	−3.35	18.99

Source: Datastream.

was also high, with the Thai market having a monthly volatility of 20%.[6] Clearly, real estate investment in Asia is anything but low risk.

Table 2 gives the estimates for the explanatory variables' slope coefficients. One can see that high short-term rates predicted lower excess returns for many Asian economies. The term-spread variable tended to predict lower excess returns in general. Appreciation in the dollar predicted lower excess returns for all the crisis economies in Asia. This should not be surprising, because the dramatic currency devaluation last year triggered a sharp fall in real estate stock prices. The dividend yields generally predicted higher excess returns. The proportion of real estate companies in the total market capitalization appears to have different effects across markets. But generally a high proportion of real estate companies in the total market capitalization tends to predict lower expected returns for the future. This should not be too surprising, because a rapidly growing real estate equity market relative to the market as a whole tends to indicate excessive development and thus lower future expected returns. Finally, the t-statistics and the adjusted R^2 indicate that the expected excess returns do vary across countries.

The top panels of Figs. 1–8 show the co-movement of excess returns, $\tilde{r}_{i,t+1}$, and the expected excess returns, $E_t(\tilde{r}_{i,t+1})$, for all the real estate stock portfolios. An inspection of these figures reveals

---

[6]In comparison to the U.S. property market, the Thai real estate market is over five times as volatile as the U.S. market.

Table 2. Unrestricted conditional risk premiums. Regression of excess returns on real estate stock portfolios at time $t+1$ on a constant, a short-term rate, the spread between long and short rate, percentage change on the dollar exchange rate, the market dividend yield in each country, and the proportion of property companies in the total market capitalization.

Country	Constant	Short	Spread	% FX	DivYld	Pmv/mv	$\bar{R}^2$
Hong Kong	3.504	− 2.278**	− 3.926**	3.808	4.461**	− 0.073	0.080
	(0.23)	(−3.52)	(−2.34)	(0.69)	(3.11)	(−0.19)	
Singapore	8.423	− 1.732**	− 3.485	−0.108	4.650*	− 0.80**	0.067
	(1.13)	(−2.37)	(−1.29)	(−0.14)	(1.95)	(−2.29)	
Indonesia	9.680	− 0.810	0.995	−1.610	1.733	− 1.642	0.168
	(0.69)	(−1.16)	(0.76)	(−1.49)	(0.25)	(−0.67)	
Malaysia	− 3.748	− 0.910	− 4.044	− 1.540**	3.180	1.438	0.080
	(−0.18)	(−0.41)	(−0.84)	(−3.11)	(1.08)	(0.49)	
Philippines	15.35**	− 0.946**	− 3.786**	−0.024	4.700*	−0.258	0.082
	(2.55)	(−2.19)	(−3.45)	(−0.06)	(1.94)	(1.65)	
Thailand	29.24	− 1.593	0.906	− 1.299**	0.692	−4.372	0.067
	(1.14)	(−0.81)	(0.69)	(−2.12)	(0.19)	(−1.46)	
Japan	−10.89	1.179	11.75	−0.096	435.8	0.106	−0.022
	(−0.55)	(0.08)	(0.38)	(−1.24)	(0.49)	(0.99)	
U.S.	10.40*	−0.835	− 0.781	0.066*	−2.622	−7.302	0.017
	(1.78)	(−0.68)	(−0.62)	(1.70)	(−0.92)	(−0.69)	

Note: * indicates significance level at 10% while ** indicate significance level at 5%.

that the conditional risk premiums for property stocks do vary over time, which accounted for a portion of the volatility in Asian real estate stocks. The predictability in expected excess returns that we document does not necessarily imply that the markets are inefficient but rather that it can reflect rational pricing in an efficient market under different business conditions. However, the huge variation in expected excess returns or the risk premiums is still astonishing, given the seemingly stable risk tolerance of market participants and the stable payoff structure for portfolio fund managers.

Table 3 presents the beta estimates for the property portfolios in the asset pricing model and performs the tests for the number of latent factors in each market. We estimate the regression system under the assumption that there is only one "priced" systematic factor (Ling and Naranjo (1997) allow for multiple risk factors), $\tilde{f}_{1,t+1}$, in the economy ($K = 1$). Here, we have normalized the single factor so that the market portfolio in each economy has a beta of 1. We find that the single-factor model cannot be rejected for most economies.

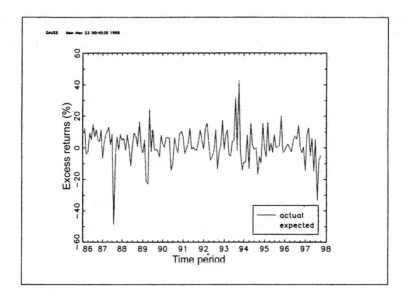

Fig. 1A.   Actual and expected returns for Hong Kong real estate stocks.

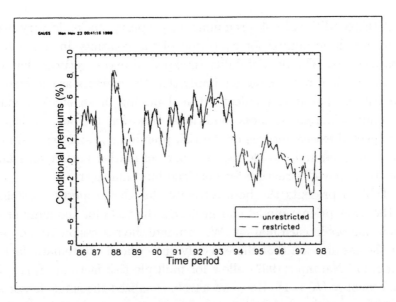

Fig. 1B.   Restricted and unrestricted risk premiums for Hong Kong real estate stocks.

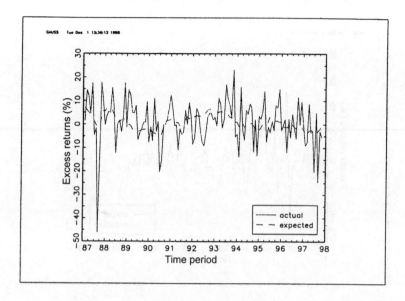

Fig. 2A.   Actual and expected returns for Singapore real estate stocks.

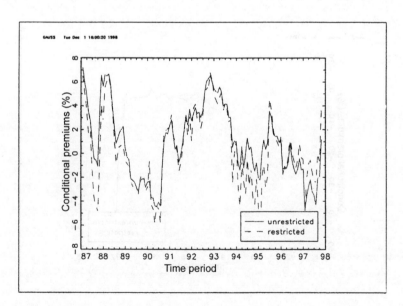

Fig. 2B.   Restricted and unrestricted risk premiums for Singapore real estate stocks.

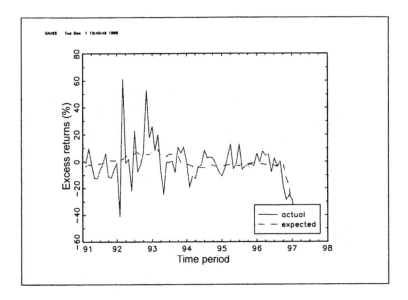

Fig. 3A.   Actual and expected returns for Indonesian real estate stocks.

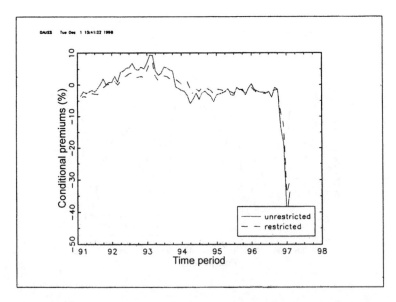

Fig. 3B.   Restricted and unrestricted risk premiums for Indonesian real estate stocks.

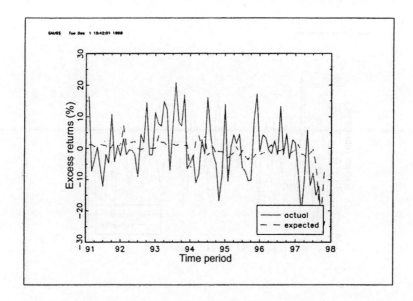

Fig. 4A.   Actual and expected returns for Malaysian real estate stocks.

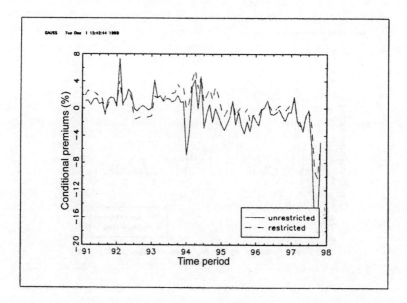

Fig. 4B.   Restricted and unrestricted risk premiums for Malaysian real estate stocks.

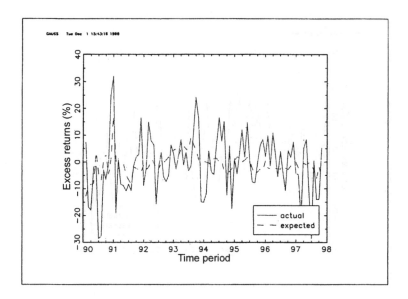

Fig. 5A.   Actual and expected returns for Philippines real estate stocks.

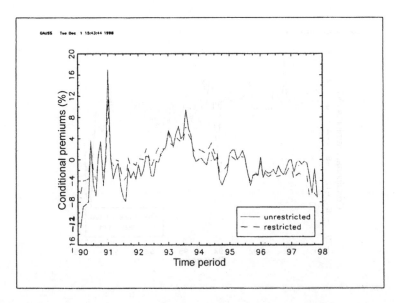

Fig. 5B.   Restricted and unrestricted risk premiums for Philippines real estate stocks.

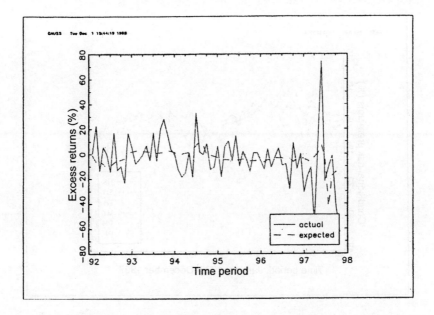

Fig. 6A.   Actual and expected returns for Thailand real estate stocks.

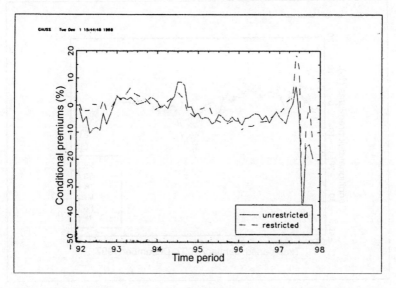

Fig. 6B.   Restricted and unrestricted risk premiums for Thailand real estate stocks.

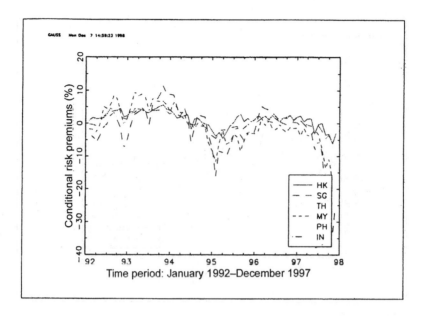

Fig. 7.   Conditional premiums in an integrated model.

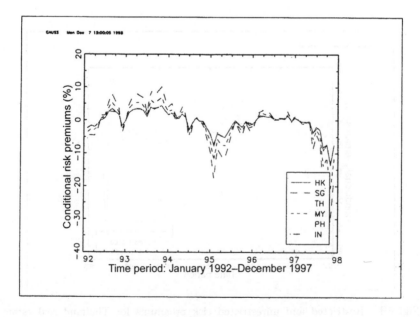

Fig. 8.   Conditional premiums in an integrated model.

Table 3. Beta for the property portfolios and test for the number of factors in each market. A single-country model is used in estimating the betas.

Country	Market beta	χ^2-Test	Significance level
Hong Kong	1.206 (0.061)	20.35 ($K = 1$)	0.727
Singapore	0.926 (0.075)	25.21 ($K = 1$)	0.450
Indonesia	1.507 (0.188)	31.53 ($K = 1$)	0.171
Malaysia	0.913 (0.162)	26.70 ($K = 1$)	0.371
Philippines	0.860 (0.122)	25.17 ($K = 1$)	0.452
Thailand	1.448 (0.204)	29.83 ($K = 1$)	0.230

Note: * Model rejected at 5% level.

Thus, we will use the single-factor model for computing restricted conditional risk premiums.

The bottom panels of Fig. 1–6 give an alternative visual presentation of the results reported in Table 3. The figures plot the unrestricted and restricted fitted values of $E_t(\tilde{r}_{i,t+1})$ for property stocks using a solid line and a dashed line, respectively. These charts show that the expected excess returns estimated under the rank restriction closely resemble those estimated without the restriction. The figures also show that the single-factor, latent-variable model provides a fairly good fit of the unrestricted conditional excess returns for most countries and results in an impressive degree of movement in conditional expected excess returns. We can see that while the conditional premiums were often positive for real estate investors, they also turned negative during some sample periods, offering investors inadequate compensation for risk taking. One may conclude from this that market timing based on conditional risk premium can help enhance investment returns. But it is worth noting that the transaction costs associated with the market timing strategy are often quite high in emerging markets.

10.4 The Multi-Country Model

While the single-country model allows us to examine conditional risk premiums of all industries in a single country, it does not permit us to examine the co-movement of property shares across countries. To solve this problem. we begin by assuming that the property markets of the above six countries are integrated and that a multi-factor asset pricing model applies. As a result, we can use the latent-variable model to examine the conditional premiums for real estate portfolios across different markets.[7] It also allows us to estimate the sensitivities of real estate stock returns to domestic factors. The forecasting variables used here include a constant term, the yield on HK 1-month deposit rate, the spread between the yields on 1-year deposit rate and 1-month deposit rate in HK, the percentage change in the yen exchange rate in dollars, the price–earnings ratio and dividend yields on a southeast Asian property portfolio constructed by Datastream. The 1-month deposit rate describes the short-term interest rate. The spread variable tells us the term structure of interest rates. The P/E ratio and dividend yield variables are used to capture information on expectations about future cash flows and required returns in the property market. These variables have been used by Campbell (1987), Campbell and Hamao (1992), Fama and French (1988, 1989), Ferson (1989), Ferson and Harvey (1993), Ling and Naranjo (1997), among others.[8]

Table 4 gives the parameter estimates for the unrestricted conditional risk premium on property portfolios based on Eq. (10.4'). It is interesting to see that high HK short-term rates predicted lower excess returns for many Asian economies. None of the other variables appears to explain much of the variation in Asian property expected returns, including the yen-dollar exchange rates. Finally, a joint F-test of all the parameters indicates that the coefficients of the regression parameters are not all zero, suggesting that expected excess returns do vary over time.

---

[7]Formally testing whether these markets are integrated or not is beyond the scope of this paper, because the data series are too short to perform an integration test such as those of Bekaert and Harvey (1997).

[8]Fama and French (1989) also uses the spread between yields of a low-grade, long-term corporate bond and a long-term Treasury bond to capture the default risk in the financial market. But they find the variable to be capturing the same information as the dividend yield. Thus, we include only dividend yield in the study.

Table 4. Unrestricted conditional risk premiums in a multi-country model. Regression of excess returns on real estate returns on real estate stock portfolios at time $t + 1$ on a constant, 1-month HK deposit rate, the spread between the yields on 1-year deposit rate and 1-month deposit rate in HK, the percentage change in the yen exchange rate in dollars, the price–earnings ratio and dividend yields on Southeast Asian property portfolios constructed by Datastream.

Country	Constant	ImDr	Spread	% FX	P/E	DivYld	$\bar{R}^2$
Hong Kong	19.73	− 2.504	− 0.699	0.316	−0.113	− 1.856	0.011
	(1.11)	(−1.65)	(−0.24)	(0.77)	(−0.40)	(−0.49)	
Singapore	18.19	− 2.471*	− 1.384	−0.126	−0.084	− 1.726	0.136
	(1.21)	(−1.91)	(−0.55)	(−0.36)	(−0.35)	(−0.53)	
Thailand	−4.099	− 3.569	− 5.207	−1.046	0.735	1.622	0.157
	(−0.14)	(−1.39)	(−1.05)	(−1.49)	(1.55)	(0.25)	
Malaysia	37.12*	− 5.432**	− 1.182	−0.344	−0.197	− 3.525	0.450
	(1.92)	(−3.28)	(−0.37)	(−0.76)	(−0.64)	(−0.85)	
Philippines	18.87	− 2.705*	0.964	−0.300	−0.007	− 3.939	0.241
	(1.10)	(−1.84)	(0.34)	(−0.75)	(−0.03)	(−1.07)	
Indonesia	62.75**	− 7.917**	− 0.130	0.261	−0.258	− 12.38**	0.402
	(2.99)	(−4.41)	(−0.04)	(0.53)	(−0.78)	(−2.74)	

Note: *indicates significance level at 10% while asterisks ** indicate significance level at 5%.

Figure 7 shows the co-movement of expected excess return (unrestricted), $E_t(\tilde{r}_{i,t+1})$, for the real estate stock portfolios of Hong Kong, Singapore, Indonesia, Malaysia, the Philippines, and Thailand. Here, the conditional excess returns appear to move quite closely with each other. This supports the hypothesis that the risk premiums in these four markets move closely over time. As a result, they provide an explanation of market contagion across these markets. This conclusion is further confirmed by the bottom panel of Table 4, which tests the hypothesis that there is only one "priced" systematic factor, $\tilde{f}_{1,t+1}$, in the economy ($K = 1$). Here, we have normalized the single factor so that the U.S. property portfolio has a beta of 1). We find that the single-factor model is not rejected by the data. Thus, we cannot reject the hypothesis that a single-factor model drives restricted conditional risk premiums across all Asian markets. Figure 8 shows the co-movement of expected excess return (restricted), $E_t(\tilde{r}_{i,t+1})$, for the six real estate stock portfolios. By comparing Figs. 7 and 8, we can see that the one-factor model (Fig. 8) provides an adequate description of the unrestricted conditional premium in Fig. 7. Thus, our result is consistent with the view that Asian real estate security markets are integrated, because the law of one price (risk premium) seems to hold.

10.5   Summary and Conclusions

This paper uses a multi-factor, latent-variable model to examine the time variation of expected returns on Asian property stocks. Using data from 1990 to 1997, we find strong evidence of time-varying risk premium, suggesting that property development based on constant discount rate may misspecify the cost of capital. A further study using a multi-country model suggests that conditional excess returns of many crisis economies appear to move quite closely with one another. This supports the hypothesis that the risk premiums in these Asian markets move closely over time. As a result, they provide a partial explanation of market contagion in the region. Moreover, graphical evidence indicates that risk premiums vary substantially over time and suggests that market timing may be a fruitful endeavor.

References

Bekaert, G. and C.R. Harvey, 1995, Time-Varying World Market Integration, *Journal of Finance*, **50**(2), 403–444.

Bekaert, G. and C.R. Harvey, 1997, Emerging Equity Market Volatility, *Journal of Financial Economics* **43**(1), 27–77.

Bessler, W. and G. Booth, 1994, Interest Rate Sensitivity of Bank Stock Returns in a Universal Banking System, *Journal of International Financial Markets, Institutions and Money* **3**(3–4), 117–36.

Campbell, J., 1987, Stock Returns and the Term Structure, *Journal of Financial Economics* **18**, 373–399.

Campbell, J., 1993, Intertemporal Asset Pricing without consumption Data, *American Economic Review* **83**, 487–512.

Campbell, J. and Y. Hamao, 1992, Predictable Returns in the United states and Japan: A Study of Long-Term Capital Markets Integration, *Journal of Finance* **47**(1), 43–70.

Fama, E. and K. French, 1988, Dividend Yields and Expected Stock Returns, *Journal of Financial Economics* **22**(1), 3–25.

Fama, E. and K. French, 1989, Business Conditions and Expected Returns on Stocks and Bonds, *Journal of Financial Economics* **25**(1), 23–49.

Ferson, W.E. 1989, Changes in Expected Security Returns, Risk and Level of Interest Rates, *Journal of Finance*, **44**, 1191–1217.

Ferson, W.E. and C.R. Harvey, 1993, The Risk and Predictability of International Equity Returns, *Review of Financial Studies* **6**(3), 527–566.

Gibbons, M. and W.E. Ferson, 1985, Testing Asset Pricing Models with Changing Expectations and an Unobservable Market Portfolio, *Journal of Financial Economics* **14**(2), 217–236.

Hansen, L. and R. Hodrick, 1980, Forward Exchange Rate as Optimal Predictors of Future Spot Rates: An Econometric Analysis, *The Journal of Political Economy* **88** (5), 829–853.

Harvey, C. 1995. Predictable Risk and Returns in Emerging Markets, *Review of Financial Studies*, 773–816.

Krugman, P. 1998 Will Asia Bounce Back? Speech for CFFB, Hong Kong.

Ling, D. and A. Naranjo, 1997, Economic Risk Factors and Commercial Real Estate Returns, *Journal of Real Estate Finance and Economics* **14**(3), 283–307.

Ling, D. and A. Naranjo, 1999, The Integration of Commercial Real Estate Markets and Stock Markets, *Real Estate Economics* **27**(3), 483–515.

Liu, C. and J.P. Mei, 1998, The Predictability of International Real Estate Markets, Exchange Rate Risks and Diversification Consequences, *Real Estate Economics* **26**(1), 3–39.

Malkiel, B. and J.P. Mei, 1998, Global Bargain Hunting, Simon and Schuster.

Ross, S., 1976, The Arbitrage Theory of Capital Asset Pricing, *Journal of Economic Theory* **13**, 341–360.

CHAPTER 11

Institutional Factors and Real Estate Returns: A Cross-Country Study

HSIEN-HSING LIAO*

Associate Professor, Department of Finance, National Taiwan University, Taipei, Taiwan

JIANPING (J.P.) MEI[†]

Associate Professor, Department of International Business, New York University, New York, NY 10012

This chapter provides an empirical study of the relationship between institutional factors and real estate returns. Using data from both developed and emerging market countries, our empirical results show that institutional factors do influence real estate returns and that these factors may not be fully priced. We find that when controlling return volatility and level of economic growth, a higher property return is expected in countries where the economic growth, a higher property return is expected in countries where the economy is more efficient and has more economic freedom. Our results support the view that the combination of "lumpiness" of real estate investment and the volatile nature of international capital flows may expose property investors to extra investors to extra investment risk, which needs to be compensated. Our results also indicate that an improvement in a country's economic efficiency and economic freedom may reduce property variance risk.

*E-mail: hliao@ccms.ntu.edu.tw. The author acknowledges the financial support of the National Science Council of Taiwan.

[†]Phone: (212) 998-0354, E-mail: jmei@stern.nyu.edu.

238

11.1 Introduction

The importance of institutional factors in economic activities has been extensively discussed. There is a growing literature on the economics of law. Researchers are examining how laws influence the economic environment. Most of the existing literature of law and economics focus on the relationship between the legal systems and economic efficiency. They include the interdependency between legal system (or political system) and the economic system;[1] the relationship between laws and social welfare;[2] and the impact of government intervention on economic development.[3] Most studies argue that a well-established institutional framework is essential for both economic efficiency and development. Among the literature, two studies are worth noting. Jaffe and Louziotis (1996) conducted a detailed survey on the issue of property right and economic efficiency. They also linked their discussion with real estate investment. Scully (1988) showed empirical evidence of the relationship between institutional framework and economic development. These studies provide some guidelines on the methodology for empirically examining the relationship between institutional framework and other economic activities.

Because of the immobility of real property and the complexity of real estate transactions, a real estate investor needs more legal protection on property rights. It makes sense to hypothesize that institutional factors may exert more influence on real estate markets than other markets (Jaffe and Louziotis, 1996). Despite the huge potential impact of institutional factors on real estate markets, there has been little empirical study on the effects of these factors on real

---

[1]To sum up, literature in this area shows that the legal system has a crucial influence on the economic system or economic performance. See Streit (1992), Grossekettler (1996), Meijer (1996), Roe (1994) and Allen (1995).

[2]Overall, this literature emphasizes the crucial role of contract laws and property right structure in a market operation. See Jaffe and Louziots (1996), Coleman (1992), Geistfeld (1994), Trebilcock (1993) and Ayres (1995).

[3]These studies emphasize the role of government whose policies or legislative efforts will influence the development of an economic system. See Lipton (1995) and Clague *et al.* (1996).

estate returns and volatility.[4] Only Geurts and Jaffe (1996) provide some preliminary empirical investigation of this issue. However, they examine only the institutional characteristics for the potential of international diversification. While they do not address the risk/return relationship empirically and discuss only correlation among various risk measures, their discussion on the possible risk variables in international real estate investment has provided some background for the current study.

Though there are theoretical reasons to believe that institutional factors should impact the real estate market, it is not clear how important these factors are in an asset pricing framework.[5] For example, it is not clear that poor legal protection would necessarily lead to poor returns, because poor legal protection (or poor regulations) may deter foreign competition (or foreign investors) thus giving established local firms a strategic advantage. It is also not obvious that high economic freedom would necessarily lead to good returns, because the unstable characteristic of international capital flows may increase the risk exposure of local market investors. One can also argue that although high economic efficiency can reduce transaction costs, it may accelerate asset turnover and increase volatility.

In this study, we use a simple regression model to investigate the potential market impact of institutional factors. We introduce an economic freedom index, which can be used to gauge the level of economic freedom in different countries around the world. We also use an economic efficiency index to measure the efficiency of an economy. We will examine how institutional factors affect the asset returns of real property as well as various measures of risks. We will

---

[4]Previous studies, such as Bittlingmayer (1992) and La Pona *et al.* (1996), did examine the relationship between capital structure and law. In a recent study, Wei (1997) examined the impact of corruption on foreign direct investment (FDI). Liao and Mei (1997) also examined the impact of law on security risk and returns. But they did not study the impact of law on real estate risk and returns.

[5]Here, the asset pricing framework refers to the fact that various legal and economic variables are used in explaining the *ex post* return of real estate assets. We are not implying that a formal asset pricing model, such as CAPM or APT, is used.

also examine whether economic variables, such as GDP growth and country risk rating, impact property returns and risks.

The organization of the study is as follows: Section 11.2 describes the data. Section 11.3 provides an *ex post* cross-sectional return generating model, which is designed to capture the impact of institutional factors on asset returns. Section 11.4 uses the regression model to examine the direct impact of institutional factors on property security returns together with other economic factors, such as economic growth and country risk ratings. Section 11.5 is the conclusion.

11.2 The Data

The data we use in studying the linkage between institutional factors and property stock returns are as follows:

(i) Property stock returns data derived from the total quarterly return index constructed by Datastream. The data covers 24 countries which trade property stocks in local securities markets. The return index for each country ends at the third quarter of 1997. However, according to the data availability, the beginning dates of the indices are not the same among countries. The countries included and the beginning date of the indices are stated as follows. The countries of which data begins at the first quarter of 1986 are: Australia, Belgium, Canada, France, Hong Kong, Ireland, Italy, Japan, Malaysia, Netherlands, Norway, Singapore, Sweden, U.K., and U.S. The beginning date for the others are Austria (1992 1st Q), Indonesia (1992 3rd Q), Denmark (1994 3rd Q), New Zealand (1998 1st Q), Peru (1994 1st Q), Philippines (1990 2nd Q), Portugal and Thailand (1990 1st Q), and Spain (1987 1st Q). To avoid a selection bias, we have included data from both developed and developing markets.

(ii) The rule of law index, the economic efficiency index, the corruption index, the risk of expropriation index, and the coercion of contract index are derived from the study of La Pona *et al.* (1996). The index originated from the "International Country Risk Guide". The higher the score the more favorable the situation. This index is an average of the monthly index between 1982 and 1995.

(iii) The economic freedom index derived from the joint study of Homes *et al.* (1997) on economic freedom around the world. The index is designed to provide an empirical measure of the level of economic freedom in countries of the world. The index is a weighted average of 10 sub-indices covering trade policy, taxation policy, government intervention in the economy, monetary policy, capital flows and foreign investment, banking policy, wage and price control, property rights, regulation, and black market activities. The 1995 data was used for this study. We have rescaled the data so that the variable increases with the level of economic freedom.

(iv) Mean annual GDP growth from 1986 to 1995, derived from the World Bank and IMF.

(v) Institutional Investors Country Credit Rating (IICCR) published by the Institutional Investor. IICCR is used to measure an individual country's credit risk.

In order to do cross-country analysis, all of the return series are converted into U.S. dollar returns. As a result, the study can be viewed from a U.S. investor's perspective. It has the advantage of not having to deal with individual country returns with different currencies, which are usually influenced by different inflation rates in various countries. The formula used to transform returns on foreign assets into dollar terms is as follows:

$$\$R_t = \left(\frac{X_{t-1}}{X_t}\right)[1 + R_t] - 1, \tag{11.1}$$

where X_t is the spot exchange rate (stated as units of foreign currency per dollar) at the month t. R_t denotes the local currency return and $\$R_t$ the dollar return.

11.3   Methodology

We construct two *ex post* cross-sectional regression models, which allows us to examine the relationship between various country-specific variables and both market returns and total risk (return volatility). According to Bekaert *et al.* (1997), owing to market segmentation, overall market volatility is generally more significant in explaining country expected returns rather than systematic risks; we construct the following multiple regress model:

$$\$ R_i = a + b\sigma_i + \gamma Y_i + \varepsilon_i , \qquad (11.2)$$

where $\$ R_i$ is mean dollar quarterly returns of property stock on country i during the sample period and σ_i is the standard deviation of asset returns, representing the total risk of the returns of property stock. Y_i is a vector of country-specific variables such as the freedom index, economic efficiency index, and IICCR. In this regression model, we can examine the impact of institutional variables by controlling the traditional risk measure σ_i.

To investigate the relationship between the traditional total risk measure (σ_i) and the institutional variables, we have also run the following regression:

$$\sigma_i = c + dY_i + \varepsilon_i . \qquad (11.3)$$

11.4 Empirical Results

Table 1 presents the summary statistics of the data. We can see a fairly wide variation of mean returns across countries with the average being 12.1% during the sample period. Hong Kong had the highest mean dollar return of 33.17% per annum while New Zealand lost an average of 11.7% per year during the same time period. The economic freedom index has a mean value of -2.23, with Hong Kong being the most free with an index level of -1.25 and Peru the most repressive with an index level of -2.90. There is also a wide variation of GDP growth across different countries. Regarding economic efficiency, a large variation across countries is also found. Several Asian and Western countries such as Singapore, Japan, Hong Kong, U.S., Sweden, and U.K. have the highest economic efficiency (10),

Table 1.   Summary statistics.

	Property return	Volati.	Freed index	GDP growth	Effici.	Rule of law	Corr.	Risk of Expro.	COFI	IICCR
Mean	0.121	0.187	−2.23	3.27%	8.32	8.26	7.91	8.93	8.54	73.6
S.D.	0.111	0.122	0.432	2.13%	2.33	2.29	2.21	1.34	1.43	15.4
Max.	0.337	0.617	−1.25	9.07%	10.00	10.00	10.00	9.98	9.69	91.9
Min.	−11.7	0.059	−2.90	0.37%	2.50	2.50	2.15	5.22	4.68	30.0
Correl.										
Volatility	0.384									
Freedom index	0.287	−0.313								
GDP growth	0.408	0.483	0.229							
Effici.	0.098	−0.658	0.652	−0.342						
Rule of law	0.046	−0.363	0.557	−0.224	0.736					
Corr.	0.020	−0.465	0.580	−0.319	0.874	0.906				
Risk of Expro.	0.039	−0.394	0.489	−0.192	0.666	0.941	0.848			
COFI	0.081	−0.339	0.566	−0.135	0.692	0.951	0.864	0.958		
IICCR	0.049	−0.373	0.531	−0.059	0.647	0.874	0.780	0.928	0.915	

Notes: Mean annual property stock returns are derived from the quarterly total return index of property stocks by Datastream. The data covers 24 countries. The index for each country ends at the third quarter of 1997. However, according to the data availability, the beginning date of the index are not the same among countries. The countries included and the beginning date of the indices are as follows: The data begins at the 1986 first quarter are: Australia, Belgium, Canada, France, Hong Kong, Ireland, Italy, Japan, Malaysia, Netherlands, Norway, Singapore, Sweden, U.K., and U.S. The others are Austria (1992 1st Q), Indonesia (1992 3rd Q), Denmark (1994 3rd Q), New Zealand (1998 1st Q), Peru (1994 1st Q), Philippines (1990 2nd Q), Portugal and Thailand (1990 1st Q), and Spain (1987 1st Q). The rule of law index, economic efficiency index, corruption index, risk of expropriation index, and coercion of contract index are derived from the study of La Pona *et al.* (1996). The indices originated from *International Country Risk Guide.* This index is an average of the monthly index between 1982 and 1995. The economic freedom index is derived from Homes *et al.*'s joint study (1997) on economic freedom around the world. The index is designed to provide an empirical measure of the level of economic freedom in countries of the world. The index is a weighted average of 10 sub-indices covering trade policy, taxation policy, government intervention in the economy, monetary policy, capital flows and foreign investment, banking policy, wage and price control, property rights, regulation, and black market activities. the 1995 data was used for this study. We have rescaled the data so that the variable increases with the level of economic freedom. Mean annual GDP growth from 1986 to 1995, derived from the World Bank and IMF. Institutional Investors Country Credit Rating (IICCR) is taken from the *Institutional Investor*, March 1996.

while Peru has the least efficiency (2.5). We can also see a large variation in the degree of rule of law across different countries, with several Western countries such as Australia and the U.S. having the most rigorous rule of law (10) and Peru having the least respect for rule of law (2.5). Table 1 also shows a wide variation of several risk measures across different countries, such as the corruption index, the risk of expropriation index, the coercion of contract index, IICCR, and individual market volatility.

Table 1 also presents the correlation matrix among the variables. We can see a few interesting numbers. First of all, the group of variables, including the rule of law index, the corruption index, the risk of expropriation index, the coercion of contract index, and IICCR are strongly and positively correlated to each other within a country. The correlation coefficients among the group of variables are almost all above 0.8, and a large part of them are even greater than 0.9. This is expected because respect for the rule of law naturally leads to less corruption, less risk of government expropriation, and strong coercion of contract. It is also expected that a better situation in former variables causes a better rating in IICCR. From an investment risk perspective, since the group of variables have high positive relationship with IICCR (0.874, 0.780, 0.928, and 0.915, respectively), this indicates that a country can improve its credit ratings by making improvements in these three variables and therefore can help reduce its international borrowing cost. In addition, it is worth noting that economic efficiency has a fairly high correlation with the above group of variables. It suggests that a well-established legal system may be an important foundation for economic efficiency. From Table 1, a fairly high correlation is also found between economic freedom and the above risk-related variables. This is interesting because it suggests that instead of being an impediment to economic freedom, respect for the rule of law may actually be an important condition for economic freedom.

The high correlation among risk-related variables (the rule of law, the corruption index, the risk of expropriation index, the coercion of contract index, and IICCR) shown in Table 1 may cause a multicollinearity problem in a multiple regression analysis. To reduce the problem we retain only the credit rating variable in the following re-

Table 2.   Regression of property returns on institutional variable, controlling volatility.

Regression	Constant	Volatility	Institutional variables	Name of institutional var.	$R^2(\%)$ (adjusted)
(1)	0.014	0.087			10.9
	(1.39)	(1.95)**	–		
(2)	0.073	0.120	0.029		
	(2.79)**	(2.80)**	(2.40)**	Freedom index	26.8
VIF†		1.1	1.1		
(3)	−0.065	0.180	0.007		
	(−2.11)**	(3.42)**	(2.68)**	Eco. efficiency	14.2
VIF		1.8	1.8		
(4)	−0.019	0.106	0.001		
	(−0.59)	(2.21)**	(1.05)	IICCR	11.3
VIF		1.2	1.2		
(5)	0.007	0.056	0.004		
	(0.07)	(1.10)	(1.31)	GDP growth	13.7
VIF		1.3	1.3		
Overall	0.164	0.892	0.039		
stocks	(2.73)**	(1.44)	(1.36)	Freedom index	3.1

Note: † VIF indicates variance inflation factor; number in parenthesis represents t-statistics; * indicates a 10% significant level; ** indicates a 5% significant level.

gression analysis without loss of much information.[6] The other four variables are dropped from the dependent variable set. The reason for retaining the credit rating variable is that IICCR is a well-known risk measure widely used by international investors.

Table 2 presents the results of the return regression, as shown in Eq. (11.2), and assumes the right-hand variables as being exogenous. We ran five regressions. In the first regression, we put only return volatility as an explaining variable. To examine the impact of individual institutional variables, in the other four regressions, we

---

[6]We conduct a principal component analysis of these five variables. The results show that the first component includes all the five variables with similar loadings (−0.455, −0.428, −0.456, −0.457, −0.438) and accounts for 92% of the variance of their correlation matrix). In addition, only the eigenvalue of the first component (4.589) is greater than 1 and is much greater than that of the second component (0.243). It should lose little information to retain only one of the five variables in the following analysis.

put one institutional variable in each regression as well as the return volatility.

From Table 2, except for the first regression, the small values of variance inflation factors (VIF) of all the explaining variables indicate that there is little multicollinearity problem. We can see that controlling return volatility, both the economic freedom variable and the economic efficiency variable have a significant and positive impact on the property stock returns. It means that with the same level of total risk, a higher property stock return is expected in a more efficient economy or in a country with a higher level of economic freedom. The results are interesting and worth further discussion. In the property market, making or adjusting an investment decision can take a much longer time than other financial assets. In a more efficient economic environment, the time allowed to react to new information is much shorter. However, for property investors, it is very hard to adjust their investment decisions in a short period. This inertial characteristic (lumpiness or illiquidity) of real estate investment decisions make the property investors more likely to be exposed to the risk of wrong investment decisions. On the other hand, in a less efficient environment, the property investors may be allowed a longer time to react to new information. Therefore, the property investors require a higher return to compensate the additional risk exposure.

In an economy with a higher degree of economic freedom, international capital flow is much easier to get in and out. Therefore the local property market is more likely to be influenced by the uncertainty of capital flow.

The recent Asian financial crisis is a case in point. Hong Kong real estate price dropped about 50% during the crisis, whereas the Chinese real estate market was less affected. In addition, owing to the inertial characteristics of real estate investment decisions, property investors find it difficult to move in and out to alter their portfolio quickly. In comparison to other financial assets, property investors are exposed to extra liquidity risk. To confirm the deduction, we regress the security market returns on its volatility and the freedom index (see last row of Table 2). The result shows that economic

Table 3.   Regression of property returns on each institutional variable, controlling volatility and GDP growth.

Regression	Constant	Volatility	GDP growth	Institutional variables	Name of institutional var.	$R^2(\%)$ (adjusted)
(1)	0.066	0.108	0.001	0.027		
	(2.06)**	(1.98)**	(0.36)	(1.93)**	Freedom index	23.6
VIF[†]		1.7	1.6	1.4		
(2)	−0.020	0.075	0.003	0.001		
	(−0.60)	(1.35)	(1.16)	(0.88)	IICCR	12.7
VIF		1.5	1.3	1.2		
(3)	−0.738	0.148	0.004	0.008		
	(−2.45)**	(2.72)**	(1.62)	(2.83)**	Eco. efficiency	35.4
VIF		2.0	1.3	1.8		

Note: [†] VIF indicates variance inflation factor; number in parenthesis represents *t*-statistics; * indicates a 10% significant level; ** indicates a 5% significant level.

freedom does significantly influence the expected return.[7] It is hardly surprising that credit rating and GDP growth have no significant explanatory power. This may suggest that these developments are largely expected by investors and priced into property stocks so that they have no impact on future returns.

To separate the influence of stage of economic growth, we also ran the regression by controlling both the return volatility and GDP growth. The results are exhibited in Table 3. The results are similar to Table 2. The level of economic freedom and economic efficiency are still positively and significantly influenced by property returns. It indicates that the above two risks are also priced under the same stage of economic growth. In short, from Tables 2 and 3, we can conclude that the "lumpiness" of real estate investment and the volatile nature of international capital flows may expose property investors to extra investment risk (which needs to be compensated). It also confirms that institutional factors do influence real estate returns and the risks are reflected in their prices.

---

[7]Another explanation is that higher level of economic efficiency probably contributed to high *ex post* real estate returns through profit factors other than GDP growth.

Table 4. The statistical determinants of property return volatility, controlling GDP growth.

Regression	Constant	GDP growth	Institutional variables	Name of institutional var.	$R^2(\%)$ (adjusted)
(1)	0.096	0.028	–		
	(2.31)**	(2.58)**			19.8
(2)	−0.206	0.034	−0.127		
	(−1.70)	(3.43)**	(−2.63)**	Freedom index	36.8
(3)	0.303	0.027	−0.003		
	(2.70)**	(2.63)**	(−1.96)**	IICCR	29.0
(4)	0.376	0.017	−0.029		
	(4.25)**	(1.79)*	(−3.43)**	Eco. efficiency	14.1

Note: Number in parenthesis represents t-statistics; * indicates a 10% significant level; ** indicates a 5% significant level.

Table 4 presents the results of the relationship between the institutional variables and return volatility controlling GDP growth. From Table 4, we can see that GDP positively influences property stock return volatility. This is to be expected. Most countries with high economic growth are developing countries. their capital markets are known to be more volatile. On the other hand, most Western countries have more mature economies and do not have fluctuating economic growth. Their capital markets are less volatile.

Second, from Table 4, we find that all three institutional variables have negative an significant impact on property return volatility. Since crediting rating agencies usually award better rating to economies with lower return volatility, it is not surprising that the crediting variable has a negative impact on property stock return volatility. But it is little surprising that the impact of economic freedom and efficiency variables are negative. Considering the results of the return and the volatility regressions together, we find that these two institutional variables play two different roles in property stock pricing. This implies that an improvement in these two institutional dimensions on the one hand reduces property variance risk and on the other may enhance *ex post* real estate returns.[8]

---

[8]It is also true for market return volatility. We also regress the same model using market return volatility as an independent variable. The t-values for coefficients of economic freedom, IICCR, and economic efficiency are −2.86, −4.84, and

11.5   Conclusion

This chapter provides an empirical study of the relationship between institutional factors and real estate returns. We use data from both developed and emerging market countries. Our empirical results show that institutional factors do influence real estate returns and that these factors are probably not fully priced. We find that when controlling return volatility and level of economic growth, a higher property return is expected in countries where the economy is more efficiency and has more economic freedom. Our results support the view that the combination of "lumpiness" of real estate investment and the volatile nature of international capital flows may expose property investors to extra investment risk, which needs to be compensated. Our results also indicate that an improvement in a country's economic efficiency and economic freedom may reduce property variance risk.

References

Allen, F., 1995, Review of: Strong Managers, Weak Owners: The Political Roots of American Corporate Finance (by Roe, M.J.), *Journal of Economic Literature* **33**(4), 1994–1996.

Ayres, I., 1995, Review of: The Limits of Freedom of Contract (by Trebilcock, M.J.), *Journal of Economic Literature* **33**(2), 865–866.

Bekaert, G. and C. Harvey, 1997, Emerging Equity Market Volatility, *Journal of Financial Economics* **43** (1), 29–78.

Bekaert, G., C. Erb, C. Harvey, and T. Viskanta, 1997, The Cross-Sectional Determinants of Emerging Equity Market Returns, in P. Carman (ed.), *Quantitative Investing for the Globe Markets*, Chicago and London: Fitzroy Dearborn Publisher.

Bittlingmayer, G., 1992, Stock Returns, Real Activity, and the Trust Question, *Journal of Finance* **47**(5), 1701–1730.

Clague, C., P. Keefer, S. Knack and M. Olson, 1996, Property and Contract Rights in Autocracies and Democracies, *Journal of Economic Growth* **1**(2), 243–276.

−3.52. The adjusted R^2s for each regression are 27.3%, 52.2%, and 36.5%. This also confirms the findings of Erb *et al.* (1996) that volatility is negatively related to a country's risk ratings.

Coleman, J., 1992, *Risks and Wrongs*, Cambridge Studies in Philosophy and Law, Cambridge, New York and Melbourne: Cambridge University Press.

Erb, C., C. Harvey, and T. Viskanta, 1996, Political Risk, Economic Risk and Financial Risk, *Financial Analysts Journal* **52** (6), 29–47.

Geistfeld, M., 1994, Review of: Risks and Wrongs (by Coleman, J.L.), *Journal of Economic Literature* **32**(3), 1263–1265.

Geurts, T. and A. Jaffe, 1996, Risk and Real Estate Investment: An International Perspective, *Journal of Real Estate Research* **11**(2), 117–130.

Grossekettler, H., 1996, Franz Bohm as a Pioneering Champion of an Economic Theory of Legislative Science, *European Journal of Law and Economics* **3**(4), 309–329.

Homes, K., B. Johnson, and M. Kirkpatrick, 1997, 1997 Index of Economic Freedom, Washington, D.C.: The Heritage Foundation, and New York: the *Wall Street Journal*.

Jaffe, A. and D. Louziotis Jr., 1996, Property Rights and Economic Efficiency: A Survey of Institutional Factors, *Journal of Real Estate Literature* **4**(2), 137–159.

Knack, S. and P. Keefer, 1995, Institutions and Economic Performance: Cross-Country Tests Using Alternative Institutional Measures, *Economics and Politics* **7**(3), 207–227.

La Pona, R., F. Lopez-de-Silanes, A. Shleifer and R. Vishny, 1998, Law and Finance, *The Journal of Political Economy* **106** (6), 1113–1156.

Liao, H.-H. and J.P. Mei, 1997, Why Should We Care about Law and Order — An Asset Pricing Perspective, Working Paper.

Lipton, M., 1995, Market, Redistributive and Proto-reform: Can Liberalization Help the Poor?, *Asian Development Review* **13**(1), 1–35.

Meijer, G., 1996, Co-determination and the Market Economy, *European Journal of Law and Economics* **3**(4), 361–368.

Roe, M., 1994, *Strong Managers, Weak Owners: The Political Roots of American Corporate Finance*, Princeton, N.J.: Princeton University Press.

Scully, G., 1988, The Institutional Framework and Economic Development, *Journal of Political Economy* **96**(3), 652–662.

Streit, M., 1992, Economic Order, Private Law and Public Policy: The Freiburg School of Law and Economics in Perspective, *Journal of Institutional and Theoretical Economics* **148**(4), 675–704.

Trebilcock, M., 1993, *The Limits of Freedom of Contract*, Cambridge and London: Harvard University Press.

Wei, S.-J., 1997, How Reluctant are Nations in Global Integration? Unpublished, Kennedy School of Government, Harvard University.

World Bank, 1995, *World Development Report 1995*, Oxford University Press.

Index